When The Trumpet Sounds

Studies on the Second Coming of Jesus Christ

Dr. Ken Chant

When The Trumpet Sounds

Studies on the Second Coming of Jesus Christ

By Ken Chant

Copyright © 2013 Ken Chant

ISBN 978-1-61529-095-6

Vision Publishing
1672 Main Street E 109
Ramona, CA 92065
1 800-9-VISION
www.booksbyvision.com

All rights reserved worldwide. No part of this book may be reproduced in any manner without the written permission of the author except in brief quotations embodied in critical articles or reviews.

A NOTE ON GENDER

The English language unfortunately does not contain an adequate generic term (especially in the singular number) that includes without bias both male and female. So "he, him, his, man, mankind," with their plurals, must do the work for both sexes. Accordingly, wherever it is appropriate to do so in the following pages, please include the feminine gender in the masculine, and vice versa.

FOOTNOTES

A work once fully referenced will thereafter be noted throughout the remainder of the book either by *"ibid"* (the same) or *"op. cit."* (a work previously cited).

Contents

One PROMISE 9
Two PROOF 25
Three IMMINENCE 47
Four TIME 61
Five INDICATIONS 73
ADDENDUM 95
Six SCHOOLS 99
Seven METHOD 119
Addendum SEEMINGLY UNFULFILLED ORACLES 137
Eight RESURRECTION 155
Nine RAPTURE 165
Ten IMMORTALITY 179
Eleven HADES 199
Tweleve TOMORROW 211
Thirteen BEMA 225
Fourteen JUDGMENT 245
Addendum – ON HELL DOLEFUL DUNGEONS OF DARKNESS!... 275
Fifteen ETERNITY 285
Addendum THE "SEVENTY WEEKS" PROPHECY 291
PART TWO ORACLES GALORE! 303
SOOTHSAYERS EVERYWHERE! 304

ABBREVIATIONS

Abbreviations commonly used for the books of the Bible are

Genesis	Ge	Habakkuk	Hb
Exodus	Ex	Zephaniah	Zp
Leviticus	Le	Haggai	Hg
Numbers	Nu	Zechariah	Zc
Deuteronomy	De	Malachi	Mal
Joshua	Js		
Judges	Jg		
Ruth	Ru	Matthew	Mt
1 Samuel	1 Sa	Mark	Mk
2 Samuel	2 Sa	Luke	Lu
1 Kings	1 Kg	John	Jn
2 Kings	2 Kg	Acts	Ac
1 Chronicles	1 Ch	Romans	Ro
2 Chronicles	2 Ch	1 Corinthians	1 Co
Ezra	Ezr	2 Corinthians	2 Co
Nehemiah	Ne	Galatians	Ga
Esther	Es	Ephesians	Ep
Job	Jb	Philippians	Ph
Psalm	Ps	Colossians	Cl
Proverbs	Pr	1 Thessalonians	1 Th
Ecclesiastes	Ec	2 Thessalonians	2 Th
Song of Songs	Ca *	1 Timothy	1 Ti
Isaiah	Is	2 Timothy	2 Ti
Jeremiah	Je	Titus	Tit
Lamentations	La	Philemon	Phm
Ezekiel	Ez	Hebrews	He
Daniel	Da	James	Ja
Hosea	Ho	1 Peter	1 Pe
Joel	Jl	2 Peter	2 Pe
Amos	Am	1 John	1 Jn
Obadiah	Ob	2 John	2 Jn
Jonah	Jo	3 John	3 Jn
Micah	Mi	Jude	Ju
Nahum	Na	Revelation	Re

* *Ca* is an abbreviation of *Canticles*, a derivative of the Latin name of the *Song of Solomon*, which is sometimes also called the *Song of Songs*.

* Scripture translations, unless otherwise stated, are my own.

ADVANCE WARNING!

An old Jewish story tells of a Russian Jew who was paid a ruble a month by the community council to stand at the outskirts of town so that he could be the first person to greet the Messiah upon his arrival. When a friend said to him, "But the pay is so low," the man replied, "True, but the job is permanent." (1)

He was a man who had no expectancy of the coming of Messiah. This book is the opposite. It ripples on every page with an assurance that the Messiah, Jesus Christ our Lord, will one day appear again in the clouds, and all the holy angels with him, coming to exact divine vengeance on a rebellious world, to rescue his church, and to establish a new heaven and a new earth in which righteousness will reign for ever.

Thus far, so good.

But having begun well, I have to say that as you read on you may be infuriated, surprised, delighted, or awed by this book. It all depends on what you already know or believe about the return of Christ.

You will probably find here some things that will draw from you a hearty assent, and others that will make you yearn to burn a certain heretic at the nearest stake!

No other area of Bible study is so fraught with peril and rich with promise, so prone to make enemies and win friends, as the

---

(1) Jewish Literacy, by Rabbi Joseph Telushkin; William Morrow & Co Inc, NY, 1991; pg 545.

study of eschatology! (2)

A vast disparity exists between the views various Christians have on certain aspects of eschatology. Each "school" of prophecy has its erudite proponents and opponents. Each arouses fierce support from its protagonists and ferocious opposition from its antagonists. The factions struggle mightily against each other until neutrality becomes almost an impossibility. Entire denominations have been built around a particular view of Bible prophecy, with adherence to that view being mandatory for membership.

However, I have observed that many Christians hold tenaciously to a particular eschatology simply because they are not aware of any viable alternatives, or because the alternatives have been presented in such poor light that they seem unworthy of further study.

So my aim in writing these chapters has not been to *convince* you so much as to *inform* you. Hence, I have tried to present clearly those aspects of eschatology on which evangelical Christians agree and also those on which they disagree. I do not personally belong to any particular "school" (3) of prophecy; nonetheless, I do have a viewpoint on the subject, and this book necessarily presents that view. It will show that I do not adhere to the *Post-Millennial* school, nor I do I have much agreement with *Praeterism*, except in certain areas. I am probably something of a mixture of *A-Millennialism* and *Pre-Millennialism*, with sundry objections to elements of both those schools!

Mostly, my desire is to let each passage of scripture speak for

---

(2) "Eschatology" means the study of "the last things", especially in connection with biblical prophecies and statements about the return of Christ, the end of the world, and the coming new heaven and new earth.

(3) See below, the chapter headed Schools.

itself, without trying to force them into an artificial framework. Whether or not I have achieved that aim, is for you to decide.

In any case, I hope that my opinions are not *too* intrusive, and that you will find space here to formulate your own ideas.

Your study of these pages should be exciting and rewarding. Even more, may they leave you better fitted to meet the Lord with joy when he comes!

One

PROMISE

An American preacher a few years ago called the USA the "false prophet" of the Apocalypse. He claimed to have seen a vision and heard a voice that told him so. *The Doomsday Globe* was published in 1978, confidently predicting that Armageddon would begin in October 1979, with the Second Advent occurring twelve months later.

A travelling evangelist visited the city of Adelaide in the 1970s. I heard him say that Christ had spoken to him in a vision, telling him to evangelise Australia quickly. Why? Because within three years the Second Advent would occur. As I write these words, forty years have passed, and still there is no sign of Christ's return!

But then, a *hundred* years ago people were saying that Christ would come soon, and a hundred years before that, and a hundred years before that .... Go back as far as you like in church history, and in every generation Christian soothsayers were convinced Jesus would come back to the earth in their lifetime.

I have taken that journey, and I have compiled scores of references, from nearly every century since the first; yet my list contains only a small part of the total number of predictions countless preachers have made about the nearness of Christ's return. [4]

They are still busy soothsaying. As Solomon said, *"there is nothing new under the sun"*! (Ec 1:9-10)

---

(4)   See below, Part Two of this book, Oracles Galore.

But should we not try to *"discern the times"*? (Lu 12:56). Should we not search for signs of his coming? (Mt 24:33, 42-44). Are there no indications that Christ is coming soon? Are all the preachers wrong? Those questions deserve a serious answer, which I hope the following chapters will provide.

THE PROMISE REVEALED

Above all, every oracle in the Bible is ultimately focussed on Christ –

THE GLORIOUS KING

The pages of Bible prophecy contain no greater portrayal of the return of Christ than the vision John saw on the Isle of Patmos. Along with the vision, he received a command –

> *Write what you have seen, what is now, and what is to take place hereafter (1:19).*

John wrote what he saw, and created the most dramatic book in the whole world. In older versions of the Bible this book is called *"The Revelation of St. John the Divine,"* but it is more accurately called *"The Revelation of Jesus Christ"* (1:1); for across every page the voice of the risen Christ sounds in divine authority. Sometimes, too, based on its title in Greek, John's vision is called *The Apocalypse*.

We believe the *Apocalypse* is true. We embrace its promise –

> *Happy are those who read these words ... and happy are those who hear, and who observe what is written here; for the time is near (1:3).*

And we respect its curse –

> *I warn everyone who hears the words of the prophecy in this book: if anyone adds to them, God will add to him the plagues described in this book, and if anyone takes away from the words of this book of prophecy, God will take away his*

> *share in the tree of life and in the holy city (22:18-19).*

With that stern warning ringing in our ears, we should be careful not to wrest from the *Apocalypse* its greatest prediction – **the promise of Christ's return**. In fact, four times in its pages the Lord of glory himself speaks the exciting words

> *Behold, I am coming soon! (3:10-11; 22:6-7, 10-12, 20).*

But how do we know that this promise is true? How can we be sure that the hope of Christ's return is not vain? And what does he mean by *"soon"*?

THE RESURRECTION, PROOF OF CHRIST'S RETURN

During his ministry in Palestine the Lord Jesus Christ often spoke of his going back to heaven and then of his coming again to earth. He said –

> *In my Father's house are many mansions. If this were not so, I would have told you. I go to prepare a place for you, and **if I go** and prepare a place for you, **I will come again**, and receive you unto myself, that where I am there ye may be also* (Jn 14:1-3, KJV).

Notice how Jesus placed the proof of his return on the fact of his resurrection and ascension. He said, **"If I go ... I will come again."**

Did he go?

Then he will come again!

The resurrection of Christ is one of the most well attested facts in all history. But quite apart from historical evidence, the doctrine itself is one of the strongest arguments for its truth. Here is a doctrine completely foreign to every other trend of religious teaching. How can anyone explain its existence apart from its truth?

All the great religious leaders of the world – Buddha, Mahomet, Confucius – were deeply venerated by their followers. Tremendous pains were taken to preserve the mortal remains of these famed leaders. There are magnificent temples in India which enshrine one of the Buddha's teeth. The same human characteristic can be seen in the Orthodox and Catholic bodies of Christendom. How greatly people honour the relics of the saints – they revere all manner of robes, statues, and ancient articles. This world-wide and prolific testimony to the ordinary trend of human nature leaves no doubt at all that, had it been possible to do the same with the body of Jesus, it too would have been preserved and venerated (cp Jn 20:11-15).

But there are no relics of Jesus. His tomb was empty on resurrection morning!

If Jesus, therefore, was true in prophesying his death and resurrection, he must have been true also in prophesying his return to the earth in power and glory, for it is hardly likely that he would be correct in the first prediction but wrong in the second. The marvel of his return is not greater than the marvel of his victory over death!

THE KING WHO IS COMING

Who is this Christ who is *"coming soon"*? John said –

> *I saw heaven opened, and behold, a white horse! He who sat upon it is called Faithful and True, and in righteousness he judges and makes war. His eyes burn like a bright flame, and many crowns are on his head. And a name is written on him that no one knows but himself ... And name is inscribed upon his robe and upon his thigh – King of Kings and Lord of Lords* (Re 19:11-16).

With trembling awe the prophet Daniel wrote –

> *As I looked, thrones were placed and one that was ancient of days took his seat; his raiment was white as snow ... his throne was fiery flames ... a stream of fire issued and came forth from before him; a thousand served him, and ten thousand times ten thousand stood before him; the court sat in judgment, and the books were opened.* (7:9-10, RSV)

And again Daniel dreamed and saw

> *visions during the night, and behold, with the clouds of heaven One came who was like the son of man ... and to him was given dominion ... which shall not pass away, and his kingdom is one that shall never be destroyed* (vs. 13-14, RSV).

With intense excitement, Paul wrote –

> *The Lord Jesus himself will come down from heaven with his mighty angels, surrounded by blazing fire. Then he will exact vengeance upon those who refused to know God ... And on that day of his coming, he will be glorified in his saints, and all who believe in him will be filled with wonder* (2 Th 1:7-10).

Those glowing testimonies could be multiplied many times, all of them telling of the amazing glory, the indescribable majesty, of the day when Christ returns. Possessing a sure hope of the dawning of that great day, we rejoice!

THE PROMISE CONFIRMED

How certain is the promise of Christ's return? How will he come? What does "soon" mean? What will be the result? So many questions! But they do have answers –

A CLEAR PROMISE

If you doubt that Christ ever did promise one day to return to this earth, you should read the following: Mt 24:30; 25:31; Mk 8:38; 1 Th 3:13; 4:15-16; 2 Th 1:7; Tit 2:13; He 9:28; Ju 14, 15; Re 1:7; 16:15; and many others.

It seems hardly possible for language to be any clearer! How can it be reasonable to deny that Christ, who meant exactly what he said about his *going* back to heaven, also meant exactly what he said about his *coming* back to earth? Yet there are those who do doubt it, and who try to alter the impact of the promise –

AN EVADED PROMISE

Many attempts have been made to *"spiritualise"* the promise of Christ's return. While some of the prophecies *are* set in a figurative or symbolic framework, (5) it is unreasonable to deny the solid fact that lies behind the symbolism. Some of the common spiritualisations are –

EVERY TIME A CHRISTIAN DIES, CHRIST RETURNS

Against this, we object that –

- The events described in 1 Th 4:16-17 do not occur at death.

- The statements in 1 Co 15:51 are flatly contradicted if the return of Christ means death.

- The Second Advent is a comforting hope (1 Th 4:18; Tit 2:13), whereas death is a bitter enemy (1 Co 15:26; Re 20:14).

---

(5) For example, references to the "trumpet" of God, and the like.

- At death we go to be with the Lord (Ph 1:23); but at the Second Advent Christ will come for us (Jn 14:3).

- Death and the return of Christ are clearly distinguished (Jn 21:23).

- Substitute the word "death" and many passages that speak of the Second Advent become meaningless (Mt 16:28; Ph 3:20; etc).

THE SECOND ADVENT OCCURRED ON THE DAY OF PENTECOST

This is partly true, as shown by Mt 16:28; Jn 14:1-3 ,18; etc. However, *all* the Second Advent promises contained in the NT letters were made *after* the day of Pentecost, nor is there any suggestion in those references that they refer back to the day of Pentecost.

THE SECOND ADVENT OCCURRED WHEN JERUSALEM WAS DESTROYED BY THE ROMANS IN 70 AD

Even the early church experienced some confusion over this, because of the way these two events are mingled in Jesus' *Olivet Discourse*. [6] Nonetheless –

- The overthrow of Jerusalem was a time of awful suffering, which led to the enlargement of the Roman Empire; but the return of Christ will be a glad time, both for Israel and the church, leading to the establishment of the kingdom of God.

- The events of 1 Th 4:16-17, etc, did not take place at that time.

---

(6)   Matthew 24:3 ff., etc.

- The Second Advent promises found in the letters of John and in the Apocalypse were all written after 70 A.D.

CHRIST COMES BACK IN CONJUNCTION WITH EACH HUMAN CRISIS

That is, whenever there is a great event in history, a disaster, a sweeping revival, or some spiritual crisis in a person, church, or community, Christ has come.

No doubt there is a sense in which that is true. But such "spiritual" comings of Christ fall far short of the stunning event described in scripture.

THE PROMISE WILL BE FULFILLED BY THE CHURCH

That is, the Second Advent promises are symbols of the victory Christ is gaining through his church. The church, they say, will succeed in its missionary mandate and will itself bring in the kingdom of God on earth.

However, the "remnant" [7] concept shows that the church will not be ultimately successful in "Christianising" the world; on the contrary, the scene at the very end is that of the church struggling to avoid being overcome *by* the world (Mt 13:24-30, 36-43; 24:9-13, 37-39; 25:31-33; and cp. also Ac 15:14).

THE PROMISE WILL BE FULFILLED IN HEAVEN

It is said that the Second Advent promises are symbols of the ultimate gathering together of the church in heaven, redeemed and glorified; that they refer to the distant future beyond the grave; that they will not have any specific fulfilment on earth; that human life will continue on this planet indefinitely, or

---

(7) 2 Kg 19:31; Is 1:9; 10:20-22; 11:11, 16; 37:31-32; Je 23:3; 31:7; Ez 14:22; Jl 2:32; Mi 5:7-8; Ro 9:27-28; 11:5; Re 12:17.

until humanity eventually perishes from natural causes.

Against those ideas we object –

- the present heavens and the earth are to perish, not by natural dissolution, but by a sudden cataclysm called *"The Day Of The Lord"* (2 Pe 3:10). They will be replaced by a *"new heavens and a new earth"*, within which the kingdom of God will be established for ever.

- time is not endless; it is distinct from eternity (cp Is 57:15); it is part of the created order, and it has a God-ordained terminus (cp 2 Pe 3:8-9). The biblical perspective on time is that it is neither random, nor cyclic, but linear, with both its beginning and end fixed by God [8]

THE PROMISE FULFILLED

Paul gives a graphic summary in *1 Thessalonians 4:16-17* ...

THE LORD HIMSELF SHALL DESCEND FROM HEAVEN

"THE LORD HIMSELF"

Paul is careful to declare that he means Christ in person. The Greek text is emphatic, as indeed is its English translation. Who is coming? It is *"the Lord himself!"* Language could hardly be plainer. He is not describing the believer's death, nor the day of Pentecost, nor any other event that people may suggest as the Second Advent of Christ. He is talking about *the Lord himself* coming in an advent that will be visible, definite, and at once recognisable as the actual return of Christ (cp also Ac 1:11).

---

(8)   See further comments below on the nature of time.

"Shall Descend"

This expression, *"shall descend"*, shows beyond any doubt that Christ will return from heaven to this earth. The scene of his humiliation is now to become the centre of his honour. He who carried the cross will now, in the same land, wear the crown (Zc 14:4-9).

"From Heaven"

The descent of Christ from *"heaven"* shows us – (9)

His Divine Right To Rule Over All The Earth

Christ will appear in the glorious majesty of the heavens, King of kings and Lord of lords. All terrestrial governments and thrones and rulers will be compelled to yield before him.

He Will Appear First In The Sky

Christ will in *"the clouds of heaven"* (Da 7:13; Mt 24:30).

- **To the ungodly**, they will be clouds of judgment, dark and lowering (Je 4:13; Mt 26:64; Re 1:7).

- **To the godly**, those same clouds will be swift chariots (Ps 104:3) conveying them to the Lord of all glory and mercy (Na 1:3, 7). They will be the blazoning symbols of his marvellous salvation (Is 44:22-23a), and of healing and deliverance (Is 25:4-8).

---

(9) I am treating the Second Advent as a single event, as indeed the Bible itself does. Some of the church Fathers did separate Daniel's 70th Week from the other "weeks", but the idea of dividing the return of Christ into two parts (pre- and post-tribulation) did not exist until the 19th century. These ideas are taken up in more detail below.

He Will Come With Power And Great Glory

Not this time the swaddling clothes of a helpless babe! Not this time the lowly manger! Not this time poverty and pain! No! When Christ appears the second time:

- it will be with great power; Mt 24:30; Lu 21:27.
- he will lead the massed armies of heaven; Re 19:14.
- he will be invested with superb majesty and military might; Re 19:11, 15.
- he will surge across the heavens in flaming fire, driving all before the glory of his power; 2 Th 1:8, 9.
- he will be pronounced King of kings and Lord of lords; Re 19:16.
- he will be crowned with many crowns; Re 19:12.
- he will be surrounded by the brilliant glory of God; Is 2:10, 19, 21; Lu 9:26; 1 Ch 29:11; Da 7:14.

Thus will *"the Lord himself descend from heaven"*!

"He Will Come With A Shout"

Not this time will he appear as the Christ of the child's lisping prayer, *"Gentle Jesus, meek and mild ..."* His coming on that day will be with supernal power and overwhelming majesty. Beforehand it was said of him,

> *He will not strive, nor cry; neither will anyone hear his voice in the streets* (Mt 12:19-20).

But now he is *"sending forth judgment unto victory"*, and he is silent no longer in the face of human sin.

In particular, this stupendous, awe-inspiring, heaven-rending, earth-shaking SHOUT of the Son of God will signify –

His Shout of TRIUMPH

- the exultant cry of an all-conquering Warrior; the calling of the nations to judgment (Ps 47:1-5).

His Answer to ISRAEL

- responding to their joyful acclamation of their Sovereign (Is 12:6; Zp 3:14-17).

His Cry of Victory Over DEATH

- as he awakens the righteous dead in preparation for the resurrection (Jn 5:25-29).

HE WILL COME WITH THE VOICE OF THE ARCHANGEL

Since the dawn of world history the angels have been silent. They have ministered to the heirs of salvation (He 1:14; Lu 1:26-27); but they have remained otherwise unseen and unheard. Hence the ungodly have scoffed at their existence. But now, at the hour of Christ's coming, with an awful declamation, the thunder of the archangel's voice will roar across the skies and resound around the earth. With startled ears and astonished eyes, men and women will witness the mystery of heaven being laid open!

How the angels must yearn to shout! What would you and I say if we had a place to stand and a voice to cry to the whole earth? *"A voice said, 'Cry!' and I said, 'What shall I cry?' 'All flesh is grass ... and the grass withers!'"* (Is 40:6).

But at last the restraint will be removed, and the mighty archangel of God will *shout*!

What will that immense Voice achieve?

IT WILL GATHER THE HOST OF HEAVEN

From every quarter of the universe, in serried ranks, *"all the holy angels"* will attend the Lord Jesus when he comes (Da 7:10); Mt 25:31; 2 Th 1:7). Their number beyond the multitude of the stars, they will come with Christ, not in ministering mercy, but in military might, to execute judgment upon the ungodly (2 Th 1:7-8; Jude 14, 15).

IT WILL BE THE VOICE OF A ROYAL HERALD

That Voice will call the heavens and the earth to make way for the Great King. It will cleave a passage through the skies, compelling all the nations to bend before Christ like dry grass before a summer gale (Is 64:1-2). How great the contrast with that former herald, who cried alone in the wilderness! (Mk 1:3).

IT WILL FORCE THE DOOM OF GOD

The wrath of heaven will fall upon the enemies of Israel while the voice of the archangel bids that ancient race rejoice, for their salvation is at hand. Thus Armageddon will be brought to an end. That Voice will desolate *Gog* and *Magog*, and bring to Israel the fulfilment of her promised redemption. For this is not the voice of Gabriel, the gentle messenger of mercy (Lu 1:26); it is the voice of that mighty and resplendent prince of battle, *Michael* (Jude 8), who has a special function as the Protector of Israel. His God-given charge in the latter days is to stand on Israel's side and to wage war on her behalf (Da 10:13; 12:1).

HE WILL COME WITH THE TRUMPET OF GOD

Who can imagine the terror that will chill the hearts of men when they hear the heavens torn open by the dread blare of that supernatural trumpet? What will it signify to the stupefied minds of the ungodly? What echo will it have in the leaping hearts of the godly?

IT WILL HAVE AN IMPACT UPON THE NATIONS

- compelling the attention of the whole earth (Is 18:3), creating alarm and dismay (Zp 1:14-16); for it is the war-cry of the Almighty against the peoples (Jl 2:1-2); and it heralds the imminent appearing of the Lord God himself (Re 1:10; 4:1; Ex 19:16-17).

IT WILL HAVE AN IMPACT UPON ISRAEL

- for it will be the final prophetic fulfilment of the ancient feast of trumpets (Le 23:23-25; Nu 29:1-6).

At the beginning of Israel's sacred year, the *Passover Feast* was observed; which typified the sacrifice of Christ upon the cross.

After fifty days, the *Feast of Pentecost* was observed; which typified the giving of the Holy Spirit to the church, and the fruitful missionary harvest promised by God.

Then came a long break until the wine harvest was gathered home; which typified the work of the Holy Spirit during this gospel age.

Finally, in the seventh month of the sacred year, at the end of the wine harvest, the *Feast of Trumpets* was celebrated. This feast ushered in the new civil year, picturing the establishment of a new era, the next stage in the development of God's eternal kingdom.

For the <u>church</u>, this feast typifies the completion of the gospel harvest, the joyful celebration of the ingathering of all whom God has chosen.

For <u>Israel</u>, in the latter days, the sound of the trumpet will draw that nation to its final discovery of the Lord's atonement for her sins, and it will inaugurate the last great time of Jubilee, bringing liberty, rest, and joy (Le 25:9-10; Is 27:13; 62:2 ff. – the *"acceptable year"* is the *Year of Jubilee*).

ABOVE ALL, IT WILL HAVE AN IMPACT UPON THE CHURCH

- for it will call the dead in Christ from their graves, and will cause the translation of all living believers, so that together they will be caught up to meet the Lord in glory (1 Th 4:16; 1 Co 15:52; Mt 24:31; Is 35:10; Mk 13:13, 27).

<u>This then is the manner of Christ's return.</u> It will be an event of incredible splendour, the glorious consummation of the age-old purpose of God, an utterly transcendent demonstration of the Lord's immense power and limitless sovereignty. Little wonder the apostle says –

> *Whatever we have to go through now is less than nothing compared with the magnificent future God has planned for us. The whole creation is on tip-toe to see the wonderful sight of the sons of God coming into their own"* (Ro 8:18-25, JBP).

How can we do otherwise than "*love his appearing*" (2 Ti 4:8), "*waiting for and hastening the coming of the day of God!*" (2 Pe 3:12, RSV).

Two

PROOF

Dr. Paul E. Little has written –

> *Both friends and enemies of the Christian faith have recognised that the resurrection of Christ is the foundation stone of Christianity ... either he did or he didn't rise from the dead. If he did, it was the most sensational event in all history, and we have conclusive answers to the profound questions of our existence: Where have we come from? Why are we here? Where are we going? If Christ rose, we know with certainty that God exists ... and the universe takes on meaning and purpose ... on the other hand, if Christ did not rise from the dead, Christianity is an interesting museum piece – nothing more."* (10)

And I would add, if Christ did not conquer death, then all hope of his return is obviously vain. If he did not rise, he cannot return! If he did rise, he will certainly return!

The unbreakable link between Christ's resurrection and his Second Advent was mentioned briefly in the last chapter. Here I want to look at some common objections to the resurrection of Christ, and then to examine the evidence in favour of the empty tomb. If we can establish beyond reasonable doubt that Jesus truly did rise from the dead, and ascended back into heaven, then we gain mighty confidence in the promise of his return.

---

(10) Know Why You Believe; Scripture Press Pub. Inc., Wheaton, Illinois; 1968; pg 26.

SOME COMMON OBJECTIONS

Here are some of the most common ways of avoiding what is clearly stated in scripture, that Jesus rose bodily from the grave after lying there, dead, from Friday afternoon to Sunday morning –

A SPIRITUAL RESURRECTION

Some scholars reject the idea that Jesus rose physically from the grave, and claim that the resurrection must be understood only in a spiritual sense. They try to retain the *values* of the resurrection, while denying the *event*. They describe the gospel stories as "symbols" used by the apostles to describe their *spiritual* experience of the glorified Christ.

But Christianity is unique in this: it is firmly rooted in historical fact, not abstract speculation. Our faith is not based upon great *ideas*, but upon what God has actually *done* in history. In the gospel, fact and faith are inseparable. The claims of the gospel are rooted in objective evidence, not in the clever imagination of a few pious thinkers; they deal with reality, not myth, and with observation, not fiction.

This objectivity sets Christianity apart from all other faiths. Other religions may be able to survive on the shifting foundation of human imagination, speculation, and invention. But our religion is inescapably based upon God's actions among men. If the history is wrong, then the doctrine is wrong. The integrity of Christianity, the validity of its claims, the authority of the gospel, all depend finally upon the fact of the empty tomb.

What eternal value could anyone gain from a mere legend? The benefit of an apple, for example, lies in the fact that it exists – an imaginary apple nourishes no-one! So the merit of the resurrection lies in the fact of its occurrence. To pretend otherwise is to live in a fool's paradise.

MIRACLES JUST DON'T HAPPEN

"Miracles do not happen!" So wrote the 19th century British philosopher, Matthew Arnold. His judgment is shared by many modern scholars. Their attitude is simply, nature is everywhere uniform; therefore, any event discontinuous with ordinary human experience is impossible. Such things just don't happen! Those who hold this view cannot accept the testimony of scripture on the resurrection of Christ. They openly discard that testimony, refusing even to consider it.

But we may well ask: does our philosophy determine what happened in history, or should history determine our philosophy? After all, if a man *has* risen from the dead, then that event becomes part of human experience; therefore it cannot be said to violate that experience.

The fact that an event has occurred only once in history (to the present date) does not discount it. How often must an action occur before it becomes acceptable? There are many things other men have experienced that have not been a part of my life. Does that invalidate them? Hardly! The fact is, whether or not the resurrection took place is a historical question – all the philosophical presuppositions in the world cannot alter what has indeed happened!

That miracles are impossible is an unproved assumption. The most any person can say is that he has never observed a miracle. But other reliable and honest witnesses say that they *have* observed miracles. Which witness is believed must be determined by criteria more substantial than intellectual prejudice.

Even if the theory of the uniformity of nature could be objectively proved (and proof continues to elude scholars [11]), it

---

(11) The "uniformity of nature throughout all its parts" (including the most distant galaxies) is unproved and unprovable scientifically (if by "science" we mean a theory that can be tested by personal

Continued on next page ....

would show that miracles are impossible only if it could also show that all the reports of miracles, which abound in both secular and sacred history, are false. But that is an impossible task! As Professor Clark H. Pinnock has pointed out, no historian can begin his work by dictating what history can contain. The historian must be open to whatever the witnesses report.

Again, is nature really so fixed and uniform that nothing outside our present or past experience can take place? How sparse our knowledge really is! Who is bold enough to say that he knows all the limits that gird natural law? Must the normal be measured strictly within the bounds of our experience to the present date? Yet how many of us would dare to predict the future? Many things have been achieved in our time that earlier generations would have reckoned fantastic! We cannot be sure that our experience is universal enough, nor our knowledge complete enough, to determine what may or may not be a possible happening in the past, present, or future.

So in the case of Jesus we may say –

- the question of whether he did or did not rise from the dead must be decided by the historian, working with the evidence provided by the Bible and by contemporary witnesses, not by the philosopher.

If history shows that Christ did rise from the dead, then the philosopher must adjust himself to this fact.

---

experiment). The "uniformity" proposition remains a philosophical assertion. It could be objectively proved only if someone were personally able to visit every single part of the universe, and conduct in each place a series of practical tests – which, of course, is absurd. The theory is no doubt true. But in the end, we affirm its truth only because God is consistent in all his behaviour (neither capricious nor arbitrary), and therefore his creation reflects the same orderly consistency. The universe itself offers no such absolute proof.

- no serious scholar doubts that Jesus of Nazareth lived in Judea in the first three decades of our era, and that he was crucified by the Romans at the instigation of the Jewish religious leaders.

Yet once that fact is accepted , we are faced with a life and character marvellously unique. No other like him has lived either before or since. Given this uniqueness, *his* resurrection may have been a perfectly natural event, in no way discontinuous with the laws of nature (cp Ac 2:24).

- the life, death, and resurrection of Jesus have been a part of nature since the first promise of Ge 3:15.

So the resurrection of Christ, while it was a unique event, was neither isolated nor unannounced. It was instead the necessary culmination of a series of events going right back to the beginning of creation. In that sense, far from being discontinuous with nature, the resurrection of Jesus has its roots in the very dawn of human history.

So, rejection of the resurrection of Christ simply on the grounds of a philosophical presupposition reveals, not balanced wisdom, but unwarranted bias.

THE GOSPEL NARRATIVES ARE LEGENDARY

Those who argue that the gospels are fiction usually presuppose that they were all written long after the death of Christ. Even if that contention could be established, the same cannot be said of the New Testament letters. For example, Paul's *Letter to the Corinthians* , in which he mentions all the salient features of the life, death, and resurrection of Christ, was written within 30 years of those events. Legends require more than three decades in which to grow. Remember also, when Paul wrote his letter, there were still hundreds of living witnesses of the events he describes (1 Co 15:1-8).

> *What gives a special authority to (Paul's) list as historical evidence is the reference to most of the*

five hundred brethren being still alive. St. Paul says in effect, "If you do not believe me, you can ask them." Such a statement, in an admittedly genuine letter written within thirty years of the event, is almost as strong evidence as one could hope to get for something that happened nearly two thousand years ago." (12)

THE APOSTLES WERE DECEIVERS

It may be that in the history of the race, individual men have been found who, swept by some fanaticism, have been willing to die for fraud ... But (the church) is not a case of isolated individuals, but of a whole company and society of men and women and children, ever increasing in number, all of them having to suffer ... All of the apostles save one died violent deaths, and he was exiled to a lonely island ... It is not within the compass of rational consideration to believe that men who so suffered, suffered for a story they themselves had invented. (13)

To argue that the early Christians perpetrated a deliberate fraud poses a psychological and ethical problem that is greater than the problem of the resurrection. How could good people have built a gospel, so forceful for truth, upon a deliberate lie? How could they have suffered torture and death so gladly,

---

(12) Quotation by professor William Lillie, taken from an article by professor E. M. Yamauchi, in Christianity Today magazine, March 29th, 1974, pg. 14. The original quotation comes from "The Empty Tomb and the Resurrection," a chapter in the symposium, "Historicity and Chronology in the New Testament;" 1965; pg. 125.

(13) Dr. G. Campbell Morgan. The source of this quotation is unknown to me.

knowing all the time that the message for which they were suffering was nonsense? How could they be supposed to have acted in a manner so foreign to all that we know about their character? Perhaps one man might be so fanatical; but how could there have been *four* such writers? Whatever else the apostles may have been, it is impossible to picture them as deliberate liars.

Nor is there any sign of collusion among the four evangelists, which you would certainly expect if the gospel stories were fictitious. On the contrary, the gospels are remarkable, not only for their likeness, but equally for their difference. Luke explains why – they were written at different times, by different men, for different reasons (Lu 1:1-4).

Even more telling, the numerous apocryphal gospels show what kind of stories imposters would have written. (14)

THE APOSTLES WERE DECEIVED

"I allow," says someone, "that the apostles were not liars. But they may well have been deceived. No doubt they were convinced themselves that Christ was risen from the dead; but they were suffering from a delusion. Perhaps, under the severe emotional stress of the crucifixion and the events surrounding it, they experienced a psychological trauma and saw an apparition of Christ."

Others add that, because of the intense longing they had for their Lord to rise from the dead, a mental hallucination came upon the disciples. They saw what they desperately *wanted* to see.

---

(14) Among many others, cp The Gospel of Peter, dated c. 150. Note there especially the claim that the soldiers actually saw Jesus come out of the tomb – an obvious attempt to lend authenticity to the story. By comparison, the canonical gospels are sober and restrained.

Those arguments can be easily dismissed –

- Modern psychology has shown that such shared hallucinations are common only to certain types of people.

They could not have been experienced by the large number of diverse people who claimed to be eyewitnesses, either of the resurrection itself or of Jesus' various post resurrection appearances. Paul boldly insists that 500 people at one time saw the risen Christ (1 Co 15:6).

- The suggestion that the resurrection appearances of Christ were no more than apparitions, caused by the overwrought disciples seeing what they craved eagerly to see, ignores one plain fact – the disciples had not the slightest expectation of seeing Jesus again!

Even when confronted with overwhelming proof that the Lord was indeed risen from the dead, they could hardly be persuaded to believe! (cp Mk 16:14). They even failed to recognise him when he did appear to them! (Lu 24:13-31; Jn 20:15; 21:4)

- It may have been possible for one or two of the Lord's closest disciples to have been deceived by some kind of visionary wish-fulfilment, but how can that be said of all the other post resurrection appearances of Christ?

Sometimes those appearances were witnessed by individuals, sometimes by small or large companies; and they were well separated in time and place.

Edwin Yamauchi writes –

> *Hallucinations do play a major role in religious cultures, but they are induced either by drugs or by the extreme deprivation of food, drink, and sleep ... These factors were not present in the various appearances of the risen Christ to his*

disciples ... The variety of conditions under which Christ appeared also militate against hallucination. The appearances to Mary Magdalene, to Cleopas, to the disciples on the shore of Galilee, to Paul on the road to Damascus, all differ in their circumstances. C. S. Lewis suggests – "... any theory of hallucination breaks down on the fact (and if it is invention it is the oddest invention that ever entered the mind of man) that on three separate occasions this hallucination was not immediately recognised as Jesus (Lu 24:13-31; Jn 20:15; 21:4)" (Miracles, 1947, pg 153) ... Finally, what rules out the theory of hallucinations is the fact that the disciples were thoroughly dejected at the death of Christ and were not, despite Christ's predictions, expecting a resurrection of their leader." [15]

CHRIST REVIVED FROM A SWOON

Here is a miracle greater than the resurrection! Jesus, we are told, recovered from a swoon, staggered out of the tomb, and convinced his disciples he had conquered death! How could such an absurd theory ever have gained any credence? Who could believe that a man exhausted from pain and loss of blood, brutally mutilated by the lash and the thorns, wounded by the nails and spear, could survive three days in the tomb? That by itself would be amazing. But we are asked to accept even more wonderful things! This man, bloodless, suffering toxic shock, broken and torn, was still strong enough to push away the great stone, scatter the armed guard, and majestically persuade 500 witnesses that he had trodden death under foot. Only

---

(15) "Easter – Myth, Hallucination, or History;" article in Christianity Today, March 15, 1974, pg 6.

prejudiced folly could believe such nonsense.

But let us suppose the swoon theory is indeed true. What then? Even if Jesus had performed the astonishing feat of reviving from a swoon, persuading everyone he had actually died, but was now alive again, he must eventually have died. His later inevitable death would have shattered any claim that he had ever been victorious over the grave.

The "swoon" theory requires us to believe that Jesus, who claimed to embody all that is true, and whose influence for truth has been and is incalculable, conspired with his disciples to deceive the world. Together, we are told, that group of men perpetrated a monumental fraud, unequalled in history. Only someone who refuses to see, hear, or understand, could take such monstrous silliness seriously.

The fact is, if Jesus was crucified on that Friday in old Jerusalem (and no one doubts that he was), he is either still buried, or he is alive for ever. Scripture is unanimous in asserting the latter. And not only so, but the writers of the New Testament speak about him (a man they had once known in human form) in the most exalted and staggering terms, despite facing torture and death. Why? How could they do so? Surely there is no sensible answer except the one they give themselves – yes, they had indeed known Jesus as a man; but then they had witnessed both his resurrection from the dead and his ascension. So now they can say no other than, he is risen, and he reigns from the most exalted throne in heaven, glorified as Lord, Saviour, and God.

THE BODY WAS STOLEN

Some writers attempt to explain the empty tomb by suggesting that the body of Jesus was stolen. But the Jews took steps to prevent this by placing a guard at the tomb (Mt 28:65, 66); thus the disciples were prevented from spiriting the body away. In any case, **to** suppose that the disciples stole the body is to involve them in a deceit that I have already shown should be impossible to believe.

Perhaps the Jews themselves stole the body? But then they could have destroyed the infant church at birth simply by producing the remains.

What about the Romans? They were not interested in the body of Jesus – they committed his body into the care of Joseph of Arimathea.

Every objection to the resurrection of Jesus that has ever been raised fails because all of them either –

- depend upon a philosophical bias that refuses to take the evidence seriously; or
- require belief in a social and psychological miracle at least as great (but not so probable) as that of the resurrection; or
- replace the resurrection with a moral and ethical absurdity.

Why do people refuse to believe that Jesus conquered death? Not because the evidence is inadequate. Rather, because for them any folly is preferred above acknowledging the lordship of the risen Christ!

THE RESURRECTION AS HISTORY

Luke was able to claim *"many infallible proofs"* that Christ was alive (Ac 1:3, KJV). How do we stand? Consider the following –

NOTHING ELSE EXPLAINS THE DOCTRINE

Resurrection, as distinct from *resuscitation*, was a radical new idea. There is no evidence prior to the gospels of any similar idea in any other religion. Who could believe that a group of fishermen, carpenters, tax collectors, could *invent* such an extraordinary story? But if it was not invented, what was its source? Surely nothing less than a simple record of what those men and women actually saw, heard, and felt (1 Jn 1:1-3).

A religion without *relics* was also a startling innovation. The later history of the church, the reverence people showed to any kind of relic of a martyr, the sacrifices they made, the wars they fought, the perjury they committed, just to get a relic, shows the natural bent of the human spirit. Throughout the ancient world, relics added authority and authenticity to a religion. The lack of relics of Christ was reckoned a scandal by later generations of superstitious Christians and their pagan neighbours. But why was there a lack? Had there been any possibility of a relic of Christ (for example, his grave clothes), the ancients would have seized it with joy.

There were no relics, first, because Jesus was risen; second, because the apostles, having seen the risen Christ, scorned any other memento of their Lord. His garments, his possessions, things he had handled – all were discarded as worthless. Christ *himself* was with them. What need had they of bits and pieces!

Later generations, who had lost that marvellous sense of the presence of the glorious Lord, craved every token they could seize. But the apostles present us with the wonder of a faith devoid of relics – a mystery that remains inexplicable apart from the resurrection of Christ.

NOTHING ELSE EXPLAINS THE CHURCH

Professor J. Pelikan, of Yale University, once claimed that

> *there are many problems ... connected with the reports of the Resurrection. But apologists for Christianity have maintained that none of these problems is as formidable as the problem of explaining the rise of the Christian church if there were no Resurrection. The transformation of the fleeing disciples into bold confessors was*

> *an even greater miracle than the Resurrection of Jesus Christ from the dead."* (16)

The resurrection was the only thing that made the sacrifices of the early Christians rational. If the tomb was not empty on that first Easter morning, then the disciples are made into a sorry company of clowns. Yet every page of their writings declares the opposite, that here were a group of men and women possessing astonishing spiritual power, who changed the world in their lifetime!

Nothing about the church makes any sense apart from the unshakeable faith of the first Christians that Jesus had died, then lived again three days later. As Dr. W. Pannenberg has pointed out –

> *It is hard to see what justification could be given for anyone to remain a Christian if he felt that the resurrection simply didn't take place.* (17)

Some say that any evidence brought forward to establish the resurrection, no matter how compelling it may be, is annulled by the very nature of the event. When confronted by such an amazing happening, isn't it more likely that the evidence is false, or has been misinterpreted? Which is more probable? That the resurrection occurred, or that the disciples were mistaken?

At first sight, that argument appears strong. But Dr. L. Burkholder has shown that it loses force in one particular circumstance – when the testimony is of such a nature that its falsehood would be more miraculous than the fact it endeavours to establish. I have shown above that this is certainly the case with the witness of the early churches about

---

(16)   Article, "Jesus Christ," Encyclopedia Britannica, 1963 ed., Vol.13.
(17)   I have lost the source of this quote.

the resurrection of Christ. (18)

The church has depended for its growth, not upon the sword (as, for example, in Islam), but upon the integrity of its witnesses (1 Jn 1:1-3; 1 Co 15:14-15). If those witnesses were fraudulent, how can the phenomenal expansion of the church be explained? It defies canons of logic, it violates the dynamics of life, to suppose that something whose growth depends upon truth, finds its actual increase through a lie.

NOTHING ELSE EXPLAINS THE EMPTY TOMB

Neither the Jewish leaders nor the Romans disputed that the tomb was empty, they merely gave another explanation of the awkward fact (Mt 28:11-15). However, if the tomb was empty because the disciples had hidden the body of Jesus, how were they able to preach with such passion and die with such courage? All for a lie? And it still has to be shown how they managed to overcome the Roman soldiers and roll back the stone. For men so distraught, so shattered, as the disciples were at that time, those very actions would have been miracles more improbable than the resurrection!

Other critics agree that the tomb the disciples visited was empty, but, they say, it was the wrong tomb! In the misty dawn, the women first, and then the men, mistook another empty tomb for the place where Jesus had been laid. But Joseph of Arimathea, in whose tomb the body had been sealed, would soon have rectified that mistake, not to mention the Jewish authorities, who had everything to gain by producing the body.

The critics also ignore the clear testimony of the disciples that they saw lying on the slab of stone the linen cloths in which the body had been wrapped (Lu 24:12; Jn. 20:4-10).

---

(18)   Ibid.

NOTHING ELSE SATISFIES THE APOSTOLIC MESSAGE

Many scholars, disliking anything that seems miraculous, say the resurrection was *"spiritual,"* that the *body* of Jesus did not rise, but only his *soul*. But if that were so, why did the early Christians use the physical terminology found everywhere in the NT? Simply because, in the Jewish mind of that time, resurrection from death could be thought of only in a bodily form; a so-called *"spiritual"* resurrection would have been inconceivable – see Jn 5:28-29; Mt 27:62-66; 1 Th 4:16-17; and cp the analogy of Jonah, Mt 12:40.

When Paul (the earliest writer we have who witnesses to the resurrection) asserts his belief that Christ rose from the dead, could he have done so without implying as self-evident that the tomb was empty, and that Jesus had risen bodily from the grave?

NOTHING ELSE EXPLAINS THE APOSTOLIC UNANIMITY

There is not a hint anywhere in the NT that any of the leaders of the early church ever questioned the resurrection. True, they began by mocking the report as an *"idle tale, and they did not believe the women"* (Lu 24:11); [19] but their early scepticism quickly gave way before the *"many infallible proofs"* of Jesus' triumph over death. From that time on they all bore witness to the resurrection with compelling certainty. They argued about many things, but never about this!

---

(19)   Both E. M. Yamauchi, and C. F. D. Moule comment on "the striking fact that the first appearances of the risen Christ were not to the apostles but instead to women." According to Jewish principles of evidence in those days, women were reckoned to be "notoriously invalid witnesses." If the resurrection story was a later Christian invention, composed in order to justify the message the church was preaching, the story would have been framed to avoid initial dependence upon female witnesses.

So firm was their conviction, they willingly submitted to hideous tortures and violent death rather than abandon their allegiance to the living Christ.

Men, women, and children do not easily sacrifice themselves for an idea unless they are assured of its absolute truth. A man might be willing to sacrifice himself for a belief that is flawed; but will he stand by and watch his wife, his little ones, be torn apart by wild animals, devoured by flames, sold into slavery, and made to suffer every kind of bestiality? Perhaps a lunatic fanatic might. But if there were even a shadow of doubt, any ordinary man would recant and save his loved ones. Yet the staggering truth remains that thousands of ordinary people, sensible, upright citizens, young and old, yielded themselves and those they loved to unspeakable torments rather than deny that Christ was risen. [20] They could not deny it. They knew it was true.

Could such unanimity, such absolute assurance, such unshakeable devotion, among so many, in so many different places, and from so many walks of life, have been established on the basis of a lie, a delusion, a fantasy?

NOTHING ELSE EXPLAINS THE DAY OF PENTECOST

The extraordinary events of the day of Pentecost (Ac 2:1-4, ff) were explained by Peter as a direct result of the resurrection of Christ (vs. 23, 24, 32-36). The evidence was so compelling that 3,000 people were at once converted, and their number continued to increase (vs. 41, 47); even *"a great many of the priests were obedient to the faith"* (6:7).

There was no city in the world more improbable than Jerusalem as the birthplace of Christianity. This new religion demanded the worship of a man who was presumed to have

---

(20)   Cp Eusebius, <u>Church History</u>, Bk 6, ch 41, 42, 43

been executed as a blasphemer and traitor, and who was now supposed to be risen from the dead. Further, his disciples were proclaiming him the only Saviour of mankind, the Creator of heaven and earth, the only Son of God. How contrary to the perception Jerusalem had of itself!

The Jews were fiercely monotheistic; yet Peter commanded them to recognise the deity of Christ (2:25-26). They revered Moses as their leader and David as their king; but now they must follow a labourer, Jesus of Nazareth (vs. 29-31). They were looking for a Messiah who would lead them to military victory over the Romans and create a great Jewish Empire; but now they are accused of murdering that same Messiah (vs. 23). They looked for an earthly king; but now they are told that he has ascended into heaven, and that his kingdom is not of this world (vs. 32-35).

No community on earth was less likely to believe the stunning declaration: *"Therefore you should know – and never doubt it – that God has made this Jesus, whom you crucified, both Lord and Christ!"* (vs. 36).

Yet thousands of them *did* believe, from prince to pauper, from priest to peasant. They believed because of the amazing happenings on the day of Pentecost, which proved to them beyond doubt that Jesus of Nazareth was indeed alive from the dead. Watching prophecy being fulfilled before their eyes, they could not resist the claim that Jesus of Nazareth was *"the Holy One of God"* who could not be imprisoned by death (vs. 27).

NOTHING ELSE SATISFIES BIBLICAL PREDICTIONS

Each of the following scripture references, by prophecy or type, portrays the resurrection of Christ in terms that demand his physical, literal triumph over death – Jn 2:19-22; Mt 12:40; Le 23:11; Ps 16:8-11 (cp Ac 2:24-28). See also Jn 5:24-29; 10:17-18. Jesus' resurrection was also prefigured by the several people he himself raised from the dead, notably Lazarus (Jn 11:1-44).

NOTHING ELSE EXPLAINS THE TRANSFORMED DISCIPLES

History contains no more enthralling record than the story of the millions of people, beginning with the first disciples, who have been transformed by the power of the gospel –

> *The psychological change in the disciples is striking. What transformed Peter, the man who could be unhinged by questions from a servant girl, into so bold a spokesman for the faith that the whole Sanhedrin could not silence him? ... The transformation of James the Just, Jesus' doubting brother, and of Paul, a convinced enemy of the fledgling church, is even more striking ... One of the Jewish beliefs held with most tenacity is observance of the Sabbath, and yet Christian Jews transferred their worship from Saturday to Sunday, which they termed "the Lord's day". Only some drastic consideration would have introduced this change – their weekly celebration of the Resurrection.* [21]

Perhaps the most dramatic change of all was wrought in Thomas (Jn 20:26-29). A dogmatic sceptic became a convinced believer! A thorough Jew, to whom anything even hinting polytheism or blasphemy was absolute anathema, falls on his face before Jesus of Nazareth crying, *"My Lord and my God!"*

The same proof is being offered today – the transformed lives of countless men and women, people who have found pardon, healing, liberation, renewal, in Christ, bear witness that he lives!

---

(21) Paul E. Maier, "The Empty Tomb as History," article in Christianity Today, March, 1975, pg 5

Did you notice in the quote above, that before the year 100 even *Jewish* Christians had forsaken the Jewish Sabbath, and were worshiping on Sunday, *"the eighth day ... the Lord's Day,"* the day of the resurrection. [22] What force was powerful enough to persuade those Jews to abandon centuries of tradition, to endure, when they worshipped on Sunday, the hatred and persecution of their neighbours? Nobody has ever been able to offer a better explanation than the one given in scripture – the resurrection of Christ established a new dynamic in the earth, and a new day of rest and celebration.

Think, too, about the scant success people have had when they tried to persuade the larger community to go back to worshipping on the seventh day, Saturday! And imagine what would happen if any attempt were made to force such a change upon the nation! People today cling to their traditions as fiercely as ever they did in the first century. Only something as cataclysmic as the resurrection can force such radical changes, especially on people who are deeply devout.

NOTHING ELSE SATISFIES THE CANONS OF HISTORY

If we cannot accept the witness of history to the resurrection of Christ, then we have little reason to accept the factuality of any event of those times.

Canon Westcott wrote –

> *Indeed, taking all the evidence together, it is not too much to say that there is no historical*

---

(22)   Cp the account of Sunday worship in Justin Martyr, <u>Apology</u> Bk 1, ch 45-47 (Bettenson, pg 66, 67).

> *incident better or more variously supported than the resurrection of Christ.* (23)

Professor F. F. Bruce insisted there is more contemporary evidence in support of the resurrection of Christ than there is of Julius Caesar's visit to Gaul, for which the primary source is his own (rather biased) book, *Commentaries on the Gallic Wars*! Nor did Caesar face any peril in writing his book. Nor did any dare contest his claims – at least, not in his lifetime! How different the status and trustworthiness of the writers of the four Gospels!

THE RESURRECTION AS AN ACT OF FAITH

It is true to say that the evidence of the resurrection does not establish it with mathematical certainty. Why is that? Why didn't God provide compelling, undeniable proof that the tomb was empty? Why didn't he demonstrate beyond all possible dispute that Christ is risen? Simply, because the evidence stops at a point that leaves room either for faith or for unbelief. God requires a moral choice here, as in every matter dealing with his revelation of himself to man.

Nonetheless, the evidence does create a high degree of probability for the event. And when faith responds to that evidence, personal experience of the power of Christ's resurrection makes the fact unassailable! (Ga 2:20) We believe; therefore we *know!* (24)

So then, confessing with our lips that Jesus Christ is Lord, and believing in our hearts that God has raised him from the dead, we discover his wonderful salvation – a salvation that will have

---

(23) Other aspects of the Resurrection of Christ, and more proofs of its historicity, are given in my book, <u>The Cross and the Crown</u>, Vision Publishing, Ramona, CA.

(24) He 11:3; Greek, pistei nooumen = "by faith we know", in the sense of "understand deeply", "perceive inwardly"; "grasp fully".

its glorious consummation when

> *Christ, once having been offered to bear the sins of many, will come a second time, not to deal with sin, but to save those who are eagerly waiting for him* (He 9:28; Ro 10:9).

Three

IMMINENCE

(People say) to themselves in their deluded way: "Our life is short and full of trouble, and when a man comes to his end there is no remedy; no man was ever known to return from the grave. By mere chance were we born, and afterwards we shall be as though we had never been, for the breath in our nostrils is but a wisp of smoke; our reason is a mere spark kept alive by the beating of our hearts, and when that goes out, our body will turn to ashes and the breath of our life disperse like empty air. Our names will be forgotten with the passing of time, and no one will remember anything we did. Our life will blow over like the last vestige of a cloud; and as a mist is chased away by the sun's rays and overborn by its heat, so will it too be dispersed. A passing shadow – such is our life, and there is no postponement of our end; a man's fate is sealed, and none returns." (25)

What a bleak and dismal view of life and of human destiny! It sounds as modern as tomorrow's secular newspaper article, yet it was written more than 2000 years ago! But what else can anyone say about life, whether then or now, if indeed it is true that *"no one has ever come back from the dead"*, that we have no hope beyond the grave, no destiny but worms?

---

(25) *From the OT apocryphal book The Wisdom of Solomon (2:1-6, NEB). The words are quoted to express the attitude of the ungodly, which the author rightly scorns.*

Happily, we Christians sing a different song – not a lament, but a refrain of laughing joy, for we *know* that Christ has conquered death, and that he is coming again to receive us into his glorious kingdom. The dead in Christ will be first to rise, then those who are alive and on earth when Jesus comes, for they too will be caught up with them into the air to meet the Lord, and so shall we ever be with the Lord! (1 Th 4:13-18).

That certainty has been the chief joy and hope of the church for twenty centuries. But is our hope valid? Will the Lord really come again?

To answer those questions, let me ask another: *what will result if Christ fails to come?* The answer: *CHAOS*! If the Second Advent does not take place, the plan of God will fail, for the return of Christ is the goal toward which the entire creation is straining (Ro 8:19-23). If Christ does not return, history will lose its purpose, and hope will vanish.

THE NECESSITY OF CHRIST'S RETURN

BIBLICAL INTEGRITY DEMANDS CHRIST'S RETURN

What is the most prominent doctrine in the Bible? The promise of Christ's return! Someone has calculated that this great event is mentioned in the Bible more than 300 times. In the OT there are 20 times as many references to Christ's return in glory as there are to his first coming in humility. Someone has said that one fifth of the Bible is prophecy, and that one third of prophecy relates to the return of Christ. The Second Advent is mentioned twice as often as the atonement.

I cannot either prove or disprove those claims, for to do so would take more time than I am willing to devote to the task. But after reading the Bible right through some 40 times, or more, I have no doubt that they are true in their general impact – that is, the doctrine of the Second Advent is not hidden in some dark corner of scripture, but stands boldly and prominently upon its pages in both testaments.

Such strong testimony binds the integrity of the entire Bible inextricably to the promise of Christ's return. If he does not come again the Word of God will be made a lie, human destiny will lack fulfilment, the consummation of God's glory will be denied, and the very foundations of the universe will be uprooted! (Mk 13:31; He 11:3).

OUR SALVATION DEPENDS UPON HIS RETURN

Undeniably, we still live in *"mortal and corruptible"* bodies; a state that will not be changed until Christ returns (1 Co 15:51-54). We read also –

> *Christ will appear a second time, not to deal with sin, <u>but to save</u> those who are eagerly waiting for him* (He 9:28) ... and again: *Our commonwealth is in heaven, and from it we await a Saviour, the Lord Jesus Christ, who shall change our lowly body to be like his glorious body* (Ph 3:20-21; see also 1 Jn 3:2).

So there is a definite *future aspect* of salvation that constitutes the great hope of the Christian. And this hope will not, cannot, be realised *until we hear the trumpet sound and see the Lord returning in glory* –

> *Let us put on the breastplate of faith and love, and for a helmet, <u>the hope of salvation</u>* (1 Th 5:8).

Faith and love, to be effective, must be crowned by **hope** – perhaps the loveliest word in our language. When *hope* is linked with the gospel it shows our certainty that Christ will come again. It looks toward the future consummation of our salvation. How empty *faith* and *love* would be if they were not crowned by the splendour of a joyful *hope* in the return of Christ!

See also Mt 10:22; Ro 13:11-12; 2 Ti 2:10; 1 Pe 1:3-5; along with Paul's dramatic saying –

> *If Christ has not been raised then our preaching is worthless, and your faith is useless ... you are still in your sins. Also, those who have fallen asleep in Christ have irrevocably perished. If we have hope in Christ only during this present life, then we are the most pitiable of all creatures.* (1 Co 15:14-20).

The resurrection of the dead is an essential part of our Christian faith. If there is no day of resurrection then we gain no advantage from Christ, and we may as well *"eat and drink, for tomorrow we die"* (vs. 32). So our great hope of a future completion of salvation can be realised only by a day of resurrection. *But when will this day be?* Only at the Second Coming of Christ! See 1 Co 15:51-58; and the related passage in 1 Th 4:13-18.

WORLD DESTINY DEPENDS ON HIS RETURN

Where is humanity heading? What is the goal of mankind? Will all things continue as they have from the beginning? What lies before us? If the promise of Christ's return is invalid, then we face millions upon millions of dreary years. Endless! Unchanging! Multiple centuries piling up with no discernible purpose, meaning, or value, until our planet is engulfed in some natural disaster and all life perishes.

Suppose the prospect facing humanity is nothing more than an infinite succession of generations. Suppose God does not intend to intervene in the course of human affairs. What then? At once a doom of eventual total extinction is pronounced upon the human race. Sooner or later, if the nations are left to control their own destiny, they will destroy both themselves and the earth. The past ten thousand years have seen no real change in human nature; there is little reason to suppose that the next ten thousand will be any more fruitful!

But quite apart from human action, current scientific thought proposes several ways in which the planet must one day inevitably be utterly destroyed – a large asteroid striking us; an ice age that will engulf all but a narrow equatorial strip under a sheet of ice three kilometres thick; massive earthquakes caused by colliding tectonic plates on the earth's surface; catastrophic climate change, caused by both human activity and natural factors; swallowed up by the sun when it finally turns into a red giant; and some other possible ways of ruin. Simply, one way or another, the planet is irresistibly doomed, and all life with it, unless God intervenes.

But suppose none of that were true. Suppose time and the earth will go on for ever. To look into the future and see nothing but an unending succession of hours, days, weeks, months, years, and generations, is an appalling prospect. Such a view leaves humanity with no true goal, no enchanting vision. Here is a recipe for despair. What else but frustration and futility can result from all the struggle and pain of the millennia leading nowhere? Must we say bleakly that eventually the world and all its inhabitants must live endlessly without destiny or purpose, except to survive? Will all human life just decay into final mindless ruin? Must we, and all those who have gone before us, and who will come after us, perish without hope, without meaning, our lives and efforts wasted and worthless?

Thank God, he *has* promised to intervene! *Christ is coming back to take the government upon his own shoulder*. Our faith is not vain! The world has a goal in the future: it is *moving toward the kingdom of God*. The works of man will not fall into empty oblivion. God, through the Second Advent of Christ, will draw all things together to his own glory and to the magnificent fulfilment of mankind's proper destiny.

CHRISTIAN INTEGRITY DEPENDS ON HIS RETURN

The entire Christian message irrevocably stands or falls on the doctrine of the Second Advent. This doctrine filled the minds and ministry of the early Christians. Again and again, as they faced the hostile might of the Roman Empire, and as they pitted themselves against the powers of darkness, they returned to this doctrine for renewed strength and courage.

Professor W. M. Arnett has written that the tremendous importance of the Second Advent is –

> *observed in the fact that it is bound up with the great doctrines of the Christian faith, such as the Deity of Christ (Mt 26:63-64); the Atonement (He 9:13-28); Sonship with God (1 Jn 3:1-2); Sanctification (1 Th 3:12-13; 5:23); the Resurrection (1 Co 15:23); Final Judgment (2 Ti 4:1); and the Promise of Rewards (2 Ti 4:7-8; Re 22:12; 1 Pe 5:4). Above all, its importance is seen in the fact that Christ declared it (e.g., Mt 24:25; Lu 21; Mk 13; Jn 14).* [26]

Furthermore, Dr J. Dwight Pentecost has pointed out the many practical exhortations that the New Testament draws from the doctrine of the Second Advent. Here are some of them –

- the doctrine is used as an exhortation to:

Watchfulness (Mt 25:13)	Sobriety (1 Th 5:2-6)
Repentance (Ac 3:19-21)	Fidelity (Mt 25:19-21)
Boldness (Mk 8:38)	Consecration (Mt 16:26-27)
Moderation (Ph 4:5)	Patience (He 10:36-37)
Self-denial (Cl 3:3-5)	Sincerity (Ph 1:9-10)
Endurance (1 Pe 1:7)	Holiness (2 Pe 3:11-13)
Brotherly Love (1 Th 3:12-13)	Heavenly Mindedness (Ph 3:20-21)
Assurance (Ph 1:6)	Hold Fast (Re 3:11)
Separation (Ti 2:11-13)	Carefulness (1 Co 4:5)
Hope (Mt 19:27-28)	Comfort (1 Th 4:14-18)

- and many others. [27]

---

(26) I have lost the source of this quote.

(27) Pentecost, J. Dwight; <u>Things to Come</u>; Dunham Pub. Co., Findlay, Ohio; 1959.

In other words, remove the hope of the Second Advent from the fabric of Christianity and the rest will fall apart. The hope of Christ's return gives substance and reality to all the doctrines of the gospel. This hope is the consummation of them all. Without it, they are made pointless, irrelevant, dull and deceptive.

Therefore, Christ must come. His coming will be the climax of world history, the culmination of the earthly pilgrimage of the church, and the inauguration of a glorious new era.

THE TIME OF CHRIST'S RETURN

See *2 Peter 3:1-13*. Have you ever been embarrassed by people who mock the promise of Christ's return? Peter faced the same problem. What was his response? All the arguments that have ever been raised against the Second Advent, says Peter, can be condensed into two objections –

THE PROMISE IS UNRELIABLE

Peter quotes the critics as saying, *"Where is the promise of his coming?"* In the idiom of the day, that was not a question, but a mocking denial that the event would ever occur. But why would people want to deny the promise? Mostly because of its apparent failure to be fulfilled on time. How common that protest is in our time! People deride us – *"Twenty centuries have passed and Christ has not come. How can you hold on to such a threadbare hope?"*

What *does* the Bible say about the time of Christ's return? Are there any signs we can observe? Should we say that many prophecies remain to be fulfilled before he can come? Should we expect his return at any moment? Is his coming imminent or distant?

AN EARLY DISAPPOINTMENT

Jesus himself taught that certain things had to happen before his Second Advent could occur –

- the Comforter had to come (Jn 14:26)
- the gospel had to be preached throughout the world (Mt 24:14; Ac 1:8)
- Paul was given certain duties and promises (Ac 9:15; 23:11; 27:14)
- Peter must first die (Jn 21:18-19)
- Jerusalem must fall (Lu 21:6, 20-22)
- an apostasy must first occur (2 Th 2:2)
- Christ must be absent for *"a long time"* (Mt 25:19; Lu 19:11). (28)

Nevertheless, all of that was seemingly fulfilled within a generation of the resurrection –

- the gospel had been carried to the ends of the Roman Empire, and beyond (Cl 1:6, 23)
- Jerusalem had been destroyed by the Romans (c. 70 AD)
- Peter and Paul had been martyred
- Christ left the time of his return open in his last conversation with his disciples, neither affirming nor denying that his kingdom would be swiftly established (Ac 1:6-7).
- similarly, Jesus left open the possibility that he would return before the death of John (Jn 21:20-23).

Many early Christians interpreted that possibility as a

---

(28) From a list given in The Imminent Appearing of Christ, by J. Barton Payne; Eerdman's Pub. Co, Michigan, 1962.

certainty. Their disappointment became bitter when the decades rolled by with no sign of Jesus coming upon the clouds of heaven.

Try to imagine also the impact of the following sayings upon their original hearers. If you had been standing among those crowds, you too would have thought, *"There will only be a short delay before the sky tears apart and Christ appears in his glory!"* – Mt 16:28; 24:33-34, 42-44; Mk 13:33-37; Lu 12:35-40; 21:34-36; Ac 1:6-7.

So, for many reasons, there was a fervent expectancy in the early church that the Second Advent would soon occur – if not with the death of John, at least, not long after. Note the sense of imminence in the following – Ro 13:11-12; 1 Co 1:7-8; 7:26, 29, 31; 10:11; 11:26; 15:51; 2 Co 4:14; Ph 1:10; 3:20-21; 4:5; 1 Th 1:9-10; 4:15; 5:1, 2, 10; 1 Ti 6:14; Tit 2:12-13; Ja 5:8, 9; 1 Pe 1:20; 4:7; 1 Jn 2:18; Re 1:3; 3:11; 22:7, 12.

Just a casual scan of those verses is enough to show that the apostles generally expected the return of Christ to happen soon, probably within their own lifetime. Everywhere you turn in the NT you find this sense of imminence, sometimes plainly stated, sometimes implied – for example, Paul, when he included himself in the phrase *"we who are still alive"*, must have been expecting the rapture to occur before his death (1 Th 4:15). If he had thought, when he wrote to the Thessalonians, that the coming of Christ was still far distant, he would have used the pronoun *"they"*, not *"we"*.

Desiring to be rid of the trammels and struggles of the flesh, Paul was not waiting for death, but rather for the coming of Christ (Ro 8:19, 23, 25; Ph 3:20-21). He held to a firm hope, at least during the early years of his ministry, that Christ would come in his life-time. That hope must have been legitimate, or it would not be recorded in scripture. Notice also the almost complete silence in the NT on the question, *"Where are the dead?"* In the one place where Paul had an ideal opportunity to express his views on this matter, he chose to ignore it altogether (1 Th 4:13-18). Rather, he focussed the attention of the Thessalonians on the Second Advent. The impression conveyed is that *"where are the dead?"* was not a major problem for the early Christians. Why not? Because they possessed such a vivid hope of the nearness of Christ's return!

Later Peter (2 Pe 1:14), and then Paul (2 Ti 4:6), realised that they would die before the Second Advent; but they still reckoned the return of Christ would not be long delayed (cp 1 Ti 4:1; 2 Ti 3:1; 4:1-5). Even He 10:25, 37, written after most of the apostles had died, still beats with hope of the quick coming of Christ. The author could see *"the Day"* of Jerusalem's downfall approaching, and was convinced that the Second Advent must follow soon after. Finally, the one "sign" remaining was that of the apostle John. His approaching death brought the hope of Christ's near return to a fever pitch. When he died, toward the end of the first century, without the promise being fulfilled, many people began to question whether Christ would ever come. Indeed, after the turn of the century there was a great falling-away from the church. Multitudes of people felt the gospel could no longer be trusted.

A C*ONTEMPORARY* D*ISAPPOINTMENT*

We faced a similar crisis

Millions of people during the early decades of the 20th century fervently expected the return of Christ. They were influenced by various popular preachers, widely sold books on Bible prophecy, the Scofield reference Bible, and, of course, by the awful cataclysms of World Wars I & II.

Many of the more pious refused to buy or build houses; they scorned education, reckoning the time was too short; they rented halls rather than build churches; they withdrew from university and college, and years later died frustrated and unhappy in low-paying jobs. Some borrowed heavily, thinking they would never have to repay the loans, and were crushed by debt, bringing shame both upon themselves and the gospel. They hindered their daughters from marrying (Lu 21:23); they postponed having children; they retreated to the mountains or the desert, hoping to wait out the "Great Tribulation".

They all died with their hope unfulfilled. The books they wrote, full of "signs of the times" now collect dust.

I once talked with an elderly Swede, who was 85 in 1982. He told me about his father, now long dead, who was an early Pentecostal preacher. He still remembered his father's fervent sermons on the nearness of Christ's return, and how sure the old man was that he would live to see the Lord coming upon the clouds of heaven. Now the fiery preacher's son has himself joined his father in heaven. And Christ still delays his return.

Such stories could be repeated a million times, from every part of the evangelical and Pentecostal world. Indeed disappointed hope led many during the middle part of the century to abandon the church and the gospel. Yet that may be a slight trouble compared with the on-going disillusionment that many continue to experience now that the 21st century is well under way without any sign of the arrival of the Last Day. The problem arises from

Unwarranted and Unwise Predictions

During the last half of the 20th century many books, preachers, conferences, and magazine articles, boldly declared that *"the very last of the last days"* had come. At various times, by various "authorities" the years 1953, 1965, 1975, 1982, 1985, 1992, and others, were declared in advance to be key terminal points. If those years did not actually bring the Second Advent, it was said, they would at least launch *Armageddon*! Of course every one of those foolish soothsayers was left floundering when the 21st century dawned without any unusual cataclysm occurring.

Yet millions of Christians still remain sure that the Christian era cannot continue beyond this present century. They remain certain that Christ will return before the year 2100. Those expectations, of course, may yet prove to be correct! But what if they are wrong? It is not difficult to see disappointed hope crushing the faith of multitudes.

What went wrong for the early church, for many in the last century, and perhaps for many at the end of this? Is the promise false? Or is the common interpretation of the promise mistaken? Before answering those questions, let us look at the *second objection* people have raised against the promise –

THE PROMISE IS IMPOSSIBLE

Peter, you may remember, quoted the objectors as saying: *"All things continue as they have from the beginning."* You have probably heard similar cavils, for that same argument is echoed by sundry philosophers and scientists in our time, who talk endlessly about *"a stable and closed natural system ... the uniform and unchanging pattern of natural law,"* and so on.

The jargon used today is different, but the meaning is the same. It is the old refrain intoned by Peter's opponents: *"The world is the same today as it has always been; ergo, the Second Advent is impossible, for such an event would introduce an unnatural discontinuity, a violation of the proper order of things."*

Summary thus far: notice that the two arguments cited by Peter are all that can be said against the promise of Christ's return; that is

- you can reject the idea of a Second Advent because of a presumed failure of the promise; or
- you can reject it because of a presumed philosophical or scientific impossibility.

Peter had an answer for both of those objections –

TWO REASONS FOR AFFIRMING THE PROMISE

See *2 Peter 3:5-7*. Peter derides those who say that all things have continued unchanged from the beginning. They wilfully ignore, says he, God's two earlier radical interruptions of an existing state –

- ***first,*** when he acted to create the physical universe
- ***second,*** when he acted to bring judgment upon the world through the Flood (an event that has been strikingly confirmed by modern archaeology).

Peter then says, <u>the same word of God</u> that worked then, is now at work again, preparing the world for a final judgment by "fire". As surely as the Lord God fulfilled his plan to create the heavens and the earth and all that is in them, and as surely as he brought down the waters in judgment upon a corrupt civilisation, so he will fulfil his announced intention for the age to come.

Nothing can prevent Christ from appearing at the appointed hour. The day of redemption will dawn for his church. The day of judgment will glower upon the ungodly. God has spoken. His word cannot be turned back.

Someone cries out, *"But <u>when</u> will these things happen?"* Peter gives a remarkable answer (vs. 8, 9). Far from being dismayed by an apparently inexplicable delay in the coming of Christ, we should learn to count the years as God counts them, for whom a thousand years is like a mere day!

But can God bend time like that? Can even the almighty be so cavalier about the passage of centuries, as if they were nothing?

Let us explore this mystery.

Four

TIME

> Go, and catch a falling star,
> Get with child a mandrake root,
> Tell me where all past years are,
> Or who cleft the Devil's foot ... [29]

"Tell me where all past years are?" cried the poet, and voiced one of the greatest mysteries of human experience. What happened to the world that existed just a moment ago? This present world is not the same as the one that was here in the past second. But where did that one go? And from where does the world come that we shall enter in the next moment? The world's deepest thinkers have been baffled by the mystery of time. Even Solomon had to admit ignorance –

> *God has made everything to harmonise with its own time; thus he has given to men and women an awareness of the passage of time. Yet they are unable to grasp how God's work begins, nor how it will end.* (Ec 3:11).

In our science, time is joined with space as one of the two basic building blocks of the universe. Nonetheless, as far as we know, in the entire universe only we humans are conscious of time. Even on Earth, time is a concept found only in fairly advanced cultures; among primitives it has little meaning, and often their languages lack any past tense. Primitive peoples appear to live – as do other sensate beings – in a kind of timeless present. Thus time is basically an abstract riddle that exists only in

---

(29)   The opening lines of John Donne's poem, Go, and Catch a Falling Star.

certain human minds; it has no concrete reality of its own.

In our culture, time is a familiar measuring tool. But what are we measuring? We all know what it is – until somebody asks us to explain it! We *sense* what time is much better than we can *show* what it is! Thus **Augustine** asked (c. 400 A.D.) –

> *What is time? Who can easily and briefly explain it? Who can ever begin to understand it, let alone speak a sensible word about it! Yet in daily conversation there is nothing we refer to more familiarly and knowingly than time. We know just what we mean when we speak about time, and we know what others mean when they speak about time to us. What then is time? If no-one asks me, I know; but if I am asked to explain time, then I no longer know.* (30)

Time is essentially a perception of movement. But from what, to what? The past has no existence, except in our memories (otherwise everyone would be condemned for ever to keep on doing everything they have ever done!) The future has no existence, except in our imagination, our anticipation of it. We have only the present moment, which we cannot find any way to grasp. Not even our clocks can seize the present. They show us, not what the time is now, but what it was an instant ago. This idea of movement, along with the mystery of from where to where, is expressed in this poem by Samuel Coleridge –

> On the wide level of a mountain's head
> (I knew not where, but 'twas some faery place),
> Their pinions, ostrich-like, for sails outspread,
> Two lovely children run an endless race,
> A sister and a brother!
> This far outstripp'd the other;

---

(30) Confessions, Bk 11.14.17; paraphrase mine.

> Yet ever runs she with reverted face,
> And looks and listens for the boy behind:
> For he, alas! is blind!
> O'er rough and smooth with even step he pass'd,
> And knows not whether he be first or last. (31)

The problem of the infinite divisibility of time was pondered by a 5th century BC Greek, **_Zeno of Elea_**. He wondered how a second could consist of smaller intervals, which themselves could be broken up into still smaller ones, and so on without end. Many thinkers have grappled in vain with this paradox.

Perhaps time is simply moving from the present into the present; but that doesn't make much sense, for then time would cease to exist altogether, and become eternity.

So **_Augustine_** again –

> *I say with confidence that I know that if nothing passed away there would not be past time; and if nothing were coming, there would not be future time; and if nothing were, there would not be present time. Those two times, therefore, past and future, how can they be, when even the past now is not, and the future is not as yet? But should the present be always present, and should it not pass into time past, time truly could not be, but eternity.* (32)
>
> *That I measure time, I know. But I do not measure the future, for it does not yet exist; nor do I measure the present, because it occupies no*

---

(31) Samuel Taylor Coleridge (1634-1693), Time, Real and Imaginary – An Allegory. Coleridge said that he was trying to express the difference between "time real and time felt", that is, between "time objective and subjective".

(32) Op. cit.

> *measurable space; nor do I measure the past, because it has gone out of existence.*

What therefore do I measure? (33)

> *In what part of space, then, do we measure passing time? Do we measure time in the future, for the present moment has come out of the future? But the future as yet does not exist, so how can we measure it? Or do we measure time in the present, through which it is passing? But neither does the present moment occupy any space – for as soon as the moment arrives, it is gone again; it lingers not at all. Or do we measure time in the past, into which it passes? But how can we measure that which has no existence, except in memory? ...*

> *My soul yearns to know this most tangled enigma ... I confess unto thee, O Lord, that I am as yet ignorant as to what time is; and again I confess unto thee, O Lord, that I know that I speak these things in time, and that I have already long spoken of time. How then do I do this, when I know not what time is?* (34)

Augustine claimed that the universe and time were created together, but he saw time as a distinct entity. He disputed the idea that time is actually dependent upon the physical creation, and that it is marked by the motions of the universe. He was wrong of course, because modern science has shown the unbreakable link between the universe, time, and motion through space. (35)

---

(33) Ibid. ch, 26.
(34) Ibid, ch 21, paraphrased; ch 22; ch 25
(35) City of God, ch 6; and Confessions, Bk 11.23.29.

- ***John Hobbes*** (17th century English philosopher) claimed that only the present has any existence in nature; the past exists only in memory; the future has no existence at all.

- ***William James*** (late 19th century American philosopher) –

  Let anyone try, I will not say to arrest, but simply to notice or attend to the present moment. One of the most baffling experiences occurs. Where is it, this present moment? It has melted in our grasp, fled ere we could touch it, gone in the instant of becoming! (36)

- ***Richard P. Feynman***, American physicist and Nobel Laureate –

  What is time? We physicists work with it every day, but don't ask me what it is. It's just too difficult to think about! ...

  The Western idea that past, present, and future are arranged in a straight line – that time does not repeat – seems to have grown out of a Judeo-Christian tradition, in which events like the creation and Christ's resurrection take on special meaning because they occur in a sequence. It may also lead to a belief in life after death, rather than in earthly re-incarnation.

  Today when we glance at the clock and rush out the door, we are running our lives by a system of Babylonian numerology, coupled with Egyptian technology, within the framework of an Old Testament creation epic – all synchro-

---

(36)   Principles Of Psychology, ch 15.

> *nised by a technology that can split a second into unlimited pieces. ...*
>
> *Clocks and calendars create the illusion that we live in a world of mathematically measured segments of time.* (37)

Our concept of linear time has had a profound impact upon our culture, shaping our ideas of progress, and also (more destructively) creating in us a compulsion to cram everything possible into our lifetime, since there will be no other opportunity. Other cultures, where time is viewed as a repeating cycle, have not been driven by the same sense of urgent need to utilise effectively every moment.

Yet in reality, the only thing we can logically demonstrate is that we live in a kind of continuous flowing present, consisting of a few seconds before and behind each event. The present cannot be a hard, measurable instant, with clear boundaries. It must have a kind of "sponginess" about it, a vague definition. If it were only instantaneous, quite distinct from the moment before and after, we would not be able to make the necessary connections between such things as words in a sentence, or notes in a piece of music. Only as we are able to connect these things one with the other can they be transformed into coherent and continuous experiences – (38)

> *You would measure time the measureless and the immeasurable.*
> *You would adjust your conduct and even direct the course of your spirit according to hours and seasons.*
> *Of time you would make a stream upon whose bank you would sit and watch its flowing.*

---

(37)   National Geographic magazine, March 1990; pg. 109, 128, 129.
(38)   Ibid.

> *Yet the timeless in you is aware of*
> *life's timelessness,*
> *And knows that yesterday is but today's*
> *memory and tomorrow is today's dream.*
> *And that that which sings and contemplates in*
> *you is still dwelling within the bounds of that*
> *first moment which scattered the stars*
> *into space.*
> *Who among you does not feel that his power to*
> *love is boundless?*
> *And yet, who does not feel that very love,*
> *though boundless, encompassed within the*
> *centre of his being, and moving not from love*
> *thought to love thought, nor from love deeds to*
> *other love deeds?*
> *And is not time even as love is, undivided*
> *and spaceless?*
> *But if in your thought you must measure time*
> *into seasons, let each season encircle all the*
> *other seasons,*
> *And let today embrace the past with*
> *remembrance and the future with longing.* (39)

In the end we must turn back to scripture, where we learn that time was created by God, who inhabits eternity (Is 57:15), and he is not under time's compulsion, as we are.

We must learn to see time as God sees it, and to realise that time is the vehicle that carries us irresistibly on into the purpose of God. This is admittedly a great mystery, which Peter expressed simply in his saying: *"One day is to the Lord a thousand years, and a thousand years is one day!"* (2 Pe 3:8)

He means that in the economy of God there is neither delay nor

---

(39)   Kahlil Gibran, <u>The Prophet</u>; Alfred A. Knopf, New York, 1968; pg. 62, 63.

haste. What may seem premature to us, is delayed to God; what seems delayed to us, is premature to God – except that, in reality, *with God everything is simply right on time!*

Hence we are called to steadfast patience (He 10:35-39). Did you notice in that passage the seeming conflict between *"he is coming soon"* and *"you must be patient"*? The first is spoken from God's perspective, and the second from ours. But however we view it, Christ will assuredly come at the time appointed by the Father.

THEORIES OF TIME

Still, despite our confidence that *"our times are in his hand"* (Ps 31:15), the nature of time remains one of the deepest mysteries in life. Philosophers have wrestled with it for centuries, yet today are no closer to understanding time than they were ten thousand years ago.

There are four major theories about the passage of time –

THE RANDOM THEORY

This is the view of the existentialist and atheist, that every event is unplanned, unguided, without purpose or form; a view sternly castigated in scripture (cp Je 50:45-46). It could be diagrammed thus, as a collection of random points without any borders –

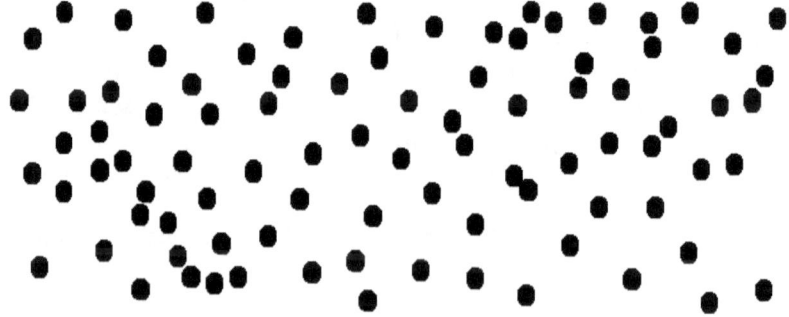

THE INFINITE THEORY

Aristotle argued for this view, by contending that every "now" implies a "before"; therefore time had no beginning, and probably will have no end. Tatian (an Assyrian Christian apologist, c. 150 A.D.) retorted –

> *Why do you Greeks divide time, saying that one part is past, and another is present, and another future? For how can the future be passing when the present exists? As those who are sailing imagine in their ignorance, as the ship is borne along, that the hills are in motion, so you do not know that it is you who are passing along, but that time remains present as long as the Creator wills it to exist.* (40)

Tatian's argument has its own weakness, as we shall see later; but the Assyrian was certainly closer to scripture than were the Greeks. Against the ancient Greek opinion stand the ideas in Re 21:6; 22:13, and other passages.

The *Infinite View* of time could be diagrammed as a line extending endlessly in either direction –

THE CYCLIC THEORY

Other Greeks held the view that time is an endless repetition of identical cycles, a view that is also held by Buddhists, and by a number of modern scientists. Heraclitus (c. 500 B.C) thought that the cycles of time were built around a cosmic year of 360 generations, which he calculated as 10,800 years. The ancient

---

(40)   Address To The Greeks, Ch 26.

Chinese taught a 129,800 year cycle.

The 3rd century B.C. Greek Stoic philosopher Chrysippus (who wrote 700 books, of which only a few fragments now remain) held to this cyclic view. William Barclay writes –

> *The Stoics believed that there are certain fixed periods, that at the end of each period the world is destroyed in a great conflagration, and that the same story in every littlest detail takes place all over again. As Chrysippus had it:*
>
> *Then again the world is restored anew in a precisely similar arrangement as before. The stars move again in their orbits, each performing the same revolutions as in the former period, without any variation. Socrates and Plato, and each individual man, will live again, with the same friends and fellow-citizens. They will go through the same experiences and the same activities. Every city and village and field will be restored, just as it was. And this restoration of the universe takes place, not once, but over and over again – indeed, to all eternity, without end.* (41)

The prophets, however, did not agree (Is 45:16-17). They rejoiced in the ongoing purpose of God that reaches irresistibly into eternity.

The cyclic view could be diagrammed thus –

---

(41) <u>The Daily Study Bible</u> – Matthew Vol. Two; St Andrew Press, Edinburgh; 1965. Commenting on Matthew 24:3, 14, 27, 28.

THE LINEAR THEORY

This is the biblical view, and indeed, would not exist without the witness of scripture (2 Pe 3:8-9). It teaches that time has an origin and a terminus in the creative purpose of God. The Bible insists that we are destined to escape the confines of time, and to enter the realm where God dwells, that is, eternity. We are therefore called to live with a goal (Ph 3:13-14).

This biblical, linear view of time could be diagrammed as a straight line with a clearly marked beginning and end, except that the line is complete only to the present moment –

THE MYSTERY OF TIME

So we must learn to see time as God sees it. He is not under time's compulsion, as we are. He dwells beyond time, inhabiting eternity (Is 57:15).

We are therefore called to steadfast patience (He 10:35-39). Christ will surely come at the time appointed by the Father.

When will that time be?

That question is taken up in the next chapter.

Five

INDICATIONS

See *2 Peter 3:9-15.*

WHY THE SECOND ADVENT IS DELAYED

Do you wonder why God has so long delayed the return of Christ? What is the Father waiting for? Are there any signs to tell whether or not the hour is near?

Scripture shows that certain *principles* are at work, controlling the time of Christ's return, and determining the attitude we should have toward that great event –

THE PRINCIPLE OF CERTAINTY

Let us begin by ridding our minds of all doubt about the event itself. Nothing is so emphatically declared in scripture as the fact of Christ's return. What could be stronger than Peter's declaration –

> *The day of the Lord <u>will</u> come like a thief, in which the heavens will pass away with a thunderous roar, and the elements will undergo a fiery dissolution, and the earth and everything on it will be burned up* (vs. 10).

If you know anything at all, you should know this: **that day <u>will</u> come!** And if God doesn't bring it on, nature will. For science has shown us that eventually our sun will begin to expand, and the earth will indeed grow so hot that even the vast mountains will turn into molten lava. All life will be extinguished. We had better hope that the Lord will act first!

But *when* will it come?

No one knows.

The year, the day, the hour – in fact, the century – are locked within the mystery of God's purpose. All attempts to predict the time of Christ's return have failed in the past, they are failing now, and they will fail in the future. The reason for this failure lies in –

THE PRINCIPLE OF UNCERTAINTY

Many Potential Fulfilments

I have written above that the early church, for a short period, could not have expected an imminent return of Christ. Certain things had to happen before Jesus could appear again in his glory. But that period soon passed, and from then onward devout Christians everywhere lived in daily anticipation of the coming of their Lord.

We too should maintain a joyful expectation of seeing Christ appear in the clouds of heaven – not tomorrow, but *today*!

But at once we face a problem. How can we live with a sense of the imminent appearing of Christ when many people claim there is still a large body of prophecy to be fulfilled, antecedent to his return?

You may find an answer in the following –

Repeating Patterns

The main events foretold, so far as they have been understood by each generation, have always had in current events a potential fulfilment. For example, every age has had its "Antichrist". One generation found him in the Roman Caesars; another in the Muslim Caliph; the Reformers saw him in the Papacy; another in Napoleon Bonaparte, or in one of the dictators of our time.

From our vantage point we can see how those old interpretations were wrong. We chuckle at our forefathers eager expectation of the Lord's near return. But although their hope was not fulfilled, within the limits of their contemporary knowledge and experience, it was justified. It served them well, by bringing them great comfort and incentive to righteousness. (42)

---

(42)   Lalage Pulvertaft writes: "(In the Germany of the 15th and 16th centuries A.D.) there was an absolute belief in Hell fire, (and) the end of the world was a real fear... (When) it had not arrived at 1000 A.D., it was expected at 1500 ... In 1525, the constellations moved into Pisces, and the Deluge was imminently expected. People took lodgings in the tops of houses, there was serious talk of moving the government into the mountains." (International History Magazine, June, 1973.)

The fears of medieval Europe proved groundless. The end of the world did not come, and life continued as before. Tertullian, one of the church fathers, who lived around 200 A.D., thought that the only thing keeping the world from coming to an end was the might of the Roman Empire. But the empire fell, and the world struggled on! At the approach of the year 1000 A.D., millions were sure that the end of the world was nigh. As the Black Death plague ravaged Europe, people who read their Bibles were certain that this was a sign of Christ's return. Martin Luther, commenting on what he believed were "the signs of the times" in his day, wrote: " ... the day of judgment is not far off. Christ's words and these signs move me so to believe. For whatever chronicles we may read of the time of Christ until now, we shall not find a parallel to the present century ... The world has reached its culmination in what relates to temporal interests or what Christ called the cares of this life, eating, drinking, building, planting, buying, selling, marrying and caring for children, and the like ... Whoever considers must acknowledge that this cannot hold much longer." (From Plain Truth Magazine, December, 1973.)

Encyclopedia Britannica, Vol. 15, pg. 496, ed. 1963, points out that expectation of the millennium was strong among "the leading sectors from the 13th to the 15th centuries ... and in the revolutionary movements of the 15th and 16th centuries – especially in the Anabaptist movements ... The German and Swiss reformers also believed that the end of the world was near."

Continued on next page ....

Ambiguous Oracles

Even in the clearest prophecies there is an element of uncertainty, which was no doubt designed by God to leave room for faith and to keep us alert. Here are some examples –

- Christ's suggestion that John might live to see the Second Advent (Jn 21:22-23)

- the kingdom of God can be hastened through prayer and spreading the gospel (Mt 6:10; 24:14), which means the time cannot be absolutely fixed in advance. In some mysterious way the church itself is a partner with God in determining both the course of the future and the hour of Christ's return.

- some of the Lord's statements to his disciples are clearly ambiguous; see Ac 1:6-7; Mt 10:23; 16:28; Lu 9:27; 21:28, 31-32.

Many believe that Jesus' statement, *"this generation shall not pass away"* (Lu 21:32), leaps across the centuries to our own time, or perhaps to a time still future. They may be right. But, as I have suggested above, if you had been there when Jesus addressed the crowds, what would you have thought of his constant use of the pronoun *"you"*? Surely you would have accepted without hesitation that he was speaking to *you* and to *your* generation? His manner, the language he used, the way he phrased his words, all gave his hearers good cause to conclude

---

I have a couple of 19th century studies on Bible prophecy on my bookshelves, whose authors marshalled the signs of the times and confidently predicted that Christ would return before the 20th century dawned. Over the years I have read several other old books in which similar predictions were made. The hope behind those predictions was valid, and in harmony with scripture, although the writers all proved to be in error concerning the actual time of Christ's return. See also Part Two, below, Oracles Galore, for a more comprehensive list of failed predictions.

that they were the generation of which he was speaking.

- Jesus said that Jerusalem must be *"trodden down until the times of the gentiles are fulfilled,"* but he gave no indication how long this would be (Lu 21:24).
- the phrase *"the last days"* is ambiguous.

While this expression unquestionably refers to the days right at the end of the age, just prior to the coming of the Christ, and therefore may actually be yet future, it was also used to describe the days of the early church. Its use by the first Christians reveals their conviction that they were witnessing events to which the phrase could be applied, and that all the prophecies relevant to the *"last days"* could be fulfilled in their time. See Ac 2:17; He 1:2; 1 Pe 1:20; 1 Jn 2:18; Jude 18. Also other passages, while pointing to a future time, are still placed in such a context as to indicate that the writers were expecting a fairly rapid fulfilment (1 Ti 4:1; 2 Ti 3:1; 2 Pe 3:3).

- the Lord's promise to *"shorten the days"* (Mt 24:22) destroys the foundation of any attempt to set a narrow date for his Second Advent .

So it can be said that every age (insofar as the people of that time were able to understand Bible prophecy and the nature of contemporary events) has had within it a potential of fulfilled prophecy, and therefore of Christ's imminent return.

Thus while we accept that all the prophesied antecedents to Christ's return must be fulfilled before he can return, we also accept that his return is potentially imminent and that we must be ever alert for his coming.

That is why Peter (in our text) urged his readers to *"wait"* and *"look"* for that day (vs. 12) every day, for who can tell whether or not Christ will come *today*!

Yet it does apparently lie in our power to *"hasten"* the last day (vs. 12) – and see again my note on the Lord's Prayer above.

Hence, despite popular opinion, there can be <u>no</u> certain signs that the day is near. History surely demonstrates that counting up *"signs of the times"*, and using them to predict the nearness of Christ's return, is futile. Generation after generation of sign-watchers has been wrong. And also foolish, for the Bible itself says there will be no certain signs to tell you that the last day is at hand. (43)

NO SIGNS OF THE TIMES

You may be startled by my assertion that there are no *"signs of the times"*. So many writers have listed so many *"proofs"* that we are in *"the last days"* that people can hardly imagine anything else. But think about the following scriptures:

- *Daniel 12:8, 9.* Daniel had the same trouble with his own oracles that millions have had since then. He lamented: *"I heard, but I did not understand!"* He urged the angel to explain *"the issues"* to him, but got only the firm reply: *"The words are <u>shut up</u> and <u>sealed</u> until the time of the end."*

---

(43) But we moderns are marvellously arrogant in our assumption that we are surely the last and most important generation! I once heard two men talking about Bible prophecy. One of them boldly asserted that no generation prior to ours has been able to interpret the prophecies of Daniel. Earlier generations (he said) were fully aware that the prophecies were not being fulfilled in their time, and therefore could not be understood by them. He reckoned that our full comprehension of the prophecies is a sure sign that the end of the age is upon us. What lamentable ignorance!

Even a casual glance over the shelves of any Christian book shop will show there are as many different readings of Daniel today as there have ever been. An equally casual look into older literature will show that writers in earlier times were no less bold in claiming marvellous insight into the prophet's words than are some modern writers. When it comes to irresponsible attempts to predict the future by using Bible prophecy, there really is nothing new under the sun.

If the prophecies have been locked up until *"the time of the end,"* presumably they cannot be opened *prior* to the *"end"*. The inference seems to be that nothing beyond a partial comprehension of the prophecies is available to us at the present time. They will not be fully understood until after their fulfilment.

- *Luke 17:20-21*. Christ specifically says that there will be <u>no</u> observable signs of the coming of the kingdom of God. Language could hardly be clearer!

Once the Pharisees asked Jesus, *"When will the kingdom of God come?"* He replied, *"The kingdom of God <u>will not come with signs that you can observe</u> ..."*

So anyone who waves a Bible in one hand and a newspaper in the other, saying *"Lo, here it is!"* or, *"It is there!"* is claiming to see what Jesus said could not be seen (Mt 24:23, 26; Mk 13:21; Lu 17:21, 23; 21:8). He was emphatic – *"Do not believe it! ... Do not go out looking for signs, and do not chase after such people!"*

The Lord gave two reasons for this lack of *"signs"* –

- The sovereign reign of God upon the earth has *already* come in the person of Jesus himself and in his indestructible church (Mt 16:18-19).

Despite appearances, the church of Jesus Christ has triumphed over all its foes, and will continue to do so. Despite his invisibility, and seeming inaction, Christ does rule with unassailable power, and all that he wills is done upon the earth.

- When the final manifestation of the kingdom of God does appear upon the earth, it will do so unexpectedly, with startling glory.

The suddenness of that great event precludes any sure prediction of its occurrence (Lu 17:22-24).

Therefore, we must be content to *wait* and *watch*, always

unsure whether this present day will see the appearing of the Lord, but always ready to meet him if he should suddenly come.

- *Luke 17:26-30.* Christ says that life will continue normally right up to the very last minute, with no special warning of his coming.

People will be doing the same things they have always done, natural things, everyday things, human things – buying, selling, planting, building, eating, drinking, marrying, and the like. Nothing in the world around them will alert them to prepare to meet their God. No alarming signs will disturb their daily cycle. The thunder-blast of the coming Christ, the dread shout of the Son of God, the rending blare of the trumpet, the terrifying cry of the archangel, will crash suddenly upon them with withering horror.

- *Matthew 24:3-8; Mark 13:3-8.* In both passages Christ lists six things (44) that are commonly taken as *"signs of the times"*, but which he clearly states should not be so taken.

Rather, said Jesus, such things are just ongoing symptoms of a diseased world. They will all remain part of human experience until the very time of the end. They are no better signs of the *"last day"* in our time than they were in previous generations. Yet time and again across the centuries, when any of the six disasters has ravaged the people, enthusiastic preachers have cited them as augurs of Christ's near return. But Jesus said –

> *Take heed that no one leads you astray (by these signs) ... <u>the end is not yet</u> ... these are but the*

---

(44) They are: false prophets; wars; broken alliances; earthquakes; famines; persecution.

beginning of the birth pangs (45) *... do not believe it* (when they point to the "signs") ..." (Mt 24:4, 6, 8; Mk 13:5, 7, 21).

THE PRINCIPLE OF DELAY

My surname, *"Chant"*, is French in origin. Four hundred years ago, my French Protestant forefathers were driven out of their homes by religious persecution. They had to flee their native land, and eventually settled in Somerset, in England.

Later, some of them migrated to the USA, others to Australia.

During those blood-stained decades in French history, many humble believers were robbed, raped, tortured, murdered, simply because they wanted freedom to worship God in their own way. During those anguished years thousands of them, torn by pain, broken, mutilated, rotting in foul dungeons, wept and pleaded, *"How long, O Lord, before thou wilt judge and avenge our blood on those who dwell upon the earth"* (Re 6:10). But like the saints John saw in his vision, so too my forefathers were told to *"rest a little longer, until the number of their fellow servants and their brethren should be complete"* (vs. 11). But they were not listening. They were sure that the Antichrist had seized the throne of Christ on earth. They *knew* that the last days were upon them. None of those suffering saints four centuries ago could have believed that the coming of Christ was still far distant. They yearned for God to hasten the hour, not to delay it.

Yet for all the hurt men and women have suffered since that time, none of us wish that Christ had come before the day of our own birth! I am sure you share my gratitude that the Father ignored the piteous cries of his pain-wracked people, and so

---

(45) That is, in the womb of this present age; the birth pangs that will eventually produce the new age; but how long God has decreed for the "gestation" remains unstated.

delayed the hour of judgment. I am glad he chose not to speak then the word that would have marshalled the armies of heaven to descend in awful wrath upon the earth. He *will* speak that terrible command one day (2 Th 1:7-10), but his patient long-suffering has led to our salvation!

So the apparent delay in fulfilling the promise is not therefore an act of divine weakness, as some have suggested, but rather of divine mercy. Which leads on to –

THE PRINCIPLE OF LOVE

> *The Lord is not slow about his promise as some count slowness, but is forbearing toward you, not wishing that any should perish, but that all should reach repentance ... Count the forbearance of our Lord as salvation* (2 Pe 3:9, 15).

Here is a saying you should allow the Holy Spirit to burn into your mind: on the matter of Christ's return, **the Father is not governed by a rule of <u>haste</u>, but rather by one of <u>delay</u>!**

His choice is not to send Christ back as soon as possible, **but rather to wait as long as possible!"**

What is his motive? Simply that of a Father who yearns to increase the number of his children. We humans are circumscribed by many things – finance, circumstance, health, situation – which determine the number of our children. Yet people who have a true parental heart tend always to long for more children, and would have them if they could. The Lord suffers no such restraints, and he delights to see his family ever increasing!

THE PRINCIPLE OF PERIL

Apparently a time will be reached when there is more risk of the Father's family being diminished, even destroyed, than there is promise of its continued increase. Before such blackness can engulf the earth, Jesus suggested, the Father will intervene to *"cut short"* the days. Has that time come? Is it still future? Who can tell! Only the Father knows when the harvest is reaped as fully as it can be, and the time has come to call harvest-home.

THE PRINCIPLE OF EVANGELISM

One way that the church can *"hasten"* the coming of the Lord is to fulfil its missionary mandate. In fact, this is the only sure sign of the *"end"* (Mt 24:14). We see three things here –

A Promise of the Indestructibility of the Church.

Until the *very end*, declares Christ, the church will still be bearing witness for him. That sure promise mocks every pretence of devil or man to annihilate the church of Jesus Christ. For as long as time continues, the church will stand secure upon its Rock, a light shining in the blackest night.

A Promise of Missionary Success.

The gospel **_will_** be preached in **_all_** nations. Let governments and armies raise what barriers they please, let them issue a host of decrees proscribing the gospel and its preachers. Their statutes are fences full of holes. Their walls are paper. *"He who sits in the heavens laughs, the Lord holds them in derision"* (Ps 2:1-4). They conspire in vain. They plot in ignorance. Wherever the Almighty has determined the light of the gospel shall penetrate, there it will shine, turning aside the darkness.

A Promise that Cannot be Defined.

Jesus said,

> *This gospel of the kingdom will be preached throughout the whole world as a testimony to all nations; <u>and then the end will come</u>* (Mt 24:14).

At first sight, those words seem to give a clear sign of the end – just count how many nations have heard the gospel and you will know how much time remains before *"the end"*. Indeed, many do just that; and since the sound of the gospel now reaches the ends of the earth through radio, television, the internet, and the printed page, they are sure that human history has nearly run its course.

But look again. Jesus' words are not as clear as they seem. In fact, they raise five questions –

- When is the gospel **_preached_**? Are radio, TV, literature, web pages really a sufficient witness; or does it require a living *"messenger"* with *"beautiful feet"* actually to appear upon the *"mountains"* of every nation? (Ro 10:14-17)

- When is the gospel **_sufficiently_** preached? Is it enough to appear in just a few main locations; or must it be preached in every city, village, hamlet, community, house?

- What exactly is the *"**gospel of the kingdom**"*? Probably very little of what is preached in many churches today even qualifies as the *gospel*, let alone the *gospel of the kingdom*. Finally only the Father can judge when what he calls the *gospel of the kingdom* has been preached *"throughout the whole world"*.

- What does it mean, as a "**_witness_**"? Perhaps God requires that the gospel be preached as Paul specified, by word and deed, by the power of signs and wonders, by the power of the Holy Spirit" (Ro 15:18-19). Only when he had proclaimed Christ, not just with words, but also with miracles, did the great apostle claim that he had *fully* preached the gospel. It could well be that in God's reckoning not a single nation has yet had a proper witness brought to it!

- What **_response_** must the gospel produce? How deeply must it penetrate the life and culture of each society before the justice of God will be satisfied, before the judgment of God can rightly fall upon a recalcitrant race? (cp Ge 18:23-32; Ge 15:16).

Clearly, then, Jesus' statement cannot be used as a basis upon which to count nations and missionaries in order to arrive at a *"sign"* of the end of the age. Only God knows when its provisions will be adequately fulfilled. Our task is simply to go on bearing witness for Christ until the end comes.

But two strong things, as we have seen, do come out of what Jesus said: _the indestructibility of the church_; and _the success of its missionary mandate_. Those two things demonstrate once again that the real purpose of Bible prophecy is not to satisfy curiosity about *"times and dates"* (Ac 1:6-8), but is rather an *ethical* and *moral* intent. The promise is *spiritual* in character, not *material*.

THE PRINCIPLE OF PREPAREDNESS

Peter warned his readers, *"the day of the Lord will come like a thief"*; therefore we should be constantly ready.

There is a sense in which past generations have been wrong in their interpretations of the prophecies. *But there is also another and better sense in which they were right.* If anyone had told those people that the return of Christ was still many centuries distant, they would not have believed that claim, any more than we are willing to believe it today.

Why is this?

It is because *the kingdom of God is already born within us* (Lu 17:20-21); we are already citizens of heaven; we live all the time on the edge of eternity; the rays of the rising Sun of Righteousness have already brightly touched us, and we cannot help but live with *excitement*, sensing the imminent appearing of Christ. Hence the apostle says that we *"love"* his appearing (2

Ti 4:8), and we cannot help but yearn for it and believe it to be near. (46)

NO SIGNS THAT YOU CAN OBSERVE

Instead of looking for some "sign" of the "end" drawing near, we should simply live as if *this* day is going to be the *last* day! We should, said Jesus, be like a man who actually knows when a thief intends to break into his house and is ready and waiting to apprehend the robber! Of course, we don't know – but we should behave as if we do! (Mt 24:43-44; Lu 12:39-40). We are like someone who knows that a thief is coming, but not *when*. So he resolves to be ready *every* day, lest he be caught unaware.

THE TIME AND DATE ARE UNKNOWN

Paul warns the Thessalonians that he cannot tell them either *"the time or the date"* of the Lord's return, for, far from being predictable, that Day will come as unexpectedly as a *"thief in the night"*. Therefore, says Paul, they should be wise, awake, and watching, so that, although they cannot predict *when* the Lord will come, nonetheless the day of his return will *not* surprise them like a thief (1 Th 5:1-4).

Then Paul adds this vital fact. Far from signs of the end abounding in heaven and on earth, as harbingers of the Last Day, such signs will be so lacking that everyone (except alert Christians) will be lulled into a false sense of security –

> *People will be saying, "There is peace and security." And that is just when destruction will overtake them, as suddenly as labour pains grip a pregnant woman. They will not escape. But you, dear friends, are not living in darkness,*

---

(46) Think of a young maiden, unsure when her lover will appear, but waiting keenly for the sound of his coming.

> *and that Day should not take you by surprise, like a thief* (vs. 4-5).

JUST WATCH AND BE READY

But mark again, although the church will not be surprised when the Lord comes – because we *are* expecting him – yet we are no more able to guess *when* he will come than we can tell when a thief might break into our homes. That time is known to the Father alone (Mt 24:36). Therefore Jesus warned his hearers (and us), that the Last Day will be like the time of Noah. Right up until *the very day* that the Flood burst upon them, the people lived oblivious to the approaching ruin (vs. 38-39).

Apart from the preaching of Noah, they had no sign, no hint, nothing to show them that disaster was about to strike them. Said Jesus, that is just what it will be like at the time of his return (vs. 39). His people will be ready for him, preaching about his coming, but there will be no signs to show anyone how near or how far the Day might be. Hence, he added –

> *Watch out, then, because you do not know just when your Lord will come. ... You must always be ready, because the Son of Man will come at a time <u>when you are not expecting him</u>* (vs. 42, 44; and see also 25:13; Ph 4:5 – mark how uncertain that *"soon"* makes the time of his coming! Likewise Ja 5:9).

All the above seems to me to make nonsense of the entire enterprise of trying to predict whether or not the coming of Christ is near at hand by observing what is happening in the world around us. If those scriptures mean what they say, then the more the "signs" seem to suggest his coming is near, the more unlikely it is to happen. Rather, it is when everyone is feeling safe, at a time when *no one is expecting him*, that the Lord will return. People everywhere will be happy, prosperous, enjoying domestic and commercial life to the full, with nothing to show them that disaster is rapidly approaching, until suddenly the heavens split with the awful echo of the Trump of God. Then they will see Christ will descend with flaming fire and all his holy angels, coming to take divine vengeance upon a godless race. Then also, he will catch up his church, his Bride, to share Paradise with him for ever!

WHAT YOUR RESPONSE SHOULD BE

A CALL TO HOLINESS

Peter gives a simple but emphatic response –

> *Since everything will be destroyed in this way, what kind of people ought you to be? You ought to be living holy and godly lives as you wait eagerly for the day of God to come* (2 Pe 3:11-12).

You should also remember this – no matter how far distant the coming of Christ may be in relation to the world, as far as each individual is concerned, *his coming is no further away than death*! Death, the great reaper, in the hour of his coming is described in much the same way as the hour of the Lord's return – thus the swift loosing of the silver cord of life is unpredictable, like the suddenness of the Second Advent. See Jb 7:6; Ps 39:5; Is 38:12; Ja 4:14; Ps 103:15-16.

How should you then live? Every hour, as if you know that Christ will come before this day ends!

A CALL TO CONFIDENCE

See Mk 13:1-2, 14-20, 28-31. His disciples had drawn Jesus' attention to the *"wonderful stones and marvellous buildings"* in the great Temple in Jerusalem. But the Lord's reaction was sombre. He gravely predicted, *"there is not one stone here, standing upon another, that will not be cast down."* Startled, they asked him, *"Tell us, when will this be, and what will be the sign ...?"*

The Lord was willing to answer those questions. He gave his disciples more details about the overthrow of Jerusalem, and he also told them –

THE SIGN THAT THE DAY HAD COME

When you see the desolating sacrilege set up where it ought not to be ... then ... flee to the mountains.

Most commentators believe those words describe the encircling armies of Rome. History actually records that the Christians in Jerusalem remembered Christ's words, and when they saw the soldiers approaching the city, they escaped with all haste. Not one of them perished in the fearful siege that followed. There may also be a latter day fulfilment of the oracle, if modern Jerusalem, like the ancient city, should find itself besieged. Or perhaps, today, "Jerusalem" finds its counterpart in the church (cp. Ga 4:25-26; He 12:22).

THE TIME WHEN THE DESTRUCTION WOULD OCCUR

Truly, I say to you, this generation will not pass away before all these things take place (vs. 28-31).

Jesus addressed that prediction to those who would be still alive some forty years later, when the Roman army surged into Palestine and mercilessly shattered the Jewish nation. His words were fulfilled within the time he had promised.

So the warning Christ gave to the people of his day was accomplished to the letter. Jerusalem and its Temple fell in exactly the way, and at the exact time, predicted by the Lord. The accurate fulfilment of that prophecy gives confidence that the remainder will also be fulfilled. But with this difference – the Lord specified a time limit on the Temple prophecy; but no time limit is placed on his other predictions.

A CALL TO PATIENCE

See *Mark 13:4-13*. The disciples had asked Christ only about the destruction of the Temple. He answered their immediate question; but he also enlarged his answer to include a warning about the end of the present age, and about his Second Coming.

In the Lord's remarks about the end of the age, there are four groups of sayings –

THE CHARACTER OF THE CHRISTIAN ERA

While Christ was among them, the disciples believed a wonderful new era of joy and peace was about to possess the earth. The Lord had to show them how wrong they were. So he presented six things that he said would characterise the entire Christian era (which has thus far continued for nearly twenty centuries). I have mentioned these above, but they deserve a little more comment.

Jesus said there would be–

- a succession of false prophets, claiming to be the promised King
- endless *"wars and rumours of wars"*
- continued failure to achieve lasting international alliances
- *"earthquakes in various places"*
- repeated ecological, agricultural, and climatic disasters, summed up in the one pitiless word, *"famine"*
- unbroken opposition to, and persecution of, the church.

Who can deny that those six signs do indeed epitomise the past two thousand years, and that not even 21st century man can alter them? It is as sure that these things will fill the years ahead as that they have filled the past! Only the return of Christ will finally remove those bitter pains from human experience.

THE MEANING OF THE SIX SIGNS

Three times Christ stressed that the signs he had listed must not be taken as proof that the age was coming to an end. On the contrary, he mentioned each of them for the express purpose of plucking them out of the hands of the soothsayers. He stressed that they were to be accepted as an inevitable part of the present scheme of things, and that only the actual inauguration of the kingdom of God would put an end to them. (47)

Christ is emphatic – the signs are not signs of the end, but rather that *"the end is not yet."* They are not the end of sorrow, *"but the beginning of the sufferings"* (that is, they are birth-pangs in the womb of the present time, which will ultimately bring forth the new age.) The Lord insists, if anyone says the end is at hand, or that the coming of Christ is near, *"do not believe it"* (vs. 21-23).

Christ could hardly have expressed himself any more strongly. His warning should be enough to prevent all would-be prophets from predicting a terminating point for the end of this age. He not only plucked their favourite signs right out of their hands, but insisted that preachers should be ignored if they stubbornly continued to foretell the time of his coming.

THE ATTITUDE OF THE CHRISTIAN

How should *you* view these six signs? Twice the Lord repeated two warnings –

---

(47) As mentioned in my foreword above, I am aware that these comments, and others like them scattered throughout the book, and despite my desire to be more or less neutral, do show that I am neither a Post-Millennialist nor a Praeterist, except in a few ideas (see below, the chapter headed Schools). But then, neither am I a committed A-Millennialist nor a committed Pre-Millennialist. I just take from each "school" what seems to me to fit the scriptures best.

"Take Heed!"

> *Take heed that no one leads you astray ... Take heed to yourselves!* (Mk 13:5, 9)

Mark it well: take heed, not to the *"signs,"* but *"to yourselves"*! For this is the real purpose of all Bible prophecy – not to make us watchers of newspaper headlines, but watchers of ourselves, lest the day catch us unready.

"Do Not Be Alarmed!"

> *When you hear of wars and rumours of wars, do not be alarmed ... When they bring you to trial ... do not be anxious* (vs. 7, 11).

We who believe should remain *un*troubled, whether by the troubled state of the world (vs.7), or by the troubled state of the church (vs.11) – for in both cases we can trust in the imperturbable sovereignty of God, and in his ability to care for his own people.

A CALL TO WATCHFULNESS

See *Mark 13:24-27, 32-37*. Essentially, *the only sign of the return of Christ will be his return.* The first thing people will *"see"* to warn them of the coming of Christ, will be his coming –

> *And then they will see the Son of Man coming in clouds with great power and glory.*

Therefore the Lord stressed two important rules. He said –

THE DAY IS UNKNOWN

What could be more unequivocal than this statement? –

> *Of that day or that hour no one knows, not even the angels in heaven, nor the Son, but only the Father.*

To make the statement imply that while we do not know the *day* when the Lord will come, we can still know the *decade,* or at least the *generation,* simply shows ignorance of Jewish idiom. In the speech of the day, not to know *"the day nor the hour"* meant not to know even the approximate time. It meant the time was completely unknown. Which leaves us with only one thing to do –

WATCH FOR THE DAY

Listen to these three stern admonitions –

> *Watch, for you do not know when the time will come ... Watch, for you do not know when the Master will come ... And what I say to you* (his disciples) *I say to all* (us) *– WATCH!"* (vs. 33, 35, 37)

WATCH – not for signs, but for Christ himself!
WATCH – not a troubled world, but the sure promise of God!
WATCH – not tomorrow, but today!
WATCH – for Christ will come at a time when you least expect him!
(Mt 24:44, 50; Mk 13:33; Lu 12:40, 46).

A NOBLE EXAMPLE

About 300 years before Christ there lived a banker's clerk, a Greek slave, named Hermias. By diligent labour and careful hoarding of his meagre resources, he managed to secure his freedom and become his own master. He prospered sufficiently to purchase a small mine, and again by much toil and prudent expenditure gradually amassed a fortune large enough to buy from his Persian overlords the title *"Prince"*. Along with the title came authority over a small state, Atarneus, in Asia Minor.

Hermias ruled his territory wisely, and eventually created an army and navy strong enough to enable him to achieve a large measure of independence. Admiring the arts and all learning, he gathered into his court a glittering cluster of scholars and philosophers, including the renowned Aristotle. Hermias sat humbly at the great teacher's feet, and was overjoyed when Aristotle wooed and won his adopted daughter.

The prince grew in knowledge and wisdom, and himself wrote a book, now lost, but famous in its day, called *The Immortality Of The Soul*.

After a time Hermias was accused of conspiring with the Greeks against Persia and he was betrayed into Persian hands. His captors carried him in chains to Susa and there cruelly tortured him over a long period. Through all his torments he maintained a calm demeanour, until the Persians finally wearied of their fruitless barbarity and condemned him to be crucified.

Then came one of those sublime moments that show how the character of a noble man can rise above the most deranged circumstances to reflect the dignity of God. As he was dying, Hermias spoke these last words: *"Tell my friends and companions that I have done nothing unworthy of philosophy.* [48]

May you and I also, when we stand before Christ on that day, be able to say to our righteous companions, and to our Lord: *"I have done nothing unworthy of the gospel!"*

---

[48] The story of Hermias can be found in the works of Diogenes Laertius (3rd. cent. A.D.), <u>Lives and Opinions of Eminent Philosophers</u> – The Life of Aristotle; Athenaeus of Naucrartis (late 2nd cent. A.D.), <u>The Deipnosophists</u>; and in major encyclopedias.

ADDENDUM

Since we are facing Christ's imminent return, we must be –

EXPECTANT

Make sure that you are always ready; for the Son of Man will return when you are least expecting him (Mt 24:44).

WATCHFUL

Keep watching, for you do not know when the master of the house will come; perhaps in the evening, or midnight, at dawn, or later in the morning (Mk 13:35).

ACTIVE

Calling ten of his servants, he gave each of them the same amount of money. Then he said, "Earn as much as you can with this money, until I return"' (Lu 19:13).

PATIENT

Remain patient, therefore, dear friends, until the coming of the Lord. You know how a farmer waits for his precious crop to grow, watching it patiently until it receives the autumn and spring rains. So also you must be patient. Keep your hopes high, for the coming of the Lord is at hand (Ja.5:7-8).

MERCIFUL

Do not rush in and make quick judgments. In fact, you should wait until the Lord comes, for he will bring to light whatever is now hidden in darkness, and he will expose the real motives of every heart. Then each person will receive a proper commendation from God (1 Co 4:5).

BLAMELESS

May the God of peace himself sanctify you wholly; and may your spirit, soul, and body be kept healthy and blameless until the coming of our Lord Jesus Christ (1 Th 5:23).

OBEDIENT

I charge you to keep on obeying God faithfully, free from reproach, until the day when our Lord Jesus Christ returns (1 Ti 6:14).

WAITING

Christ, having been once offered to bear the sins of many, will appear a second time, but not this time to deal with sin. Rather, he will come to save everyone who is eagerly waiting for him (He 9:28).

ABIDING

And now, dear friends, abide in him, so that when he comes again you will you be able to greet him with confidence and not shrink shamefully away from him (1 Jn 2:28). [49]

---

(49)　I think that I am the compiler of the above list, but it is possible that I have drawn it from some other source. If so, I apologise for not being able to identify the author.

Six

SCHOOLS

Do you know how many opinions Christians have about the time and manner in which Christ will come again? It would probably be impossible to count them all!

Yet surprisingly, some people, having heard only one opinion all their lives, remain blissfully unaware that there are any alternatives. If you are one of those idyllic souls, please forgive me for disturbing your comfort by presenting to you one or two other ideas!

Then there are those whose teachers *have* mentioned other viewpoints, but always with withering scorn. So they have been driven away from even considering alternative readings of the biblical oracles. Some churches preach with a vitriolic dogmatism that defies you ever to think there are any other valid ideas! If you come from such an environment, I hope this series of chapters will encourage you, if not to change your mind, at least to think more kindly about your neighbour!

However, one version that will *not* occupy much of our time denies that Christ ever promised to come again. Thus the following report was printed in various newspapers on March 7, 1989, under the heading, *"Scholars Say Jesus Never Promised To Return"* –

> *A group of biblical scholars (meeting in Sonoma, about 30 miles north of San Francisco) has overwhelmingly agreed that Jesus Christ never promised to return and usher in a new age, and would have been "appalled" about becoming a cult figure in a new religion ...*

> *About 100 scholars, theologians, and historians discussed the teachings of the historical Jesus in a three-day seminar ... 26 of the 30 scholars who voted agreed that Jesus did not promise a Second Coming in which he would bring a new age as the leader of God's kingdom.*
>
> *Gospel writers and later followers of Jesus were the ones who predicted a Second Coming of Jesus, said most of the scholars participating in the Jesus Seminar ... The group also voted overwhelmingly that the language used to describe the future kingdom of God in the New Testament is mythic and symbolic, and recommended that people should not believe in or look forward to the Second Coming and a new age ...*
>
> *The overwhelming (opinion among the scholars), said Robert Funk (the founder of the seminar), "is that Jesus had no intention of starting a new religion. Most of the fellows think Jesus led some kind of reform movement in Judaism. I'm quite certain he had no idea that a new religion would transpire, or that he would become a cult figure in it."*
>
> *(Funk) said that Jesus "didn't think of himself as divine ... He would have been appalled by it."*
>
> *The seminar's findings reflect what is being taught in most major universities and seminaries ...*

On this matter I will be as dogmatic as the preachers I criticised above. People who deny that Christ will return in glory must also deny the reliability of our NT documents. In their quest for "the historical Jesus" these scholars have rejected the very heart of the NT revelation. But for us, who hold to the integrity of scripture, the message preached by the apostles is sure – *Christ is coming back again in glory!*

However, beyond that firm statement, Christians do have many diverse views; which brings us to –

THE GREAT DEBATE

In the year 1000 A.D. the whole of Europe was in turmoil. An old order was collapsing under the savage impact of widespread plague, frequent internecine war, and shattering social unrest. A new order was being created, and many people felt that these changes were the harbinger of Christ's return. Everywhere there was an expectation that after a millennium of Christian civilisation the time had come for the kingdom of God to be inaugurated on earth.

But their desire was vain. The years rolled by in steady succession, as they had always done. Slowly the hopes of the people subsided; the nations of Europe settled into their new political and social patterns, which remained little changed for five centuries.

Then suddenly, once again it seemed that the whole world was being torn apart. The Church was in a chaos of division. The Protestant reformers thundered their startling new doctrines. Centuries-old political alliances were shredded by new groupings of nations. Commercially, philosophically, culturally, all the old patterns were being questioned, discarded, altered beyond recognition. Countless bewildered people just *knew* that the enormous social upheavals they were witnessing presaged the end of history and the beginning of the Kingdom of God!

But again they were wrong.

In fact, a study of the history of Israel and of the Church shows that in every time of deep crisis, especially when an existing order is collapsing and the future is dark with uncertainty, people have commonly reacted by yearning for God to intervene and to establish his promised Paradise on earth. And at such times, some preachers have always been willing to turn that yearning into a confident prediction that a divine utopia is surely about to dawn, and the return of Christ is certainly at hand. (50)

But Christ has not yet come.

Now this pining for the kingdom of God is not wrong. It is soundly based on the sure promise of God that the day will irrevocably dawn, when the present era will end, when Christ will come as universal King, and the nations of the world will be gathered up into the kingdom of God. The scriptures strongly encourage us to expect this event, and to look for it daily.

But what about those who are once again declaring that the cataclysmic changes that are shaking modern society to its foundations are infallible *"signs"* of the end of the age? What about those who declare that our daily headlines are sure pointers to the nearness of Christ's return? It is one thing to say that the kingdom *may* begin in our lifetime; but a very different thing to say that it *will*! Who is right?

A CLIMAXING AGE

The gospels associate several major events with the day Christ's return –

- a time of worldwide ***tribulation*** (Mt 24:21; Lu 21:25-26; etc).

The beginning and duration of the tribulation are uncertain. Did it begin in the time of the early church, or will it not begin until a few years before the Second Advent? In any case, it will end when Christ comes and imposes his rule over the earth.

---

(50) See below, Part Two of this book, Oracles Galore.

- A state of **security**, in which everybody is crying *"Peace and safety!"*, unaware that sudden disaster is about to fall upon them (1 Th 5:2-3; etc).

This aspect of the last days is often overlooked, and creates a certain ambiguity in the oracles – will the end be noted for chaos and ruin, or for peace and prosperity?

- the ***rapture*** *of the church* (Mt 24:31; Mk 13:27; Lu 21:28)

Opinions differ here, too. Will the rapture be a visible event occurring at the moment of the Second Advent, or will it be secret and invisible, occurring a few years prior to the visible coming of Christ with all his angels, and with his raptured church?

- the **Second Advent** itself (Mt 24:30; Mk 13:26; Lu 21:27).

All schools, except those who deny that Christ will come again, visibly and gloriously, agree that this marvellous event will terminate the age and begin a new era.

Most evangelical Christians accept the *fact* of those events; but there is remarkable diversity and furious debate about their *nature* and *sequence*.

There are four main *"schools"* of prophecy, each of them with a different scheme built around the central idea of the *"millennium"*. The only place in the Bible where the establishment of a *"millennium"* (a period of "one thousand years") is actually stated is *Revelation 20:4-6*. But some scholars join that passage with others to build a complex picture of the kingdom of God on earth.

Which of the four scenarios (if any) best represents biblical teaching? You must choose for yourself. I will content myself here with outlining their main themes, and then presenting a few suggestions. However, as I have already mentioned a couple of times, I am furthest away from the second and last, and closest to the first and third, while refusing to be committed to any of them.

THE PREMILLENNIAL SCHOOL

This school teaches that –

- Christ will return *before* the millennium.
- his return will mark the commencement of the millennium.
- the millennium will be a literal kingdom on earth, having national Israel as its base, ruled over by Christ and the church.
- the prophecies of the OT concerning Israel must be taken literally and can be applied only indirectly to the church.
- the state of affairs during this age will steadily worsen, culminating in a period of dire tribulation just before Christ returns.

Those who hold this view usually expect to see Bible prophecy literally fulfilled in current world events, and they are sure the Second Advent will happen soon.

Within *pre-millennialism* itself there are various schools –

- those who associate *The Great Tribulation* (Re 7:14) with a future fulfilment of *Daniel's 70th-week*, [51] against those who see the tribulation as being co-extensive with this present age.

---

(51) See the Addendum at the end of Part One of this book, "The 70 Weeks Prophecy."

- those who look for a *pre*-tribulation rapture of the church, against those who teach a *post*-tribulation, or even a *mid*-tribulation, rapture.

- those who believe that most of the book of Revelation has now been fulfilled, against those who believe that most of it still remains to be fulfilled in a future tribulation period; and so on.

The *strength* of the premillennial school lies in its high view of scripture, its determination to take the prophetic oracles seriously, and in the fact that its general plan has been the view espoused by many of the great teachers of the church since earliest times.

The *weakness* of the premillennial school lies in the very thing about which it most boasts – *a literal interpretation of the prophecies*, especially of Jesus' *Olivet Discourse* (Mt 24, Mk 13, Lu 21), various parts of the *Apocalypse*, and many OT predictions. But any attempt to be consistently literal in the interpretation of Bible prophecy requires an unwarranted and arbitrary selection of "proof texts". Every literalist is obliged to place too much emphasis on those prophecies that fit his particular scheme, while resolutely ignoring the many passages that cannot be made to fit. For some examples, see the *Addendum* to this chapter, on seemingly unfulfilled oracles.

THE POSTMILLENNIAL SCHOOL

This school teaches that –

- Christ will not come again until *after* the millennium, which means his coming is still far distant.

- the church will succeed in its missionary mandate, and will not only *evangelise* but will in fact *Christianise* the world, so that every nation on earth will call itself *"Christian"*.

- the millennium should be viewed in literal terms as an earthly empire, with Christ ruling from heaven and the saints ruling on earth; but no special place should be given to national Israel.

- the church is fulfilling the OT promises to Israel in the latter days; national Israel has no special function in God's current program.

- the millennium will dawn gradually, as the church evangelises the earth, and will then continue for an indefinite but vast period of time (signified by the symbolic expression *"a thousand years"*).

Like the first, this school depends upon a mainly literal interpretation of the biblical oracles, although it gives a symbolic or spiritual interpretation to more prophecies than *premillennialism* is willing to do.

The *strength* of *postmillennialism* lies in three things –

- it is an *optimistic* viewpoint, which seems more in harmony with scripture than the endless pessimism of *premillennialism* (which loves to harp upon the gloomy refrain of *the great tribulation*, the coming *Antichrist, wars, rumours of war, floods, famines, disasters*, and the like)

- it agrees better with the many scriptures that describe the world, just prior to the Second Advent, as enjoying peace, prosperity, and security – just as in the days of Noah – so that the Second Advent, like a thief in the night, will come upon them without warning (Mt 24:37-41; 1 Th 5:3; etc).

- it is a *simple* viewpoint; for it argues that many predictions in both the OT and NT concerning the expansion of the kingdom, when those predictions are taken at face value, contain no mention of the Second

Advent being required for their fulfilment (e.g., Is 2:2-4; Mt 13:31-33; etc).

Pre-millennialists, on the other hand, constantly carry the Second Advent into various OT passages, claiming those passages cannot be fulfilled apart from the return of Christ. They may, of course, be correct; but there is nothing in the passages themselves to show it.

The *weakness* of the *postmillennial* school lies in –

- its failure to give adequate place for predictions about *"the great tribulation"*.

- its failure to find a place for national Israel; yet, quite apart from numerous OT predictions about Israel's coming glory, Paul's words seem to demand some continuing important place for the Jews in God's plan (Ro 9, 10, 11).

- its denial of the *imminence* of Christ's return; for if Christ cannot return until *after* a vast and indefinite *millennium*, there is plainly no sense in *"watching"* and *"waiting"* for him. Yet the injunction to do both is written large in the NT.

- its undue optimism about the church succeeding in its missionary mandate, whereas Jesus several times predicted a great falling-away prior to his Second Advent (cp Mt 13:24-30; Lu 18:8; etc; and the *Apocalypse*).

THE AMILLENNIAL SCHOOL

This school teaches that –

- the millennium must be viewed in a figurative or symbolic sense; that is, it describes a spiritual, not a political kingdom.

- the millennium was inaugurated by Christ at the time of his resurrection, and the Day of Pentecost (cp Mt 16:28; Ac 2:17-21). The church has therefore lived in that millennial reign from then until now, and will continue to live in it until the time of the Second Advent.

- the OT prophecies concerning Israel in the latter days are being fulfilled exclusively in the church; the Jews no longer have any special place in the program of God.

- the state of affairs in the world at large will probably worsen until the time of Christ's return, although there will probably also be a great outpouring of the Holy Spirit (in other words, both *"the wheat and the tares"* of Jesus' parable will flourish side by side until Jesus comes).

- on the day of Christ's return the great judgment will begin, the present heavens and earth will be replaced by the new heaven and the new earth of God's promise, and the eternal kingdom of God will be inaugurated.

This school depends upon a mainly symbolic interpretation of the prophecies, although it does allow that some prophecies must be interpreted more or less literally (e.g., Jesus' prediction of the overthrow of Jerusalem; and some OT oracles).

The *strength* of amillennialism lies in –

- its generally consistent method of handling the prophecies; it avoids the strained interpretations and arbitrary selection of scriptures that tend to cloud the two previous schools.

- its freedom from confusing complexity, for it teaches just one coming of Christ, one resurrection, one judgment, and so on.

Have you noticed that in any given prophecy there is *never* any mention of more than one (or one phase) of each of those events? The various scenarios posited by some *premillennial* teachers – two comings of Christ, one secret, one visible; several judgments, separated by long intervals of time; different programs for the Jews and the church; and the like – can be constructed only by arbitrarily importing other verses into each passage.

When the prophecies are allowed to stand alone (as they were spoken by the prophets), and interpreted within their own local context, none of those scenes can be found. The picture then becomes much more like that of *amillennialism* – <u>one</u> coming of Christ; one great judgment; one company of redeemed people; and so on.

None of which means that *amillennialism* wins over *premillennialism*, but only that the latter school has a more difficult dogma to establish than does the former.

- its dismissal of the idea that there are any necessary precursors to the return of Christ; thus it can maintain a firm sense of the imminence of the Second Advent.

- its freedom to accept (with *post*-millennialism) that the church will yet enjoy great success in its missionary endeavour; plus its freedom to accept (with *pre*-millennialism) that things will also get much worse before Christ returns.

- its ability to get the best of both worlds, by avoiding (on the one hand) the pessimism and sensationalism that often plague *pre*-millennialism, and (on the other hand) the rather improbable optimism of *post*-millennialism.

The *weakness* of *amillennialism* lies in –

- its failure to find a proper place for national Israel.

- its spiritualising of prophecies which often seem to require a more literal fulfilment.

- its failure to recognise that just as surely as prophecy has been literally fulfilled in the past, so it can be literally fulfilled in the future.

However, *amillennialism* is an ancient view, going right back to some of the Fathers of the early church; and it was the view of all of the major Reformers; and it remains today the view of the majority of Christians.

Note that the <u>main difference</u> between the three schools examined thus far is the extent to which the prophecies are treated <u>literally</u> or <u>figuratively</u>. They all read some prophecies literally, and some figuratively, but differ in their choices.

Thus the first two schools prefer to read the prophecies <u>literally</u>, unless they are compelled to adopt a figurative sense; the third school prefers to read the prophecies <u>figuratively</u>, unless it is compelled to adopt a literal sense.

However, the next school, the fourth, uses an altogether different method –

THE PRAETERIST SCHOOL

The term *praeterism* is sometimes used derisively to describe the views of liberal scholars who reject the whole idea of a supernatural Bible and predictive prophecy. But *praeterism* also describes the views of a group of scholars who fully accept the veracity of the Bible, but argue that –

- the few prophecies in the Bible that are truly predictive belong in a special class, dealing mostly with the first advent of Christ;

- most OT prophecy was addressed to contemporary nations (not to future generations); but

- the prophets expressed themselves in such a way that successive and larger fulfilments of their prophecies (which were not really *predictions*) may be expected; and

- that no specific predictions remain to be fulfilled [52] except those that relate to the actual day of Christ's return, and to the events that will follow that day.

There is also a branch of praeterism that denies any literal return of Christ. It reckons that *all* the oracles that other Christians read as predicting an actual return of Christ to this earth, must be read figuratively, or symbolically. In its more extreme form, this school also denies a literal resurrection of the dead, and a literal Last Day. The dead in Christ, they say, are already in Paradise, and the present earth, indeed, the whole universe, will simply wax older and older, and eventually perish, without any particular divine intervention. It will be obvious, from what I written so far in this book, that I am not much in agreement with those notions!

The strength of praeterism lies in –

- its ability to read each prophecy as it stands, without being obliged to force the prophecies into some kind of coherent scheme;

- its treatment of Bible prophecy, not as a series of predictions about the future, but rather as a revelation of the ethical principles that govern God's dealings with mankind;

- its freedom to adopt the best from the other schools, and to reject the worse;

---

[52] "Daniel is interpreted as events that happened in the second century BC while Revelation is interpreted as events that happened in the first century AD. Preterism holds that Ancient Israel finds its continuation or fulfillment in the Christian church at the destruction of Jerusalem in AD 70." From an article on Praeterism (also spelled Preterism) in Wikipedia.

- its ability to make virtually all the biblical prophecies as relevant to the modern world as they were to the ancient one.

The weakness of praeterism lies in –

- its reluctance to accept any truly predictive element in Bible prophecy, which runs it against such specific predictions as those of Isaiah about Cyrus (41:2, 25; 45:1; 46:11; 48:14-15), and many others. The *Book of Daniel*, large parts of *Ezekiel*, a number of Jesus' predictions, many of Paul's affirmations, and the Apocalypse, cannot fit the praeterist framework unless they are stripped of all literal meaning. Thus, extreme praeterism takes even such graphic passages as *1 Thessalonians 4:14-17* and insists that they must be read figuratively, not literally.

So, are you enlightened or confused? My *disposition*, paraphrasing Shakespeare, is to say, "A plague on all your schools!" My *suggestion* is, pluck out the best from each school and cast aside the remainder; but even better, simply allow each biblical oracle to speak for itself. There really is scant need to try to compel every prophecy to fit into a single coherent scheme. If they say the same thing, fit them together. If they say different things, allow them to stand alone. And in the meantime, be content to live with a degree of darkness, for the time has not yet come for us to see everything clearly (cp. 1 Co 13:9-12).

THE RAPTURE QUESTION

Among *premillennialists* there are two different viewpoints on the *tribulation* and on the *rapture* –

THE TRIBULATION

THERE ARE THOSE WHO ARGUE THAT —

"The great tribulation" (Re 7:14) [53] is co-extensive with this present age, and will continue, with waxing and waning severity, until the actual day of Christ's return.

In this view, the *"Antichrist"* has had a number of fulfilments in history, and will probably have further fulfilments in the future; but there is no expectation of the appearance at the end of the age of a single and utterly horrific being, who will be the first and only *real* Antichrist.

This means, of course, that the church will not only go *through* the tribulation, but has *always* been going through it, and is in the midst of tribulation now. The tribulation is "great" therefore, not because of its severity, but because of its length and of its continuance until the Second Advent.

Also on this view, *Daniel's 70th Week* has long since been fulfilled (see the *Addendum* to this chapter).

THERE ARE THOSE WHO ARGUE THAT —

Daniel's 70th Week is still future, and that it will be fulfilled during the coming *"Great Tribulation"* —

- some argue also that the tribulation will endure only for half of the "week" (that is, 3½ years), while others argue for a 7-year tribulation (the full week)

- during this period, it is claimed, the Antichrist (seen as a single person) will gain power, make a covenant with the Jews, rebuild the Temple in Jerusalem; after which

---

(53) The idea of a Great Tribulation has taken a strong grip on the imaginations of many students of Bible prophecy, although it is mentioned by name only once in scripture (Re 7:14).

he will break his covenant and unleash the horrors of persecution upon the *"saints"* (variously understood as either the church, or Israel, or both).

THE RAPTURE

Most evangelical Christians believe in the *rapture* [54] of the church. But among those who believe in a *future tribulation* there is heated controversy about the time of the rapture – will it occur <u>*before*</u> or <u>*after*</u> the tribulation? The real issue then becomes whether or not the church will go *through* the tribulation or be delivered *from* it. Thus we find –

THOSE WHO CLAIM THAT —

- the rapture will take place *before* the tribulation, when Christ comes secretly (not seen by the world) *for* his church
- after that secret rapture, *the 70th week* will begin, leading into the tribulation;
- in the meantime, the church will be in heaven, being purified and made ready to return *with* Christ in glory, to destroy the Antichrist, to terminate Armageddon, and to usher in the millennium.

Thus, they say, there is a time lapse of several years between the coming of Christ *for* his church, and his later return *with* his church. Then there are

THOSE WHO CLAIM THAT —

- the church *will* go *through* the tribulation, remaining on earth throughout the entire *70th week*.

---

(54) That is, the catching up of the church into the air to meet the returning Christ.

Many schemes are suggested, which Christians are urged to implement, in order to secure their survival until the end of the tribulation.

Of course, it is taken for granted by nearly all varieties of *premillennialists* that all of these events must happen soon; for without that assurance, the entire argument becomes foolishly academic and of scant worth.

So what shall *we* do with these quarrels?

HARMONISING THE SCHOOLS

There are several other minor "schools" of prophecy, and within each school (major and minor) there are various sub-divisions, some of whom squabble furiously over the correctness of their interpretations. Exasperation with all of them, and despair at ever being able to reconcile their opposing viewpoints is not a new phenomenon. Nearly 1800 years ago Clement of Alexandria (who himself had some wild ideas about prophecy) expressed his annoyance. Talking about those with whose views he disagreed, he wrote –

> *... in the first place they will not make use of all the scriptures, and then they will not quote them entire, as the body and texture of prophecy prescribe. But, selecting ambiguous expressions, they wrest them to their own opinions, gathering a few expressions here and there, not looking to the sense, but making use of mere words ... But the truth is not found by changing the meanings ... but in consideration of what perfectly belongs to and becomes the sovereign God, and in establishing each one of the points*

> *demonstrated in the scriptures again from other scriptures!* (55)

Somewhere, too, I have read a quote from the great Augustine of Hippo (5th century), in which he expressed frustration at the impossibility of solving the conundrums raised by Jesus' *Olivet Discourse* (Mt 24:3 ff.; Mk 13:3 ff.; and cp. Lu 21:7 ff.) Some 1600 years later we are no closer to a solution than Augustine and his colleagues were! But that has not hindered some scholars from issuing dogmatic assertions about the infallibility of their own schemes. But when eschatology is being considered, the more arrogant the claim the less likely it is to be true! (56)

So I repeat my suggestion that the wisest policy, despite the fervency of their respective advocates, is to reserve judgment on all the schools of prophecy. None of them, by itself, appears to be an adequate explanation of the whole range of prophetic revelation. They all pick and choose what passages they will use, emphasise, or even ignore – of which faults some will probably accuse me, too!

Some of the prophecies are amenable to the literal approach of *premillennialism* and *postmillennialism*; others to the spiritualising approach of *amillennialism*; and others to the ethical approach of *praeterism*.

Surely it is best to avoid trying to force all the prophecies into one coherent system. The debris of failed attempts to create a single coherent interpretation of the biblical oracles lies scattered across the centuries. Scheme after scheme has been

---

(55) <u>Miscellanies</u>, Bk 7, Ch 16. For some of Clement's own extraordinary interpretations, see Bk 1, Ch 21, 5th paragraph from the end.

(56) There is a similar quote from Augustine, about his inability to decipher what Paul meant in 2 Th 2:6-7. You can find it in Part Two below, under the heading, "The Fifth Century."

discredited in the past. If Christ tarries, most of the modern fabrications will probably meet the same fate. At least, whatever faults some might find in this book, objecting to an interpretation here or there, no one will be able to accuse me of trying to create some kind of new framework into which all the oracles must be awkwardly jammed.

Rather, my aim has been to let each speak for itself, in its own context, in its own language; and apply to each prophecy whatever method makes most sense out of it, and does least violence to it.

On that basis, some things are clearly predicted in scripture, and may be confidently affirmed. Other matters are not so sure, but may be affirmed with caution. Others are still obscure, and will have to await further light from the Holy Spirit.

In the meantime, let us keep a cool spirit about them. Scholars have been debating all these issues since the time of the church Fathers without anyone yet arriving at a universally acceptable scheme. I personally think Christ may return at any time, yet it would not much surprise me to find that his return is still far distant. I live with a daily expectation of his coming, yet remain ready to die before his return.

Remember also, regardless of what school of prophecy any of us may belong to, *God will do precisely what he intends to do!* I doubt that he will consult the latest prophetic chart, drawn up by some enthusiastic eschatologist, in order to find out what his schedule should be! So do not be disturbed by the sensationalism of some modern prognosticators. They are probably as wrong as their many forerunners have been. A cautious approach is the most sensible.

But know this: **the things that <u>are</u> important are <u>sure</u>.** What are they? Just four –

Christ is coming
the church will be raptured
the judgment will follow the kingdom will be established.

The other matters, the ones that are argued about, are curious, but hardly vital.

Seven

METHOD

One can hardly refrain from feeling that Milton's lines provide an apt description of the prophetic scene –

> With ruin upon ruin, rout on rout,
> Confusion worse confounded. (57)

Such a lot of nonsense has been written! So many disparate views! No other doctrine in the Bible has been so mutilated, nor brought into so much disrespect. The worst foes of biblical eschatology have been the enthusiastic follies of its partisans.

Many Christians, disenchanted by the absurdities taught in the name of Bible prophecy, have discarded all hope of ever understanding the strange and exciting predictions spoken by the prophets of old.

Why this confusion?

The cause probably lies in the compulsive urge many modern teachers have to systematise everything they find in the Bible. It works like this –

> *"The Bible contains prophecies," they say to themselves, "and those prophecies must harmonise with each other. So I will set to and bring all the prophecies together into a coherent pattern. All the prophecies will be made to fit a single scheme; nothing will be omitted; there will be no loose ends; the entire pattern will be clearly mapped out and systematised."*

---

(57)   Paradise Lost, ii. line 996.

But that apparently worthy plan faces a serious problem: there is *no evidence* the prophets intended their oracles to be joined in such a fashion. Where does the Bible say that its prophecies provide a complete and systematic survey of coming events? On the contrary, ordinary readers get an impression that the prophecies are more like flashes of light, shining spasmodically into certain dark places of the past, present , and future (cp. 2 Pe 1:19-21).

But judge for yourself. What has been the outcome of these many earnest efforts to systematise Bible prophecy? Confusion! There are more *"schools"* of prophecy than you could pepper with a shotgun. But is God the author of confusion? [58] It seems more probable that there is something drastically wrong with the methodology adopted by the various *"schools"*.

A WRONG METHOD

Bob Ross writes –

> *I have been forced to ask why we are having so much trouble coming up with a mutually agreeable interpretation of the last things ... When it comes to some doctrine like Christology or Soteriology, evangelicals can produce a significant united front. But on eschatology we must surely be the laughing stock of unbelievers, at least of those who read what we write on the subject.*
>
> *There is, I believe, a fundamental methodological problem here that we have not confronted ... We have proceeded on the assumption that God's plans for the future are revealed in scripture something like pieces of a*

---

(58)   1 Corinthians 14:33.

giant prophetic jigsaw puzzle piled in a box. Our challenge is to sort out the pieces and put them together into a single picture with no spaces left open. If we come up with an arrangement that has an open space, we continue shuffling the pieces, perhaps surreptitiously dropping a few unwieldy ones on the floor and bending a corner here and there to get a fit.

But suppose we have only some of the pieces. Or suppose we have parts of the pieces to several different puzzles. That is, suppose that the variety of biblical material is expressive of different ways of depicting God's plans for the future, much as different artists paint their own unique pictures of a single landscape.

At any rate, prophecy is not God's crystal ball given to curious men. It is the proclamation of his sovereign, gracious will for all creation and his call to conventional fidelity to the people who are called by his name and who are ready to follow him without knowing in advance where they are going. "Hope that is seen is not hope" (Ro. 8:24). The Church today needs prophecy more than ever, not only to berate the heathen or to satisfy idle curiosity but to fire up lukewarm hearts with a vital hope in God's glorious future world, to be made known at the appearance of our Lord Jesus Christ. (59)

A BETTER METHOD

If other methods are wrong, which is the right one? That is not easy to answer. I have no wish to add another dogmatic voice to

---

(59) From a book review in Christianity Today, April 13, 1973.

the many that already clamour for attention. But perhaps I can give you something to ponder.

THE NATURE OF PROPHECY

Here is a good place to begin – biblical eschatology should be presented, not as a *system* to be studied, but as a *promise* to believe, a *power* for godly living, a *vision* to inspire dynamic faith. The prophecies of the Bible were not the products of calm reflection nor were they delivered with dispassionate, systematic logic. They were written and spoken under the impulse of an ecstatic revelation. They arose out of dreams (Da 7:1), a voice speaking in the night (Jb 4:13-16), an impulse from the Holy Spirit (2 Pe 1:21), God speaking to them (Is 38:4), and the like, and they were given to real people to answer the problems of real situations.

Must we say, then, that there is *no* system in the prophecies, nor any order or pattern to them? Is there no place for quiet meditation upon the meaning of the oracles? Did the prophets never take any notice of those who had spoken before? Such claims would be absurd. I only say that there is no *complete* system, and that any attempt to fit the prophecies into a unified scheme is doomed to fail. The end result of all these attempts has been various arid formulations that, in my opinion, can be maintained only at the expense either of tacitly ignoring or inexcusably distorting some parts of scripture.

I will explain shortly to what extent I think the biblical oracles *can* be incorporated into a pattern; but it is more important to grasp the limits imposed upon them. The prophecies were not given to provide bricks for fastidious theologians to build into logical structures. Some were given in tears to be read by a weeping people; others were spoken with laughter to be heard by the saints with joy; others arose from blazing anger against sin and idolatry; some speak to the nations, some, to Israel, some, to the church. But all were written in the bustling market of life, and they flash with a fiery conflict between righteousness and sin, heaven and earth, God and the nations. None of them was addressed to the cloistered halls of the seminary. They were forged out of the clamorous turmoil of human experience, to bring a vision of God to the multitudes struggling in *"the valley of decision"*. (60)

How can a systematic eschatology be constructed out of a partial collection of visions and inspired utterances, delivered by such a diverse group of people? Note how much they were separated –

- in *time,* by many centuries;

- in *grammar,* by a bewildering variety in their use of the same words and symbols;

- in *culture,* by differences as vast as those between the societies of Israel, Persia, Babylon, Greece, and Rome;

- in *status,* by their social position – for among them were kings, princes, priests, soldiers, peasants, theologians, laymen, some highly educated, and others scarcely literate.

To say that the Holy Spirit could override those differences and cause the prophets unwittingly to create a coherent eschatology simply begs the question; it concedes the point. For my part, after diligent study, I have concluded that James Stewart's comment on the writings of Paul is also applicable to the prophets –

> *(they) refuse to be tied down to a rigid, petty consistency.*

---

(60) Some readers may see an apparent contradiction of the foregoing in Lamentations, which has a formal acrostic structure. Yet that poetic build serves only to highlight more brilliantly the fervent passion that drenches every line with tears. The same may be said of similarly crafted passages by the prophets of Israel.

Concerning Paul's own teaching about the last things, James Stewart also says –

> *We need only compare and contrast such passages as 1 Co 15:51 ff; 2 Co 5:1 ff; 1 Th 4:13 ff; Ph 1:23; to realise ... that, for all Paul's burning interest in the world beyond death and the coming consummation of God's kingdom, he does not supply the materials for constructing anything in the nature of a scheme, far less does he attempt to reach such a construction himself.* (61)

That seems to me to be exactly true. Neither Paul, nor any of the prophets, provides enough material to build a systematic and complete system of eschatology. To attempt to do so is to attempt something the prophets themselves never dreamed of doing, and it forces the scriptures into a construction that is unnatural, artificial, and hence misleading.

UNDERSTANDING PROPHECY

How then should Bible prophecy be handled? Here are some suggestions. They do not pretend to give a complete answer to the question. But they provide guidelines for a balanced methodology –

LET EACH PROPHECY SPEAK FOR ITSELF

The various schools of prophecy usually fall into one of two faults. Either they go beyond a sound hermeneutic by over-spiritualising the scriptures, and thus distort passages which ought to be taken literally; or they fall short of a sound hermeneutic by taking too literally prophecies that need to be read figuratively.

---

(61)   I have lost the source of this quotation.

Surely each prophecy should speak for itself? If the words of Isaiah cannot be understood unless they are read in conjunction with Jeremiah or Micah; if John cannot be understood unless he is threaded into Amos and Ezekiel; then there is a fault in the reading method. Things are being sought in the prophecies that do not exist in those particular oracles.

Each prophet undoubtedly gave his message in the belief that it was complete in itself, and could be understood by itself.

Certainly, the prophets all spoke within the framework of Israel's historical and religious experience, and they made heavy use of materials, of thought-forms and imagery, that were common to that experience. In that sense the prophets illuminate one another. But surely each set of oracles must have been clear to the people to whom they were spoken, whether or not those hearers were familiar with any other oracles?

There were of course some areas (particularly messianic prophecy) where one prophet added to what another had spoken; but each part was still complete in itself, and could be read and understood within its own immediate context. Or, to express it differently, no statement in one prophecy can be altered by importing or inserting a statement from another source.

An example: some believe that the rapture of the church will occur at a *"secret"* coming of Christ some seven years before his final and public advent. One searches the Bible in vain for any passage that clearly presents such a coming of Christ, visible only to the church. It is a view based solely on a particular interpretation of Daniel's *70-weeks* prophecy. Those who teach this *"pre-tribulation secret rapture"* may be right. The events of the last days may happen just as they predict. Yet I find the view suspect, because it cannot exist apart from taking a debatable reading of Daniel and importing that reading into other prophecies. But those oracles, taken at face value, offer no suggestion of what is read into them. They can be made to teach a two-stage coming of Christ divided by seven years (or, as some would have it, 3½ years), only by forcibly expanding them to allow room for the insertion of the imported idea. My argument is that the prophecies must first be taken at face value; and only then, if their format and content demand it, should they be enriched by placing them alongside other oracles.

LITERAL OR FIGURATIVE?

Anyone who believes (as I do) that the Bible is the inspired and authoritative word of God, can hardly quarrel with the idea of interpreting the Bible literally. If the Bible is God's word, then it cannot be taken any other way. But what is meant by *"literally"*? Should the Bible be read literally in a *grammatical* sense, or in an *ideological* sense?

The basic assumption behind (at least) the *pre-millennial* view is that wherever possible the prophecies must be literally understood in a *grammatical* sense. But this leads them into grave difficulties, as I will show in a few moments. It seems far better to concentrate on the basic *idea* behind each prophecy, regardless of the dictionary meaning of the words used by the prophet (again, you will see what I mean in a few moments). Because of the peculiar nature of Hebrew apocalyptic writing, caution must be exercised even when reading apparently simple passages. It is unsafe to read Bible prophecy as you would read your daily paper. Different rules of interpretation are required. (62)

---

(62) Even a newspaper may be unintelligible to someone who knows the language but not the culture. I have often read reports or laughed at cartoons that have meaning only if one is familiar with contemporary background, substitutions, metonyms, allegories, and the like. For example, just today my local newspaper depicted the prime minister as a cricket captain, along with an array of twisted cricket terminology. The whole thing was quite meaning-
Continued on next page ....

The important thing is to discover what the prophets themselves actually meant to say. What message were they seeking to convey by the forms they used? Some examples may assist you to understand what I mean.

"Literalists" are fond of citing a rather small group of prophecies that (on the face of it) *have* had a dramatic, exact, and *"literal"* fulfilment. They quote certain oracles about the doom of Tyre, Babylon, Assyria, Edom, Egypt, and perhaps two or three others. Their argument goes thus: *"Since the predictions about these nations have had such an amazingly detailed and literal fulfilment, the same kind of fulfilment can be expected for all of the prophecies."*

Is that argument valid?

Yes, some prophecies do require, and have had or will have, this kind of specific and literal fulfilment. The major examples are prophecies about the first and Second Advents of Christ; Christ's own prophecies about the fall of Jerusalem (Mt 24; Mk 13; Lu 21; and prophecies about the resurrection of the dead, the Judgment, and the inauguration of the eternal Kingdom of God. Those prophecies stand in a class by themselves. They refer to a unique set of events and they require a unique fulfilment. (63)

However, apart from that group of special predictions, it is fair to say that the *"literal"* method of interpreting prophecy will

---

less, unless one were familiar with cricket, the state of the national cricket team (a series of dismal losses), and the current federal political scene. Against that background, the cartoon was hilarious. But anyone lacking the requisite knowledge would have reckoned the cartoonist mad. The same rules apply to reading and understanding the Bible. Parts of it have little or no meaning without at least some knowledge of the contemporary culture, the politics of the time, social mores, and the like.

(63) For further comment, see below, "Messianic Prophecies."

not work for most of the biblical oracles. I have surely already offered convincing evidence that the prophets expressed themselves in a particular prophetic style, and they did not intend their readers to look for a detailed and *"literal"* fulfilment of each detail in their predictions.

When an exact fulfilment apparently does occur it is more by an accident of history than by design of the prophet. Has there ever been an *exact* literal fulfilment of a prophecy, of the kind claimed by *"literalists"*? It is doubtful. Such fulfilments usually can be claimed only by sifting out of the prophecies all the elements that refuse to fit the fulfilment.

For example, just a couple of days before I first wrote these pages, a pamphlet came onto my desk, in which the author lauded the accurate fulfilment of every detail of Ezekiel's oracle against Tyre (26:1-28:26). But he was able to make out his case only by a cavalier use both of the prophecy and of history. Parts of the prophecy that did not suit his scheme he ignored, and he handled the history of Tyre just as carelessly.

I have seen the same folly perpetrated in connection with oracles about Babylon, Egypt, Ammon, Edom, and other OT people and nations. Assertions are made about how those oracles have been fulfilled in wonderful detail, how accurate they were, what a miracle they represent! But in every case, the assertions fail when the actual oracles themselves, and historical records, are closely examined.

At the end of this chapter you will find an *Addendum* that presents a number of oracles and shows how they have never had, and never can have, a truly *literal* fulfilment. Many more examples could be added to the list you will find there, but enough is given (I hope) to show that the literal method of handling Bible prophecy is fraught with peril.

How then should we approach the prophetic writings?

THE APOCALYPTIC STYLE

The prophets conveyed their message by using certain well recognised prophetic forms. They used set images. They spoke within a particular mental framework and a certain worldview. They employed forms of writing and a style of expression that were widely accepted as the proper manner in which inspired oracles should be given. For example, John on the Isle of Patmos used the same images Daniel had used centuries earlier, but John placed those images in a very different framework and gave them a very different meaning. John and Daniel both simply spoke in an accepted apocalyptic style, using standard forms to convey the message of God to the people. The OT prophets used this apocalyptic style in relation to Israel; the NT prophets in relation to the church.

If what I am saying is true, then there are some important corollaries –

Linear or Repetitive?

Should you expect Bible prophecy to predict a consecutive series of events, so that you can tick off the prophecies one by one as they appear to be fulfilled? That linear view of prophecy has produced some incredible textual acrobatics. Commentators who try to match their newspapers with their Bibles often display wonderful ingenuity but disappointing scholarship.

Surely it is better to meet the prophets on their own terms, to understand them within their own frame of reference. They adopted an apocalyptic style that led them, under the guidance of the Holy Spirit, to analyse their contemporary scene, to tear away the facade of their society, thus exposing its real character. They identified the spiritual forces at work in their world, using a special prophetic idiom to describe what they saw, and then predicted the inevitable outcome of all that was happening. Primarily, then, biblical prophecy has

An Ethical Thrust

The supernatural aspect of these oracles does not lie in detailed prediction of specific future events. Rather it lies in their prescience concerning the judgments of God upon certain nations, and in their repeated promises about the coming of the Messiah and of the kingdom of God.

Do the oracles have any present value? Of course they do. They still reveal the outworking of God's unchanging moral law upon the nations. Their infectious and superb optimism concerning the glorious destiny of the people of God marvellously stirs faith. And we still search them for those predictions concerning Christ that await fulfilment.

Generally speaking, then, Bible prophecy is predictive only in the sense that when the features of those ancient oracles are reflected in *our* political and/or social scene, the same outcome can be expected. In this way the prophecies have a continuing fulfilment. Hence, to quote one example, the graphic images of Revelation have been applied by succeeding generations of Christians to quite different political events. To the early Christians, *Imperial Rome* was the great persecuting power; later, it was the *Papacy*; but to us, neither of those former applications is adequate. We look for a new identity for John's visions. Yet the crucial message of the book – the triumph of the church over every adversary – has spoken vibrantly, and still speaks, to all Christians everywhere. The apocalyptic style enables the message of God to his church to be carried with equal force into each succeeding generation.

An Extravagant Style

Because their oracles were intended to have this continuing value, the prophets often used an extravagant style that far transcended the demands of describing their own contemporary world. Hyperbole was part of the apocalyptic method, a cultural imperative, but it also enabled the oracles to have lasting significance; they are applicable to many situations.

If this advice on reading Bible prophecy is adopted then it will restrain attempts to relate a prediction finally to a single political event; it will preclude any attempt to force the prophecies into a systematic structure; and it will certainly forbid the folly of trying to predict the time of the end.

MESSIANIC PROPHECIES

Messianic prophecies in general must be excluded from the restrictions I have laid down. Prophecies about the Messiah, the resurrection of the dead, and the last judgment, fall into a category that is unique. By their very nature, these events cannot be repeated. There is room in scripture for only a First and Second Advent of Christ; there can be only one last Trumpet, one Last Day, one Rapture of the church, one great final Judgment. Hence, predictions about those events are specific and definite. They are entirely a product of divine revelation. They demand the direct inspiration of God.

Of course, not all messianic and related prophecy is spoken in plain unadorned language. Rich symbolism and imagery are as common here as elsewhere. But these particular oracles are certainly more amenable to being grouped together into a more or less definite pattern.

Yet even here the materials are sparse, disconnected, and designed not to satisfy curiosity but to inspire faith. [64]

---

(64) For example: some 200 prophecies were fulfilled at the time of Christ's first advent; but what success would anyone have had, say, in 50 B.C., who might have attempted to put those prophecies together into a systematic picture of what the first coming of Christ would be like? It is inconceivable that such an attempt would have come anywhere near the truth. In fact the Messiah, when he came, was so unlike what the scholars had predicted he would be, they refused to accept him! If those early students of prophecy, who

Continued on next page ....

Cultural Barriers

Our Western society is profoundly permeated by the cultural heritage of ancient Greece. This cultural and philosophical background unconsciously leads us to accept certain presuppositions about the nature of life and of the processes of history. So deeply embedded are these assumptions that we accept them as natural, even inevitable, and we fail to realise that they may not be shared by people from other cultures.

Addicted to Order

The postulates upon which Western society is built create in us an instinctive disposition to impose order upon disorder, to leave no loose ends hanging. We take hold of our own metaphysical assumptions, and then use them as a basis on which to arrange systematically all the bits and pieces of information that come our way. Everything must fit the pattern. Even history must be viewed as a lineal sequence of events, each one arising inevitably out of the other. We are not content until we have achieved what we are pleased to call a rational explanation for every phenomenon we observe.

Yet this inner drive of ours is not so much a logical as a cultural necessity. Other peoples have not shared our compulsions, including the ancient Hebrews. Both the Old and New Testaments were written by people who had no liking for Greek culture, and who knew nothing about the philosophical foundations upon which Western society is built. Their mental framework differed from ours. To us their actions, their words, often seem illogical; but they did not seem so to them.

If this is true, then the attempt to pick out of the Bible a

---

lived within Hebrew culture and were completely familiar with its literary forms, failed so abysmally, we who live twenty centuries later ought to be doubly cautious!

detailed, consecutive, and logical pattern of events, both past and future, may not be in line with the purpose for which the scriptures were given. We in the Western world have a habit of writing things in an orderly sequence, either logically or chronologically, and we tend to assume that the Bible must be written in the same way. But this does not follow at all. Our forte is mathematics, we are masters of physical law, we major in intellectual logic. But the ancient Hebrews were poets, they understood the human soul, they lived in a world permeated by the Glory of God, they saw things through different eyes. They had no inner imperative to be logical, sequential, mathematically precise, formally accurate. Unlike the Western mind, they were more oriental in disposition, and were quite able simultaneously to hold seemingly contradictory ideas. (65)

Enraptured by Visions

For this reason, the task of sorting out the chronological sequence of the various biblical oracles has daunted the best of our theologians. The apocalyptic visions dart back and forth with a swiftness that bewilders the Western mind. The books of prophecy are pieced together in a way that often offends our sense of tidiness and order; but their authors knew nothing of such restraints. They yielded only to the demands of a magnificent poetic artistry. They were aiming for spiritual and emotional impact, not for the rational proofs of a logician.

---

(65) We actually do the same, but we seldom admit it, and become uncomfortable when we discover it. An example of people holding incompatible ideas may be seen in Christian plantation owners in the old American South, who, despite clear biblical statements, still deemed that they had a right to own slaves, sell them, flog them, and in many other ways break the second greatest commandment (Mt 12:31). Indeed, all of us, to some extent, unconsciously obey the axiom, "Don't do what I do. Do what I say." Thus we happily live with a contradiction.

The oracles of Israel may be seen as *prophetic parables* rather than as formal historical treatises, or sober predictions. They should be read as accounts that illustrate a great truth rather than as descriptions of any particular event.

True, they do describe certain happenings in history, they do deal with real nations, they do make real predictions that have come to pass. But in almost every case the actual event simply provided a peg on which the prophet could hang his apocalyptic vision. He saw and described in his own terms the awesome moral law of God and the Lord's dread judgments. And then, in the revived fortunes of Israel and other nations, the prophets saw a picture of the final sumptuous restoration of all things under the Messiah.

This approach to Bible prophecy makes it relevant to the experience of every generation. It gives abiding significance to every part of scripture.

The Church and Israel

The NT writers were Jews, writing from within a church that was mainly Jewish, surrounded by Hebrew thought and culture. They had no difficulty in seeing the church as the proper continuation of Israel, and as fulfilling all the promises made to Israel. Hence the NT abounds in quotations from the OT of promises that were in fact made to Israel, but are now applied to the church.

The apostles found it easy to transfer the promise from Israel to the church, because they expected Christ to return very soon and to bring all things to their predicted consummation. They saw no distinction between *"spiritual"* Israel and *"national"* Israel – to them there was only one Israel, the *"7,000"* who had not bowed the knee to Baal, the faithful *"remnant"* who were called out of the nation, the *"redeemed"*, who had continued in an unbroken line from Adam until the present time. Hence they spoke of the church as *"the Israel of God"*, as *"Mt Zion"*, as *"the heavenly Jerusalem"*;

and so on.

But *we* have a problem. Centuries have passed since then, and the Jews continue to exist as a separate nation. Yet if the apostles are taken at face value, surely there is only one true Israel, and that is the church. If this is so, then no prophecies concerning the Jews remain to be fulfilled save those that are common to all nations. The church alone will participate in the glorious realisation of all that the prophets spoke of, when Christ returns.

If you doubt that, ponder the following passages: Ep 2:11-13; Ro 9:1-14; 25-29; 11:1-5; 11-26.

Those passages specifically answer the question: *"If Israel <u>as a nation</u> does not obtain the promises, does this not mean that the promises have failed?"*

Paul replies, *"No!"* for the church has been brought into the Commonwealth of Israel, and the promises made to the fathers are now being fulfilled in the church. They can be fulfilled in national Israel only insofar as that nation embraces the gospel of Christ. The apostle insists –

> *It is not as though the word of God has failed. <u>For not all who are descended from Israel belong to Israel</u>, and not all are children of Abraham because they are his descendants … It is not the children of the flesh who are the children of God, but <u>the children of the promise</u> are reckoned as descendants. (Ro 9:6-8).*

Paul goes back into the distant past to illustrate this fact. He points out that although the promise of God was given to Abraham, it was channelled through only one of his sons, Isaac. Then it was passed on to only one of Isaac's sons, Jacob. The other sons remain excluded from the promise to this day.

Paul continues by claiming that God is still working by the same principle. He receives some and excludes others (because of their unbelief). Salvation is offered only to the *"remnant"* (Ro 9:25-27), and this believing *"remnant"* is now found in the church.

Some commentators construe 11:26 (*"all Israel will be saved"*) as predicting a still-future act of God that will lead to the conversion of virtually the entire nation. Not all agree with that reading of the passage, although it is probably true. Even so, note that Paul says nothing about the restoration of an earthly Davidic kingdom, nothing about the rebuilding of the temple, nothing about the reinstatement of the people in Palestine, nothing about any of those things that are an integral part of some popular prophetic scenarios.

Paul is adamant that salvation can come to Israel only upon terms that are already familiar to Christians everywhere. It will be salvation based on acceptance of the gospel. It may not take place until immediately prior to, or even after the return of Christ. But when (or if) it does take place, it will not bring the believing Israelite into an earthly paradise or material kingdom, but to the cross and to the church and to the inheritance in eternity, which is the common promise to all Christians.

Addendum

Seemingly Unfulfilled Oracles

We now understand the prophets so little because we do not understand their language; apart from this, they have spoken clearly enough. Therefore understanding them is not difficult for those who know their language and have the Spirit of God, whom all believers have. .. But if one does not understand their language and does not have the Spirit . . . the prophets appear to be intoxicated and full of wine.

Yet if we are to lack one of the two, the Spirit without a knowledge of the language would be better than a knowledge of the language without the Spirit. . . . (66)

I make no pretence to being better than anyone else in "understanding the language of the prophets", but I do have some opinions on the matter! In this *Addendum,* if you have noted my definitions of the major "schools" of prophecy, you will realise that I am departing somewhat from all of them, for it seems to me that the ancient oracles are both literal and symbolic; at the same time, they are both real predictions but also poetry. Hence, I think that both those who read the prophecies too literally and those who read them too figuratively are in error.

Any attempt to be consistently *literal* in the interpretation of Bible prophecy requires an unwarranted and arbitrary selection

---

(66)　What Luther Says Vol III; compiled by Edward M. Plass; Concordia Pub. House, Saint Louis, Missouri, 1959; selection #3665.

of "proof texts" – that is, the interpreter places too much emphasis on prophecies that fit the scheme, while ignoring the many passages that cannot be made to fit. But neither is it fair to strip the oracles of all literal intent.

The correct interpretation of Bible prophecy depends upon recognising that *the general thrust of an oracle, rather than its detail, is the important thing.* For example, see **Isaiah 10:27-32**. The predicted invasion did occur, but not in the direction nor in the sequence described by Isaiah. [67] The *intention* of his oracle was fulfilled in the mere *fact* of the invasion, which adequately satisfied the threatened divine judgment – the remainder was simply poetic and dramatic fill-in. Yet notice how little there is that is obviously symbolic in Isaiah's invasion oracle. But despite that semblance of reality, Isaiah did not expect every detail of his words to be taken literally. Instead, the prophets received their oracles by visions, dreams, revelations, and sometimes in a state of ecstasy, and then retold them in a style that is highly poetic, figurative, and symbolic (Ho 12:10). But they nonetheless had a strong literal underlay, an expectation that the predicted dooms would most certainly occur. Yet it remains misleading, or true only in a very restricted sense, to say (as some have) that prophecy is "history written beforehand".

A STRANGE EXCEPTION

The prophets of Israel were not soothsayers. They dealt with morality and righteousness, with justice and judgment, not with curious predictions. They used their dramatic oracles primarily to display the holiness of God. They assumed that their readers were familiar with the prophetic style, and that

---

(67) I cannot take space here to prove the various assertions made above, or in the remaining examples given in this Addendum. Any good commentary should be able to provide you with the necessary details.

those readers, ignoring the poetic detail, would extract from the oracles the major thrust each one contained. So much were those things true, that in one special instance – the shattering overthrow of Jerusalem by Nebuchadnezzar – when the oracles *were* unexpectedly fulfilled in hideous detail, the Jews were stricken with horror (see Jeremiah's *Lamentations*; and note also Daniel's lament: *"What has been done against Jerusalem has never before been done under the whole heaven"* [Da 9:12, NRSV]).

The level of destruction wreaked upon Jerusalem by the Babylonians went far beyond the normal practice of the time; the city and temple were reduced to piles of smoking rubble; the slaughter was merciless; havoc, ruin, devastation, misery engulfed the entire nation; it was a calamity unparalleled in the annals of the ancient world (La 1:12).

Strangely, Jeremiah's complaint seems to have been shared by God himself, who pronounced doom upon Assyria and Babylon because they brutally exceeded his mandate when they so utterly crushed Israel. (See Is 10:5-12; 37:21-22, 28-29; 47:5-6; and note the remarkable sentiment in Je 42:10c. See also Zc 1:14-15.)

Here then are some further examples of prophetic oracles that on the face of it are sober predictions, yet whose details are imaginary – [68]

LIMITED FULFILMENT

- ***Babylon (Is 13:17-22; 14:22-23; Je 50:39, 40; etc)***. As the book of *Daniel* shows, the Medes entered Babylon with ease; there was little bloodshed, and the city continued on as one of the greatest in the Persian

---

[68] The list is far from exhaustive, but I hope will be adequate to prove my point. The list is also basically the same as the one given in my book Understanding Your Bible, Vision Publishing, Ramona CA.

empire. It was later conquered by Alexander the Great, and later still became part of the Parthian Empire. In the time of Jesus (700 years after Isaiah) it was still a populous commercial centre.

Did Babylon's continuing existence embarrass the Master? No; despite Isaiah's passionate dooms, neither Jesus nor the apostles ever thought that the prophet's words had failed. They were apparently satisfied that the city's ongoing prosperity in no way diminished the truth of the ancient judgments – which shows that they did not read the oracles in the literal fashion that many moderns favour!

Soon after the time of Christ, Babylon began to decline (mainly because of changing trade routes). It was visited by the emperor Trajan in 115, who found it already partly ruined, and 84 years later was reported by the emperor Septimius Severus as being deserted. But that was nearly a millennium after Isaiah had pronounced its collapse!

Once again, must we say that the was prophet wrong? Of course not. His oracle, bared of its dramatic colouring, meant only that God would judge the proud city – an event that happened sufficiently when Babylon's pomp and power were stripped away by Cyrus the Great (539 B.C.). The provincial town that finally vanished at the end of the second century of the Christian era no longer had any connection politically, morally, or spiritually, with the arrogant imperial city of Isaiah's time.

- ***Moab (Is 15:5-9; 16:4-5, 13-14; and cp. also Zp 2:9)***. This oracle describes either an invasion by Assyria or a series of attacks by desert tribes; but there is no historical record of either event.

In any case, 200 years after Isaiah's time Moab still existed as a distinct nation, and the land remained occupied well into the Christian era. The prophet's savage indictment applied only to contemporary Moab, and it had a sufficient (though not a detailed or literal) fulfilment when Nebuchadnezzar conquered the land (in the 6th century).

Note in particular the oracle in 16:4b-5, which assures Moab, in highly idealistic (but not very realistic) language, that her only hope lay in accepting once again the sovereignty of the King of Judah (Moab had earlier thrown off the Jewish yoke).

Predictably, the Moabites refused to submit to Jewish dominance, and despite numerous invasions by various powers, continued for another thousand years, until the ravages of time finally erased the last remnants of its ancient identity.

Surprisingly, Jeremiah (48:47) predicts the restoration of Moab *"in the latter days"*, which is an oracle that much troubles various scholars. Whatever it may mean, the oracle certainly cannot be read literally, nor as applicable to ancient Moab, which has long since vanished from the earth.

Most scholars apply it either to Moabites who returned to Palestine along with the Jewish exiles, or to Moabites (or people who still resided in that area) who embraced the gospel both during apostolic times and since.

No doubt those are reasonable suggestions, but they simply confirm the fact that the prophecy did not have, and never can have, a literal fulfilment.

- ***Damascus (Is 17:1-2)***. Although Syria was invaded and crushed by the Assyrians, Damascus was never destroyed. It was later conquered again by the Babylonians, then by the Persians, Greeks, and Romans, but was still a thriving city in the time of Paul (who was led there after he was blinded on *"the road to Damascus"*).

Damascus still continues to the present day, and is possibly (despite the dooms of other prophets, e.g. Am 1:3-5) the oldest continuously inhabited city in the world.

- ***Egypt (Is 19:2-10, 17-25)***. The historical fulfilment of this oracle remains uncertain. It may refer to one of the later Assyrian invasions of Egypt (perhaps by Sargon or Esarhaddon), or to an 8th century B.C. Ethiopian invasion.

Verse 18, using normal prophetic hyperbole, probably means only that there will be substantial Jewish colonies in five cities. The "City of the Sun" was probably Heliopolis, which may have had Jewish inhabitants but was certainly never converted to Yahwism, for it was and remained the main centre of Sun worship in ancient Egypt.

In **verse 19** the *"altar"* and the *"pillar"* [69] are synonyms for a temple; however, no actual temple to Yahweh was ever built in Egypt, although large and influential colonies of Jews were later established in Alexandria and Aswan, with other groups of Jews scattered throughout the land, who remained faithful to Yahweh.

Some Egyptians were no doubt converted to Yahwism, but never to the extent implied by **verse 21**. Any attempt to apply the oracle to a date still future is precluded by the mention of *"Assyria"*, which was crushed and obliterated by the ancient Babylonians.

Ignoring then the lively, but improbable and certainly unrealistic detail, the oracle basically declares three things –

- God's judgment on ancient Egypt through civil war, drought, and invasion;
- God's control over the entire earth, every nation, and all the activities of mankind; and

---

(69) I reject as nonsense the idea that Isaiah was referring to the Pyramids.

- Yahwism would be carried to Egypt and to other lands by his scattered people.

Within those terms, the prophecy was satisfactorily accomplished.

- ***Arabia (Is 21:16-17)***. It is not possible to identify which historical invasion is referred to here; and in any case, more than 100 years later Jeremiah describes the same people as still prosperous and doomed to be conquered by Nebuchadnezzar (49:28-33).

Subsequently the tribe of Kedar dwindled in its influence and was eventually assimilated into other tribes; but by that time, for those people, Isaiah's oracles had long lost any relevance.

Whatever event the judgment referred to, it was well gone by the time the tribe finally vanished. Or, to put it differently, even if the tribe were still in existence today, the oracle would not be invalidated, for its adequate fulfilment did not depend upon every detail being literally accomplished.

- ***Tyre (Is 23:15-17)***. Tyre and Sidon were ruinously involved in a series of savage clashes between Egypt and Assyria in the middle 7th cent. B.C., and later suffered again when Nebuchadnezzar invaded the region (vs. 13). Tyre fell before the Babylonians in 572, after a gruelling 13-year siege.

Two centuries later the city angered the Persians and was conquered once more; then again by Alexander in 332; and eventually it became part of the Roman Empire. It was still a flourishing town in the time of Jesus, and has remained continuously occupied until today (despite Ez 26:13-14; 27:36;).

The "70 years" mentioned in *Isaiah 23:15* probably refers to the *total* period of Babylonian hegemony; in fact, Tyre was under immediate Babylonian dominion for only about half that period. Nor did Nebuchadnezzar actually "raze her palaces" and "make her a ruin." He did besiege and conquer Tyre; but the city remained intact and continued its commercial life under Babylonian rule.

Isaiah, by using the poetic device of "70 years" was able to indicate the approximate length of Babylonian world supremacy, and to show that after Babylon's fall Tyre's commercial supremacy would be restored. Within the prophet's intention, the prophecy was wonderfully fulfilled. But if it is taken literally it becomes deeply blemished.

- **_Edom (Is 34:5-17)_**. Although Edom suffered various invasions (mixed with periods of restored prosperity) during the centuries after Isaiah's death, at least some of her cities (e.g. Petra) were still thriving commercial centres as late as the 2nd century A.D.

Does that nullify the prophet's vision? No, but it does show that Isaiah never intended his prophecy to be taken literally. The central thrust of divine judgment upon the Edom contemporary with Isaiah was completely fulfilled. The other lurid details (e.g., vs. 9, 10) were added to intensify the warning, to give it strength, to colour it with poetic beauty and passion. (70)

The ultimate decay and disappearance of the nation was a result of altered commercial, political, and environmental factors, and could have had no reasonable connection with Isaiah's long-forgotten curse. Certainly, the extravagant details (71) of his oracles were never fulfilled. (72) (See also just

---

(70) The prophets were all as much poets as they were predictors.

(71) Streams turning into pitch, soil into sulphur, smoke rising for ever and ever, lying waste for many generations, no one ever again to pass through it, the land soaked with blood, inhabited only by goat-demons, by the demon-witch Lilith, wild creatures; and the like.

(72) The hyperbolic nature of oracles that decree a complete removal from the land of both humans and animals is suggested by
Continued on next page ....

below, under *Jeremiah 49:13, 18.*)

- **_Jerusalem_ (Je 31:40).** This passage, along with several other oracles in different places, declares that Jerusalem will be rebuilt and never again destroyed by aliens. But as Gill says in his commentary on the oracle, "certain it is, that after (Jerusalem) was rebuilt by Zerubbabel, it *was* plucked up, and thrown down by the Romans, and particularly by Hadrian, who ploughed it up, and built another city, and called it by his own name."

Gill overcomes the problem by adding, "but this figuratively rather intends the church of Christ, which is built on him the Rock, and so is immovable; and, like Mount Zion, shall abide for ever." From a Christian perspective, that is no doubt a reasonable viewpoint. But it scarcely allows for anything like a literal reading of the oracle (cp. also 33:16-18).

- **_Jewish Refugees_ (Je 42:17-18).** Despite an oracle of total annihilation, the refugees overcame sundry hardships and invasions, eventually flourished in Egypt, and developed into several prosperous communities (especially in Alexandria) that were still there in the time of Jesus (notice the amelioration tacked onto the end of *Jeremiah 44:14*, and enhanced in *vs. 28*).

- **_Egypt_ (Je 43:10-13).** Although Nebuchadnezzar did defeat Pharaoh Amasis in battle, in 566 B.C., Egypt remained independent, and apparently entered into a friendly alliance with Babylon.

Nebuchadnezzar, despite Jeremiah, did not *"smite the land of*

Jeremiah's words about Judah and Jerusalem (26:9; 36:29). Of course, as the account in Jeremiah itself makes plain, a significant number of people and flocks remained in the land after the Babylonians withdrew from Palestine.

Egypt", nor did he give the people to *"pestilence ... to captivity ... to the sword"*, nor did he *"kindle a fire in the temples of the gods of Egypt"* nor *"carry (their gods) away captive"*, nor did he *"burn (the temples of Egypt) with fire"*.

Was Jeremiah then a false prophet? No, but he would have been an astonished prophet if he had thought anyone would ever demand a strict fulfilment of every detail of his predictions!

- **_Edom_ *(Je 49:13, 18)*.** These oracles were not fulfilled literally. **Bozrah** was a powerful fortress and a royal city, well-situated to control the King's Highway (a major trade route).

Its modern name is Buseirah. Far from being turned into a *"perpetual waste"* it has remained more or less continually occupied until the present time. **Teman** (vs. 20) also still survives today as the modern town of Tawilan, about 5km east of Petra.

Edom escaped depredation at the hands of Nebuchadnezzar by becoming allied with the Babylonians. However, Jeremiah's oracles were sufficiently fulfilled by the fact that Edom later fell completely under the domination of the Nabataean Arabs. After that, the original Edomites never regained their independence.

- **_Hazor (Je 49:33)_.** The territory mentioned was never bereft of all inhabitants. Jeremiah seems rather to be using conventional terminology, a kind of apocalyptic idiom, or shorthand, that was never intended to be taken literally (cp. *"haunt of jackals"* 9:10; 10:22; 51:37; and *"desolation"* 4:27; 6:8; 9:11; 10:22; 12:10, 11; 32:43; etc; and *"no one shall dwell there"* 4:7, 29; 9:11; 26:9; 33:10; 44:22; etc).

Much the same can be said of the oracle about **_Elam_** (Persia) in *Jeremiah 49:33-39*. The land was never denuded of its entire population, it was never reduced to being *"a haunt of* *jackels, an everlasting wasteland"*, and there is no meaningful way in which ancient Elam can have its *"fortunes restored in the latter days"*.

Trying to read such oracles literally simply strips them of any valid meaning. But if they are understood within their own oracular culture, then they become passionate, vivid, dramatic, and full of pungent meaning.

- **<u>Babylon (Je 51:20-26)</u>**. As mentioned above, the description of Babylon's destruction by Cyrus was not literally fulfilled.

Cyrus actually encountered little resistance when he entered the city, so his invasion caused almost no damage. Indeed, Babylon remained a great city for several hundred more years. Its eventual decay and abandonment was an accident of changing trade patterns rather than a fulfilment of prophecy. Hence Jesus and the apostles were not troubled by the fact that Babylon was still a flourishing commercial city in their time, 600 years after Jeremiah had predicted its utter downfall.

How did the early church read the prophecy? Why were they not bothered by its apparent lack of literal fulfilment? They realised, of course, that the provincial Babylon of their time had no real connection with the great imperial city denounced eight centuries before.

Even if Babylon were still rich and prosperous today, it would not undo Jeremiah's oracle. The doom of God was sufficiently fulfilled by the crushing of Nebuchadnezzar's empire. Babylon's international dominance was humbled; she would never again be the queen city of the whole earth.

See also other oracles in *Jeremiah 4:25-29; 9:10-11; 31:40;*

32:37-41; 33:17; 46:19. [73] And for an illustration of how the fulfilment of an oracle could be considerably less draconian than the oracle itself, cp. *Jeremiah 33:10* with *39:10, 14; 40:6-12*. Note that Gedaliah was a member of the Jewish nobility, and that other commanders and nobles were left in the land after the departure of the Babylonian army. Note also the considerable number of people, leaders, and commanders, mentioned in *41:1-16*.

- **_Sodom (Ez 16:53-58)_**. This prophecy, if taken *"literally"*, predicts the restoration of Sodom and her subject cities. But even if a new city should be built on the former site of Sodom (which is still inundated by the Dead Sea), it would hardly be reasonable to equate it with the ancient city, which has now been obliterated for nearly 4,000 years.

Even in Ezekiel's day such an identification would not have been reasonable. Whatever Ezekiel meant, he was not predicting the literal resurgence of the city of Sodom. Nor did he expect his readers to approach his prophecy with such a foolish idea. But if he did not expect to be understood *"literally"* in this part of his oracle, then he probably expected also that the remainder of his oracles would be figuratively understood.

- **_Ammon & Edom (Ez 25:1-7, 10, 12-14; and cp. Zp 2:9)_**. If these oracles are taken literally, then Ezekiel contradicts Jeremiah (49:6).

As it happens, even today Ammon is still inhabited and prosperous. Likewise, the dooms of Ezekiel against Edom never

---

(73) However, by contrast, some prophecies did (and do) have a closely literal fulfilment, as, for example, Jeremiah's prediction that the Jewish captivity in Babylon would last 70 years (Je 29:10, plus other references); and note also the fulfilment of his oracle about the kings (22:10-19).

had a literal fulfilment, and many of its ancient communities remain inhabited to this day. The same can be said of his later oracles about Edom ("Mt Seir"): *"I will make Mount Seir a waste and a desolation; and I will cut off from it all who come and go. ... I will turn you into a wasteland for ever; never again will anyone dwell in your cities"* (35:7-9).

Was one prophet right and the other wrong? Of course not. The fault lies in those who try to turn the prophets into clairvoyants rather than what they were – preachers of righteousness.

Likewise, according to the ISBE, the city of Rabbah (which Ezekiel said would become a

> "pasture for camels" *25:5), and retained its importance in later times. It was captured by Ptolemy Philadelphus (285-247 BC), who called it Philadelphia. It was a member of the league of ten cities. Antiochus the Great captured it by means of treachery (Polyb. v. 71). Josephus (BJ, III, iii, 3) names it as lying East of Peraea. In the 4th century AD, it ranked with Bostra and Gerasa as one of the great fortified cities of Coele-Syria (Ritter,* Erdkunde, *XV, ii, 1154 f). It became the seat of a bishop. Abulfeda (1321 AD) says that Rabbah was in ruins at the time of the Moslem conquest.*

Notice, too, how Daniel, in an oracle that reached forward to the time of Antiochus IV Epiphanes (circa 170 B.C.), was able to describe Edom, Moab, and Ammon as still flourishing long after their utter ruin had been foretold by other prophets. Did he blush when he read their predictions? No, for he knew that within its actual intention, each prophecy had been adequately fulfilled.

- **_Tyre (Ez 26:1ff.)_.** Nebuchadnezzar (vs. 7) and his army laid siege to Tyre for 13 years (circa B.C. 567-554), but the city was not overthrown and the siege ended with a negotiated settlement (as Ezekiel himself intimates in 29:18).

Ezekiel said that Tyre would be utterly destroyed by Nebuchadnezzar, that it would *"never be rebuilt,"* that it would be engulfed by the ocean, that it would never again be inhabited, and he said, *"you shall be no more; though you be sought for, you will never be found again."* None of this was ever *"literally"* fulfilled. Nebuchadnezzar conquered, but did not destroy, Tyre. Nebuchadnezzar did not pull down its houses (26:12), nor did he turn it into a bare rock (vs. 4, 14), nor did he make any attempt to ensure that the city would be *"never rebuilt"* (vs. 14).

Some 220 years later, it was again conquered by Alexander the Great, in 332 B.C; but he did not destroy it either. Since the city still stands today, then *Ezekiel 27:36,* (74) if it were intended to be read *literally*, would be a piece of irresponsible mendacity. The truth is that in their main thrust of divine punishment upon a godless city, Ezekiel's oracles were quite fulfilled; but the ferocious details were not, and were never intended to be, fully realised.

Tyre remained a great commercial city for centuries after Babylon had fallen. The city still exists today. It was never inundated by the sea. Any tourist can easily find the modern city and the ruins of the ancient one. Does this make Ezekiel wrong? No, but it certainly makes some commentators wrong.

- ***Egypt (Ez 29:10-12; 30:6-19; 32:2ff)*** (75) What I have just said about Tyre applies equally to these

---

(74) "You have come to a dreadful end, and shall be no more forever" (NRSV).

(75) Note especially 32:7-8, in which the details are manifestly figurative. This passage shows the need to be careful about taking literally similar oracles, such as Joel 2:30-31 and Matthew 24:29, etc.

oracles. They never were, and plainly never will be done literally in all their particulars.

Thus, these things never happened – *"I will make the land of Egypt an utter waste and desolation ... No foot of man shall pass through it, and no foot of beast shall pass through it; it shall be <u>uninhabited forty years</u> ... I will scatter the Egyptians among the nations ... (Then) I will restore the fortunes of Egypt ... It shall be the most lowly of kingdoms, and never again exalt itself above the nations ..."* (see also 32:12-15) [76]

But, for all that, Ezekiel's dooms did indeed fall upon Egypt, and the nation was sufficiently judged by God.

AN IMPORTANT OBSERVATION

Did you observe, there is little in those oracles (and many others like them) that is obviously symbolic? On the contrary, they appear mostly to be factual; yet the prophets themselves apparently did not intend every detail of their words to be taken literally. Instead, they used a kind of prophetic style, or idiom, in which a central idea was proclaimed within a framework of poetic colour and standard imagery.

The ancient Jews understood this prophetic style; hence their dismay and horror, when in their case the prophecies did have an all too terrible and complete fulfilment. Despite the fearful doom predicted over and over against idolatrous Jerusalem, no-one, not even the prophets [77], ever imagined the prophecies would ever be so devastatingly accomplished. [78] As

---

(76) For further comment on this scripture, on others like it, and on the problems of reading prophecy too literally, see also above, in the "Pre-millennial School" section.

(77) Read Lamentations and see how appalled Jeremiah was at the awful fulfilment of his own predictions against Jerusalem.

(78) Even worse carnage and devastation had been pronounced upon Babylon than upon Jerusalem (cp. Is 13, and many other

Continued on next page ....

I have said above, reducing a great city to rubble, as the Babylonians did to Jerusalem, was uncommon in the ancient world. The report of it scandalised the nations. Their complaint seems to have been shared by God himself, who pronounced wreckage upon Assyria and Babylon because they went far beyond his dictate when they so utterly crushed Israel (cp Is 10:5-12; 37:21-22, 28-29; 47:5-6).

Does this mean prophecy should never be read literally? Not at all. But it does mean that caution is needed, and it does call into question the *pre-millennialist* supposition that the literal method is universally the only valid way to read the prophetic scriptures.

Lastly, there is the case of

- **_Jesus (Jn 7:27)_**. The misunderstanding among even the devout of that time about the manner of the Messiah's first appearance should make us cautious of dogmatism about his second coming!

Note also the difficulties inherent in *Matthew 10:23; 16:28*. See also *Matthew 11:14*, which shows that Jesus was quite willing to accept the fulfilment in principle of an oracle rather than a literal fulfilment.

Or look at his *Olivet Discourse* (Mt 24:3-44). Commentators have been searching out the meaning of those oracles for nearly twenty centuries and are no closer to consensus now than they were at the beginning!

The Puritan commentator Matthew Henry described the *Olivet Discourse* (Mt 24:3-51) as "dark and difficult", and reckoned that Jesus preached it, not *ad populum* – to the people, but *ad*

---

prophecies); yet Babylon and its people emerged almost unscathed from the Persian conquest, to remain largely untroubled for centuries, albeit deprived of its former pomp and power.

clerum – to the clergy (Commentary, *in. loc.*).

There is also the difficulty that some people find in Jesus' words about *"not one stone will be left standing upon another"* (Mt 24:2; Mk 13:2), when in fact, the "Wailing Wall" in Jerusalem, which was part of the very temple Jesus had just left, still has many stones *"standing one upon another"*! Does this mean that Jesus got it wrong, that he was a false prophet? Of course not. It means only that he spoke within the same sort of prophetic framework as the other prophets of Israel used, employing colourful and exaggerated imagery to state a basic truth. In this case, the oracle was more than sufficiently fulfilled when the Roman general Titus gave command for the city and temple to be razed to the ground. [79]

William E. Biederwolf says that across the centuries opinions on the first part of the *Olivet Discourse* have fallen into four groups –

- Those who think it was all fulfilled in the past at the time of the Destruction of Jerusalem.

- Those who think it is all yet to be fulfilled during the time of the great tribulation just before the coming of the Lord in glory and in judgment on the antichristian forces of the world after the Church has been caught up according to the fourth chapter of *1 Thessalonians*.

- Those who think it is being fulfilled in this present dispensation and is to find its final and more awful fulfilment in the great tribulation through which the Church herself will pass in the time of the end.

---

[79]   See the description in Josephus, The Jewish Wars 7.1.1.

- Those who see part fulfilment in the Destruction of Jerusalem and the other part in the Parousia (the second coming of Jesus) which is still in the future. [80]

- I would add a fifth common interpretation: the *idealist* view, which holds that the oracle must be read in a figurative and symbolic sense, with continual fulfilments across the centuries.

Which is the correct view? Only heaven knows! That is why St John Chrysostom (5th century) thought it safer to focus on the moral and ethical aspects of the *Discourse* than on any attempt to pinpoint the meaning of its details – an opinion with which I heartily concur *(Homilies on Matthew 24)*.

---

[80] The Second Coming Bible, Baker Book House, 1972; pg. 327.

Eight

RESURRECTION

A long time ago the wise king wrote, *"There is nothing new under the sun."* Nowhere is that rule more certain than when it is linked with human venality; thus from the dawn of history public office has been to some people the key to private treasure. Thus the man who was probably the first person ever to earn a living as a professional writer, Thomas Fuller, wrote in 1662 about the fiscal advantages available to the unscrupulous at the royal court. On being asked what the perquisites might be of the office of Lord Treasurer of England, Fuller quoted the reply of a former treasurer: "that it might be worth some thousands of pounds to him who (after death) would go instantly to heaven; twice as much to him who would go to purgatory; and a *nemo scit* (no-one knows how much) to him who would adventure to go to a worse place!" [81]

Heaven and hell! How seriously they are treated by some; how scornfully by others! The following pages concentrate on these two great themes, beginning with the still greater event that is the prelude to eternity: *the resurrection of the dead*. Three astonishing miracles are predicted in scripture for that magnificent day –

- **_first_**, the _resurrection_ of the church, which will bring all Christians out of the grave, and, as it were, stand us upon the earth again; then follows

---

(81)   From Fuller's Preface to his History of the Worthies of England; reprinted by the Folio Society, London, 1987.

- **_second_**, the _rapture_; that is, the act of catching up the entire church into the air to meet the returning Christ; [82] then follows

- **_third_**, the _resurrection_ of the rest of the dead. [83]

THE RAISING OF THE DEAD

HOW MANY WILL RISE?

ALL OF THE DEAD

Scripture states nothing more clearly than this: all who have ever died will eventually be called out of their graves by the word and power of the living God, to receive their appointed destiny (Da 12:2; Ac 24:15; Re 20:11-15; Jn 5:28-29; etc).

> *I like that ancient Saxon phrase, which calls*
> *The burial ground God's Acre! It is just;*
> *It consecrates each grave within its walls,*
> *And breathes a benison o'er the sleeping dust ...*
>
> *Into its furrow shall we all be cast,*
> *In the sure faith that we shall rise again*
> *At the great harvest, when the archangel's blast*
> *Shall winnow, like a fan, the chaff and grain ...*

---

(82) In this context, "rapture" does not carry its ordinary meaning of ecstatic joy, or transports of happiness; rather, it reaches back to a Latin word, rapere, which means to "snatch up and carry away". The past participle of rapere is raptus – hence the "rapture", in which the church will be "seized" and carried off into heaven.

(83) No one would argue with the sequence of these three events, but there is much contention over how long a gap separates the first two from the third. As you saw in the last Chapter, some would place the three events on the same day; others would separate them by at least the length of the "millennium".

With thy rude ploughshare, Death, turn up the sod,
And spread the furrow for the seed we sow;
This is the field and Acre of our God,
This is the place where human harvests grow! (84)

Truly, from the fruitful grave every human soul will rise, but not all to the same destiny. As the poet declared, this harvest, like any other, is a mixture of *"chaff and grain"*. So we find the dead called from their resting places –

IN TWO GROUPS

The Just

Whatever divisions of creed, colour, status, wealth, learning, may have separated the dead while they were living, now that they lie in the grave there are but two groups: the *just*, and the *unjust*. The first of those groups to rise from the dead will be the *just* – that is, the entire church, which means all those who have died in Christ, plus all the believers who are still alive on earth when Jesus comes. The second group to rise will be

The Unjust

That is, the remainder of humanity. (85)

HOW CAN WE BE SURE?

A friend who was an undertaker once told me a cluster of stories about the astonishing efforts people make to avoid the resurrection. One in particular sticks in my memory. A man

---

(84) H. W. Longfellow, *God's Acre*; stanzas 1, 3, 5.

(85) Note once again: I am concerned here only with the fact of the resurrection, not with its sequence. In other words, I am not dealing with the question of whether or not the resurrection and/or rapture will occur before or after the tribulation, nor whether it will occur before or after the millennium.

died, and left instructions in his will that he was to be cremated and his ashes scattered slowly from a plane flying as high as possible. He then stated his confidence that his ashes, now scattered across hundreds of square miles of land, could never again be assembled! Thus he hoped to thwart the Last Judgment!

Then there was the woman (I think a German countess) who commanded her heirs to bury her in a lead coffin, welded together, in a deep, reinforced concrete grave, bound around with steel traps. She hoped her remains would lie undisturbed for eternity. But she reckoned without the humour of the Almighty. As her stone tomb was being built, a gentle breeze lodged a tiny beech seed in one corner. The seed took root, grew irresistibly, and eventually split the concrete asunder, leaving her bones exposed to the eyes of all!

If such efforts were not so sad they would be ludicrous. If there is to be no resurrection, why make any attempt to avoid it? If the resurrection truly has been decreed by God, what human contrivance could possibly hinder the wisdom and power of the Almighty?

But some people will commit any folly in preference to yielding consent to the sovereignty of God. Others argue that a resurrection of the dead is impossible, on the following three grounds –

THE DISSIPATION OF THE BODY

Suppose *your* mortal remains were consumed to ashes and scattered across land and sea. Can God really call you together again and cause you to stand before him on Judgment day?

The Bible answer to that question is given in two affirmations –

- **<u>first</u>**: *our* resurrection has been made inescapable by the resurrection of *Christ* (1 Co 6:14; Re 1:17-18; Ac 17:31).

- **second**: God has limitless power to do this (Ac 26:8; Ph 3:21).

Since Christ is indeed risen from the dead, and since the Lord our God the Almighty reigns, why should it be thought difficult for the dead to rise? Neither flame, nor damp, nor worm, nor corruption, can defy the majesty of heaven. When the voice of God speaks, the dead will rise, no matter how finely their dust has been mingled with the elements, or even dissolved into atoms.

The second argument against the resurrection is based on –

THE LACK OF CONTINUITY

How many generations have gone before us! How many millions have perished, and earth has gone back to earth, and dust to dust, and ashes to ashes, only to surface again in the blowing winds and shifting soil of the restless planet! Who can deny that we are all a composite of the clay of countless generations? The elements that compose my body, and yours, have all been part of the flesh of thousands who now sleep in the grave.

> *"Therefore," someone argues, "if I am to rise with the same body I now have, it can only be at the cost of others whose dust is in me. If they rise, I cannot. If I rise, they cannot."* [86]

But Paul (2Co 5:1-5) shows that the resurrection does not depend upon gathering up a particular collection of molecules. He uses a remarkable illustration to show the nature and purpose of the resurrection. It has four parts –

- ***Our real "self" is distinct from the body in which it dwells.***

---

(86)   I have lost the source of this quote.

Paul describes the body as a *"tent"* in which *"we"* live while awaiting our new *"heavenly dwelling"*. We can even be *"away from the body"* (vs. 8) and still fully retain our identity, so great is the distinction between the two. Thus Paul will rise in the resurrection, and remain the same person, even though his former body has long since mingled with the dust of a million other living things.

- ***The identity of our real "self" does not depend upon it inhabiting a certain body.***

Rather, it depends upon an unbroken consciousness and memory. We have already experienced this in our present life. Probably there is today not one cell in your body remaining from when you were a baby. All the cells you were born with have been exhausted and discarded. So in that sense you have a different body from the one you first inhabited. Yet you are manifestly the same person. That is why Paul can speak about *"longing to be clothed with a heavenly dwelling"* without suggesting that the process would turn him into another man.

- ***Without a body, the real "self" is "naked" and it yearns to be "clothed" (vs2-3).***

Without a proper covering, the real self cannot fully express itself. Paul is very careful here. He does not want to go too far in separating the self from its body. He wants to avoid a pagan dualism, which views body and soul as enemies of each other. He will have nothing to do with the idea that salvation consists of crushing the body so that the soul might soar free into heaven. He makes it clear that the major function of the resurrection is to restore full body/soul harmony to the redeemed, although in a glorious new body of *"heavenly"* origin.

A soul left *"naked"* would be doomed to a wretched half-existence for all eternity. But instead, we have a joyous hope. We presently live in a ragged *"tent"*, *"groaning and burdened"*, longing for God's magnificent promise to be fulfilled. And in the resurrection our present disjunction will indeed be transformed into radiant wholeness. God will not leave us "*naked*"; rather, "*we have a building made by God, an everlasting house in heaven, not built by human hands ... God himself made us for this very purpose!*"

Now we have an answer to a problem that has puzzled many people: if the soul joins Christ in Paradise immediately after death (Lu 23:43), what is the purpose of the resurrection? The reason is clear. The soul with Christ may be in bliss; but full expression of its glory, and full possession of riches of the kingdom, depend upon the ultimate reunion of soul and body in the resurrection.

- ### *The real "self" cannot be satisfied with just any body.*

Rather, the new body that clothes the "self" must somehow be associated with the old body (vs4). If Paul had closed his argument at vs. 3, it *would* have left the impression that we shall altogether discard the old body, like a worn-out *tent*, and change it for a brand new *mansion*, with the old having no connection with the new. But that would no longer be a *resurrection*; rather, it would be a *replacement!*

How can that problem be solved? Paul does it by a surprising twist. He changes the analogy. Instead of talking about replacing a tent with a palace, he likens the resurrection to changing an old garment for a new. But he does it in a peculiar way. He visualises the old as being *incorporated into* the new; not just one garment being placed on top of another, but somehow both of them merging to form a new kind of garment, one that is both earthly and heavenly –

> We do not want to be <u>unclothed</u>, but rather to be <u>clothed over</u> with our heavenly dwelling, so that what is mortal may be swallowed up by life (vs. 4).

There is in Wisconsin (as of 2012) a famous place called the

House On The Rock, where the builder has utilised the existing rock formation and trees as part of the house. The house is not just built *around* those natural features, rather the boulders and trees are *integral* to the whole structure, its foundations, walls, and rafters.

In the same way, the resurrection will create an amalgam of the old and the new, wrought together to form *"our everlasting house in heaven, not built by human hands"* (vs. 2), but by a mystery of divine power. Thus your resurrection body must bear the stamp of your personality, the mark of your character; it must be a body in which each cell is organised according to the original pattern of your identity; yet it must be something more than a replacement, or even a replica, of the old. So, the resurrection body will be neither –

- **_a restoration of the original_** molecules, in their entirety, that were buried in the grave; nor
- **_a wholly new body_** that has no relationship to the one that was buried.

Perhaps someone will protest: "All of this sounds too much like the old absurdity Heywood raised 400 years ago: how can you both eat your cake and keep it? On the one hand you are trying to solve the problem of the destruction of the body in the grave, and you say the resurrection doesn't depend upon raising that same body. But then, on the other hand, you say there can be no resurrection without somehow incorporating the old body. Make up your mind!"

A paradox indeed! But not so puzzling as it may seem. How this paradox can be resolved is discussed below. But above all the detail stands this great fact: **the Holy Spirit is the Guarantor of this resurrection to the church** (vs. 5).

So I stand at my mother's grave, or at the grave of my infant son Gavin, and shrink from the horror of destruction that lies below me, and I begin to doubt. Suddenly, the Holy Spirit stirs within me; the word of God blazes in my soul; the resurrection power of the living Christ trembles in my flesh; and once again I *know* that the promise of God cannot fail! The dead shall live again. Death has no strength to withstand the call of the Almighty. When he speaks, all who are in the grave will come forth, willingly or not, and will be obliged to stand before their God.

How does the Holy Spirit *"guarantee what is to come"*? His special pledge is surely *glossolalia*. If anyone asks, when we speak in tongues, *"What does this mean?"* (Ac 2:12), we reply, *"This is what the prophet Joel spoke about. What you see and hear is proof that Christ is risen from the dead, and that we too shall rise in his name on the last day!"* (Ac 2:16, 33) [87] Whenever the Holy Spirit is flowing from my innermost being, like a river of living water (Jn 7:38-39), and I stand in the presence of God, praising him with *"tongues of angels and of men"* (1 Co 13:1), my heart leaps toward the Second Advent. In the sound of that heavenly language my ears hear the first echoes of the supernatural *"shout of Christ"*, the distant thunder of *"the voice of the archangel"*, and an early warning of *"the trumpet blast of God"*! (1 Th 4:16).

Having such a gift from God, rejoicing daily in such an irresistible witness, how can I doubt that Christ is coming again and that I shall rise to meet him in the air when he comes? (2 Co 5:5; 1 Th 4:16-18). So we have answered two objections to the resurrection: the barrier of bodily dissipation; and the lack of continuity between the old body and the new. But there is a third –

THE BURDEN OF A MATERIAL BODY

To some people this is an irremediable blemish on the idea of a

---

(87) Note that our text passage, 2 Co 5:1-10, was addressed to the Corinthians, the most charismatic of churches, who could hardly have understood *"the guarantee of the Spirit"* in any other than glossolalic terms.

literal resurrection of the dead. What possible benefit could there be in burdening the soul with a material body for all eternity? Should we not prefer to be like the angels, immaterial spirits? Doesn't Christ himself promise this? (Mt 22:30).

Paul's answer is expressed in a remarkable phrase, *"it is raised a spiritual body"* (1 Co 15:42-44). There is the solution. The saints in the resurrection will not merely be *"like"* the angels, rather, they will be *superior* to the angels! (1 Co 6:2, 3) The angels are presently spirits, and will always remain so. We are presently *"natural"*; but without discarding the glory of the natural, we will also assume the spiritual. No angel will ever share the splendour of this new kind of existence: *"a spiritual body"*.

So the objection is foolish, that a resurrection would "burden us with a material body." On the contrary, in the resurrection we shall assume an expressive power, a dignity and majesty, infinitely beyond anything we know now. Indeed, it will be the glory of Jesus himself! (1 Jn 3:2-3).

Nine

RAPTURE

Someone came to Paul and asked him, *"How are the dead raised?"*

To us, that seems a reasonable question. But Paul had a different opinion! His response was blunt: *"Don't be stupid!"* (1 Co 15:35a, 36a).

Nonetheless, he decided to be kind to ignorance, and graciously suggested that the answer can be found in your own garden –

THE DEATH OF THE BODY IS NO BARRIER

Here is the ancient and despairing cry: *"If a man dies, how can he live again?"* (Jb 14:14) Death seems so final, so utterly irreversible. To raise a living person into eternal life is easy to visualise. But how can those who have been dead for centuries, or even a year, ever walk and talk again?

Says Paul, walk outside, look at your garden, and you will see that very thing happening all the time – life coming out of death –

> *What you plant cannot come to life until it first dies!* (1 Co 15:36).

You plant a seed. A flower grows from it. But not until the seed has perished. So, far from bodily death hindering the resurrection, it is in fact a necessary precursor! Even those who are alive when Jesus comes must still undergo a physical change akin to death and resurrection (Ph 3:21).

THE DISSOLUTION OF THE BODY IS NO BARRIER

Again we encounter what is probably the most serious

objection to a resurrection of the dead – how can a body that has returned to its primeval elements, mingled with the dust of the earth, absorbed into plants, animals, and other human beings, ever be raised again as a single entity?

Once more, Paul finds his answer in the miracle of a garden –

> *What you sow in the ground is not the plant it will become, but a naked seed – perhaps a grain of wheat, or some other seed.* (vs. 37).

How much of the original seed would you find if you were able to dissect an adult plant down to its last cell? Nothing! The processes of germination and growth completely consume the seed; yet there remains an ineradicable link between the seed and its plant.

Likewise in human life. Nothing of the seed of life our parents gave us remains in us. Yet who can ever dissolve the bond that runs unbroken back to the moment of our conception in the womb? Even more, how much of your infant frame remains in you? Nothing! Every cell has long since been expended and discarded. Yet the links that chain you to that infant identity can never be undone.

Thus we see again what we saw above – continuity of identity does not depend upon continuity of bodily parts. Your present body may be utterly dissolved away, as a seed is in the damp earth, but a new body can arise from that same earth, indisputably linked with the one that perished. A germ of life, a mystical identity, passes from cell to cell during this earthly pilgrimage, and will do so again when the voice of God calls us from the grave.

The Division of the Body is No Barrier

"But surely," someone will protest, "the sundering of soul and body in death shatters the bond that united them, and makes a resurrection pointless?"

Paul will not allow it. So long as the germ of life and personal identity remains undestroyed, not even the sundering of body and soul can deter the resurrection. God is able to give the soul whatever body he chooses, and in the process maintain the unity of the original person –

> *God gives to every seed its own "body", whatever kind he wants it to have, and each seed has its own special "body"* (vs. 38).

That a "body" will rise from every "seed" planted in the earth, is part of the immutable law of God. Thus all who die will live again to face the judgment. Each "body" called out of the earth will be irrevocably linked with the one decomposed in the grave. This is no doubt a mystery, but it is one that is rooted in the mystery of the Father's irresistible will.

So Paul dismisses the question: *"How can the dead rise?"* But then he is at once challenged with another –

WHAT BODY WILL THE DEAD HAVE?

Once again, the great apostle is impatient. *"What a stupid question!"* was his rejoinder. (vs. 35b, 36a).

Nonetheless, he condescended to give two answers (vs. 37, 38) –

EACH SEED PRODUCES ITS OWN KIND

There is a dread finality about the laws of sowing and reaping. What each seed will produce is already determined by an inner identity. Once the seed is planted, that inner identity cannot be changed. How deceiving, also, outward appearance may be! Two seeds may look the same: yet one may produce a thorn, and the other an orchid; or, one may produce a healthy plant, and the other, a plant rotten with disease.

The resurrection will be the same. People all look much the same when they are lowered into the grave. But what a difference when they come out! Some to life, some to damnation (Jn 5:28-29). And that result is fixed at the moment of death. Those who lie in the grave have their destiny irrevocably determined, beyond remedy or change, beyond increase or decrease.

A seed may be modified before it is planted. But once it is placed in the soil nothing can change the plant that will grow out of it – *"a different kind of plant grows from each kind of seed"* (1 Co 15:38). Likewise, what you are when you sleep will determine what you will be when you awake. Now is the time to shape your destiny; then will be too late. Those who are planted ugly with sin, will arise with the same character, fully disclosed. Those who are planted in the beauty of holiness, will arise with the same fragrant loveliness radiating from their entire being. The judgment will hardly be necessary. The resurrection itself will reveal with utter clarity the true character of each person at the moment of death. The grave cannot change it. The resurrection will fully unveil it.

THE FLOWER IS MORE GLORIOUS THAN ITS SEED

Now Paul narrows his analogy to the *godly* (vs. 40-44), and shows how vast a difference exists between the natural body and the spiritual body that arises from it (cp. also vs. 37). Look at a seed (says the apostle), and then look at the plant that grows from it. How small, unprepossessing, insignificant, the seed; but how glorious the orchid! If you look at a seed, with no other knowledge of the plant, how could you ever tell what magnificence it might be hiding? So are we. Not much to look at now. But what splendour will emblazon us on that coming day! Our risen form will be as much more glorious than our present shape as the rose is to its seed. No one, looking at us now, could imagine what we shall be. But we can say two things about our coming appearance –

- we shall *all* be like Jesus (1 Jn 3:2; Re 1:12-17a); but

- we shall *not* all be like each other – for we shall differ from each other in glory, in the resurrection, as the sun differs from the moon, and the moon from the stars, and the stars from each other (1 Co 15:41).

Just as the light of all heavenly bodies is the same kind, so there will be a commonality in the radiant beauty shared by all the saints on that day. Yet as surely as the lights in the sky above us differ dramatically in their effulgence, so will saint differ from saint in shining beauty. Some will blaze like the sun; some with the serene loveliness of the moon; others like the bright constellations; but many with but a dim and feeble gleam. That is why the apostle urges each of us to strive for an *"abundant entrance"* into the kingdom of God (1 Pe 1:11).

THE RAPTURE OF THE CHURCH

RAISED WITH A "SPIRITUAL" BODY

It is time to give more attention to Paul's remarkable statement about the saints rising with a *"spiritual body"*. Please read *1 Corinthians 15:42-44*.

Some idea of the nature of this coming *"spiritual body"* can be seen from the examples of

MOSES AND ELIJAH

See **_Matthew 17:3-4_**. Although the exact nature of those apparitions on the mountain remains uncertain, and although they are not entirely parallel to the resurrection, they do suggest certain things about the resurrection –

- The disciples instantly recognised Moses and Elijah, though they had obviously never met them nor seen any likeness of them.

There will be no strangers in the resurrection; recognition of each other by all the saints will probably be intuitive, instantaneous, and total.

- Though Moses and Elijah were primarily spiritual in nature, they still had a physical, or at least a visible, form.

We shall be neither wholly ethereal nor wholly material in the resurrection; but a marvellous blending of the two, physical and spiritual, equally at home in either dimension, possessing a mysterious *"spiritual body"*.

- They were intelligent, they knew the Lord Jesus Christ, they had a clear understanding of the purpose of God, and they were able to speak with Jesus about his coming death (Lu 9:31).

Paul declares that one of the great joys of the resurrection will be this: *"we shall know fully, even as we are fully known."* (1 Co 13:12) No longer condemned to look through *"a dark glass"*! (vs. 12). No longer confined within *"partial knowledge"* and *"partial revelation"*! (vs. 9). Then our eyes will be opened to see the face of the Lord our King *"in his beauty"* (Is 33:17, 24), and to know his will and to do it with perfect joy!

- They evidently retained their distinctive personalities and characteristics.

Moses was still Moses. Elijah was still Elijah. Their passage into heaven had not changed them into other people. Our gospel is not like that of the Hindus, which imagines *Nirvana* as a state of total absorption into the divine, like a drop of spray falling back into the vast green sea. Christ did not come to obliterate us (which is the thief's work, Jn 10:10), but to make us truly ourselves – what we should have been, would have been, if sin had not so savagely marred us. Whatever nobly distinguishes you from every other person will not be eradicated in the resurrection, but rather enhanced, enriched, made even more magnificently a reflection of part of the Father's supernal radiance.

- The possession of a *"spiritual body"* enabled them to commune freely with the transfigured Christ, and it gave them access to both earth and heaven.

Thus the saints will have full access to the far-flung universe with its multitude of galaxies, and also to the furthest reaches of the angelic heavens. Whatever qualities are needed for the fullest use of both dimensions will be provided by the amazing capabilities of those incredible *"spiritual bodies"*.

THE RISEN CHRIST

The resurrection of Christ may be taken as a pattern for the resurrection of all who have found eternal life through their faith in him –

- **_He rose from the dead_** literally and physically; he was not a mere phantom, nor merely a replica of the former man (Lu 24:36; Jn 20:27).

The same Jesus who was laid in the tomb walked out of it.

- **_His resurrection body had attributes_**, form, facial features, functions, which left no doubt that it was fully continuous with his former body.

His identity was also confirmed by the wounds that were still evident, and by the empty tomb (Lu 24:39; Jn 20:27).

- **_He could be seen and handled_** in a way that would have been impossible for a purely spirit-being.

He did not merely show himself to the disciples in a visionary form, but he conversed with them, shared activities with them, entered into a relationship with them, thus demonstrating his substance. He was neither a phantom nor some kind of airy spectre. He was *real,* the same Jesus they had known and touched before Calvary. Yet he was not *fully* the same as he had been, for now he too had a *"spiritual body"*.

- **_His body was changed_**; he had entered into a new form of existence.

Jesus had *"flesh and bones"* but no blood (Lu 24:39). [88] He was the first of an entirely new race of beings: redeemed humanity, possessing in the one body all the glory of both the *"natural"* and the *"spiritual"*.

- **_He could eat_**, yet presumably with no necessity to do so (Lu 24:41-43).

The gospels describe two different kinds of resurrection appearances of Christ – *(a)* there are those in which he appeared to be just the same as he had been before, which persuaded his disciples that he was truly alive, and encouraged them not to fear him, but to relate to him as they had always done. But there were also *(b)* those in which he appeared strangely different. These induced awe in his disciples, making them realise they could not presume upon him. The second kind gradually became predominant, culminating in his ascension.

- **_His personality_** and behavioural characteristics were unchanged.

Mary recognised his voice (Jn 20:16); the disciples recognised a familiar gesture (Lu 24:31).

- **_He was not restricted_** by physical barriers, such as a closed door (Lu 24:36; Jn 20:19), or distance (Lu 24:15, 34), and he was able to appear or disappear at will (Lu 24:31, 36; Jn 20:19, 26).

- **_He could present himself_** as an ordinary person, and yet exercise extraordinary powers, being able to change

---

(88) Note that Jesus' departure from the usual formula, "flesh and blood," would have been significant to his hearers, who identified blood with the sinful life of man.

his appearance (Mk 16:12), or to prevent people from recognising him (Lu 24:15-16, 31-32; Jn 20:14-16).

- **He had unrestricted passage** between heaven and earth (Jn 20:17, 27).

In between the two incidents described by John, it seems that Jesus had returned to heaven, possibly to fulfil the OT type of the entrance of the high priest into the holiest place with the blood of the sacrifice (Le 16:17). Also, between the Lord's occasional appearances to his disciples during the forty days before his ascension, we can suppose only that he was with the Father in heaven.

All the above characteristics suggest something to us of the nature of the resurrection (although allowance must be made for the differences that obviously exist between our resurrection and his). At least they show that the resurrection is not just a *reanimation* nor a *restoration* of the former body, but must be seen as an *entirely new order of being*.

As members of that new order each saint will become *incorruptible* and *immortal* (1 Co 15:51-53), committed forever to holiness and to unbroken joy in the presence and service of God. (89)

RAISED TO BE WITH CHRIST

See *1 Thessalonians 4:17; John 14:1-3*.

The immediate result of the rapture is expressed in the words, *"so shall we always be with the Lord"*. What a power of comfort lies in that beautiful saying! To those who love the Lord, the sweetest words he ever spoke are these: *"I will come*

---

(89) Remember, though, that "eternity" in scripture is not endless time, but rather an entirely different sphere of existence, in which God dwells, and which we, in our present confines of time and space, find impossible truly to visualise.

again and take you to myself, that where I am there you may be also!"

But many other splendid blessings are associated with the joyful promise of his return. Along with the rapture, and our union with Christ, scripture describes the following treasures: (90)

- **true rest** from trouble (2 Th 1:7)
- **freedom** from corruption and pain (Ro 8:18-23)
- **deliverance** from the wrath to come (1 Th 1:10. Note: the word *"deliver"* means *"to rescue by a sudden withdrawal"*, and it probably refers here to the rapture)
- the **gathering together** of the entire church (Mt 24:31)
- **entrance** into *immortality, incorruptibility,* and *eternal life* (Mt 25:31, 34, 36; Jn 6:39, 40; 1 Co 15:53-55).

Paul stresses the idea that this great change will take place *"in the air"* (1 Th 4:17). That is important, for the Bible speaks of *"the air"* as the domain of the principalities and powers of darkness (Ep 2:2; 6:12). How great will be Satan's chagrin when this mighty demonstration of the victory of Christ takes place right in his own territory!

- **equality** with the angels (Lu 20:35-36; Mt 22:30).

---

(90) As I have mentioned already, the saints will not be equal in glory; nonetheless, they will all receive glory. That is, some blessings belong irrevocably to every member of the raptured church. In the list above, I have tried to collect all that the NT says about the common inheritance that every saint will receive. These are the wonderful benefits that will be communicated to us in the moment of the rapture.

Note: we shall not be made *into* angels, but rather shall be *"<u>as</u> the angels"*; that is, equal to them in access to the spiritual world; equal to them in freedom from the limitations of physical laws; equal to them in society and fellowship (He 12:22b). But in other respects – our union with Christ, our authority in his kingdom, our understanding of the mysteries of God (He 2:16; 1 Co 6:2-3; 1 Pe 1:12), our *"spiritual bodies"* – we shall be raised to an honour not shared by even the mightiest of the angels!

- **<u>appearing</u>** with Christ in his glory (Cl 3:4; 2 Th 2:14)
- **<u>sitting</u>** down in his kingdom (Mt 8:11; 13:43; 25:34)
- **<u>receiving</u>** our rightful inheritance (Ac 20:32; 26:18; Cl 1:5, 12; 3:24; He 9:15; 1 Pe 2:3, 4)
- **<u>gaining</u>** the City of God (He 11:16; Jn 14:1-3; Re 21:22-27)
- **<u>wearing</u>** the crown of glory (1 Pe 5:4)
- **<u>serving</u>** God in his temple and before his throne (Re 7:15-17)
- **<u>exulting</u>** at the marriage supper of the Lamb (Re 19:9).

See *Revelation 19:4-9*, which gives a picture of the raptured church at that joyous feast; and note –

- **<u>verse 4.</u>** The *24 elders* are a picture of the whole church; the *four creatures* symbolise all the angels. It is a vision of the entire host of God's servants praising their Lord.
- **<u>verse 5.</u>** The voice is not that of Christ nor of God (notice the words *"<u>our</u> God"*), but presumably that of a high angel.

The words *"small"* and *"great"* may either refer to the former social status of each saint on earth; or to their new state in heaven; thus indicating the different honour each has received in heaven [91]. Nonetheless, they are all before the throne, joyful in the presence of God.

- **verse 6, 7.** Here is the song of the heavenly host and of all the saints, singing with one mighty voice, all dissension and division gone.

They sing, *"Hallelujah!"* The four references to this word in this chapter are the only places in which it occurs in the NT. But no other setting could be more fitting!

They are praising God for what he <u>*has*</u> done (overthrowing the Harlot, vs. 1-3); and for what he is <u>*about*</u> to do (exalt his Bride).

- **verse 8.** The *"fine linen"* of the Bride starkly contrasts with the gaudy apparel of the Harlot (18:14-16).

Did you notice the subtle apposition: the garment is *"given"* to the Bride – thus she cannot boast that it is her own workmanship; yet it is also woven out of <u>her</u> *"righteous deeds"* – which enable the Father to honour and reward her. What is this robe? Nothing less than the robe of Christ's righteousness, *"imputed for justification, imparted for sanctification,"* [92] and made into a glorious garment by the Holy Spirit, without whose gracious aid none of the members of the "Bride" would ever have been a "saint". Yet without the willing and godly labours of the Bride, the Holy Spirit would not have been able to weave her beautiful garment nor clothe her so radiantly.

- **verse 9.** The Bride may be thought of as the whole church assembled together; but in this verse it is the individual Christian who is being invited to attend the wedding feast as an honoured guest.

---

(91)   See below, the chapter headed *Bema*.
(92)   Matthew Henry.

Note how solemn the setting is: *"The <u>angel</u> said to me, 'Write this ...' And he also said to me, 'These are the true words of God.'"* John was so moved, without thinking he prostrated himself (vs. 10).

Jewish marriages followed a pattern that is reflected here –

- the **<u>announcement</u>** of the marriage.

For ages the OT stood as God's written notice of the coming betrothal (cp. the many OT references to Israel as the *Bride of God*)

- the **<u>betrothal</u>**, which was much more binding than an "engagement" is with us.

A betrothed couple were legally bound to each other, and were already thought of as man and wife (cp. 2 Co 11:2).

At this time also, the prospective husband would pay the bride-price, or dowry, to the bride's father. Thus Christ betrothed himself to us when he came and lived among us, and he purchased us as his Bride when he offered his own life on the cross.

- the **<u>interval</u>**, between betrothal and the actual wedding day, which could be quite a long time.

But eventually the groom would come with his companions to fetch his bride from her home. He would find her with her maidens, dressed and ready for the nuptial feast (cp. Mt 25:1-13). We are now in this interval stage, waiting for the coming of our Bridegroom.

- the **<u>wedding feast</u>**, which might last seven days, and sometimes twice as long; but in our case, will last for ever!

There is only *one* blessed company on this planet, and that is those who have received an invitation to the marriage supper of the Lamb. Do you have that invitation? Can you see yourself among that company?

Ten

IMMORTALITY

> My rendezvous is appointed – it is certain;
> The Lord will be there, and wait till I come, on perfect terms;
> (The great Camerado, the Lover true for whom I pine, will be there) ...
> The wonder is, always and always,
> How there can be a mean man or an infidel.
> I know I am deathless;
> I know this orbit of mine cannot be swept by the carpenter's compass;
> I know I shall not pass like a child's curlicue cut with a burnt stick at night ...
> I laugh at what you call dissolution,
> And I know the amplitude of time. (93)

No other question has haunted mankind so much as the great mystery, *"Where are the dead? What lies beyond the grave?"*

Philosophers and priests of every nation have presented a host of answers, some of them ludicrous, others pitiful. The Bible alone speaks with certainty, offering a message that is stronger than death, a message that transforms the grave from a place of horror to a place of comfort –

> A glorious destiny for man is inherent in Christianity. The Christian faith includes the certainty that the God who delights in his creation purposes perfection for that creation. Mankind is either a biological accident that conferred upon senseless matter the dubious

---

(93) From Walt Whitman's (1819-1892) masterpiece, *Song of Myself.*

blessing of consciousness without significance, or the product of a creative will that designed it to enjoy a self-conscious life capable of continuing growth and enduring usefulness. The Christian faith proclaims the second alternative, and assures all believers that they are destined to glory, not to extinction ...

None of the other great religions speaks with assurance about man's future. For example, Hinduism, the traditional belief of hundreds of millions, conceives destiny as the wheel of existence, by which the soul passes through successive transmigrations until at last it is absorbed into Nirvana. As the raindrop falls into the ocean, losing its identity but not its existence, so the soul will finally be resolved into the universal being, formless and undefinable. Consciousness will be obliterated, and as desire fades into oblivion, all passion and pain will cease ...

Buddhism also, with its implicit denial of the living God, holds no hope of ultimate personal destiny ... The Greeks had a more strongly individualised idea of destiny. They believed in the survival of the individual soul after it was freed from the confines of the body. Yet their mythology represented the after-life as a cold, shadowy existence, devoid of cheer and progress, but with the persistence of personality ... In the century when Christianity was born, the average citizen seemed to have lapsed into despair ... Into the darkness of that despairing world shone the gospel of Christ. (94)

We can call upon several witnesses to strengthen our assurance of life beyond the grave –

THE WITNESS OF REASON

Death is a universal experience, yet men will not think about it until compelled to. They plead that death is incomprehensible, that there is no evidence of survival after death. They are offended by the thought of hell and embarrassed by the thought of heaven. The triumphs of modern science and the secular atheistic philosophies of life ... have produced this reaction ... Belief in immortality may not have been extinguished, but it has been eclipsed. (95)

Those pressures of modern secularism cause many people resolutely to deny any existence beyond the grave –

Here! creep
Wretch, under a comfort served in a whirlwind: all
Life death does end, and each day dies with sleep. (96)

Brief and powerless is a man's life; on him and all his race the slow sure doom falls pitiless and dark. (97)

---

(94) Merrill C. Tenney, in an essay, "The Glorious Destiny of the Believer," in a supplement to *Christianity Today*. The date is unknown to me.

(95) J. S. Thomson, in an essay, "Death and Immortality," in *Christianity Today*, Aug 3, 1962.

(96) Gerard Manley Hopkins, *No worst, there is None*.

(97) Bertrand Russell.

Must we agree with the poet and the philosopher? Can it be true that death is the annihilation of life? Very few people really *believe* that. Their denial of life beyond the grave is more a refusal to face the issue than a declaration of firm conviction. Indeed, to say that life is utterly destroyed by death usually requires an act of steely will. It goes against nature. It defies one of humanity's deepest instincts. Everything within us cries out against the idea that we have no goal beyond the grave, no destiny except decay, no end except corruption. People cannot say that death is the end without violating their own self-awareness. They have to force themselves to say it. Leave people alone, and since the dawn of history, in every nation, tribe, and tongue, they have effortlessly conceived some form of immortality.

Four thousand years before Christ, in perhaps the most ancient civilisation on earth, the Egyptians buried their dead hoping for a happy afterlife – a hope that remained constant across thirty dynasties of pharaohs. Peasant and prince alike anxiously strove to meet every detail of the required ritual, so fearful were they of losing the promise of immortality. Part of the ritual involved mummifying the deceased, a practice that reaches back to Egypt's most primitive era –

> *The earliest preservation of human remains in Egypt appears to have been accidental. Pre-dynastic burial sites consist of shallow pit graves in which the body, in curled foetal position, lay in direct contact with the sand. The combination of intense heat and dryness desiccated the bodies naturally. Since all of these burials were accompanied by grave gods, and since the face of the dead person invariably faced the west (the later traditional place of entry to the land of the dead), it is clear that the*

> *belief in some form of afterlife existed from most ancient times.* (98)

Similar things could be said of every primeval culture, and still of virtually every culture on earth today. Those who insist that nothing lies beyond the grave have always been a tiny minority.

But because an instinct is universal, does that make it valid? Perhaps the whole human race has been deceived? Can life after death be proved?

If "scientific" proof is wanted, the answer must be *"No!"* – for the question lies beyond the reach of science. The reality of a world beyond the grave will be neither proved nor disproved by scientific inquiry. It has to be a matter either of metaphysical *speculation*, or else of divine *revelation*. They both have their place. Which brings us to the first of the rational supports we have for our confidence in an afterlife –

THE ARGUMENT FROM PERFECTION AND DESIGN

Is there some over-riding purpose, some great goal toward which humanity is steadily moving, an ultimate destiny that will finally give meaning to our existence on this planet? Most people feel compelled to reply, *"Yes!"* Why? Because through both instinct and observation of life they discover evidence of purpose across the passage of the centuries. Do you deny this? Then nothing remains but mindless chaos. Life has no meaning, obliteration is the final destiny of all human life and endeavour, and we may as well *"eat, drink, and be merry, for tomorrow we die"* – for ever! (1 Co 15:32; Is 22:13).

Who can endure such bleak pessimism? Who can bear such awful futility? No! Despite all the darkness of human sin and sorrow, among all the delight of human love and laughter, we

---

(98) The World of the Pharaohs, by Christine Hobson; Thames & Hudson, New York; 1987; pg 152.

feel driven to affirm a purpose, a plan, that is moving irresistibly toward its ordained consummation.

But that is the whole point. Whatever the universe – and each of us – may be designed for, we feel that right now we can do no more than move *toward* it. Centuries of experience have shown us that the ultimate purpose of life cannot be fulfilled in the present world. Therefore, unless our deepest perceptions are a cruel mockery, that purpose must be realised in a future world beyond the grave.

Further, we also sense that there is an ultimate <u>perfection</u> in *morals*, in *art*, in *music*, in *philosophy*, in *religion*, toward which mankind is striving. Every artist feels deeply that his greatest creation still lies before him. Every thinker knows that he has scraped the surface of truth, but cannot plumb its depths. Not even the most virtuous of people imagine that they have attained the peak of moral accomplishment. Perfection of statement or of achievement always eludes us in this life. Are we then never to encounter ultimate perfection? Is the beauty we seek just a mythical illusion? Or will we discover it in a future life, in God?

To such troubling questions the atheist has no answer. But the Christian labours with contentment, joyful in the sublime promise of Christ –

> *Blessed are the pure in heart, for they shall see God!* (Mt 5:8)

They shall *see* GOD! What more could you ask? In the face of the Father lies the realisation of all beauty and truth, the fulfilment of all worship, the discovery of all grace and glory! At last we shall fully see, fully know, be fully fulfilled!

THE ARGUMENT FROM MAN'S MORAL NATURE

> *If you were to destroy in mankind the belief in immortality, not only love, but every living force maintaining the life of the world would at once*

> *be dried up. Moreover, nothing would then be immoral, everything would be permissible.* (99)

The moral principles by which we govern our personal and social lives demonstrably have a source beyond this present world. There is a moral law in people that is an inherent part of their very human nature. When people break this moral law they know they are not exercising a natural prerogative to do whatever they like. Rather, they know they are deliberately acting against a law that transcends the time-and-space world in which they live. This sense of moral law, which is instinctive in humanity,

> *commits men to living as if they were immortal. Morality means that if a man is not immortal then he ought to be.* Morality is a guarantee that life is worth living. (100)

Morality is also a guarantee that life and moral accountability do not end with the grave. Punishment and reward are not adequately satisfied in this life; inequities abound; justice is often thwarted; the wicked frequently prosper at the cost of the righteous. This imbalance demands a time when universal justice will be done. We cry out for a just tribunal where all men and women will be properly requited or recompensed for the lives they have lived.

The biblical doctrine of a future judgment, involving every person who has ever lived, offers the only satisfactory explanation of the inequalities of life.

THE ARGUMENT FROM UNIVERSAL BELIEF

Plato cited as conclusive proof of human immortality the fact that people everywhere and in every age have had a deep and

---

(99) Dostoyevsky, in <u>The Brothers Karamazov</u>.
(100) Thomson, op. cit.

instinctive belief in some form of life beyond death. The number of known tribes and nations has vastly increased since his day. Yet Plato, were he alive, could make the same observation today as he did nearly 25 centuries ago: belief in immortality is a world-wide phenomenon, and it defies reason to suppose that the human race has for so long been so wrong on such a fundamental matter.

Many other thinkers have accepted the force of that argument, and have insisted that death does not destroy the continuity of life. As an infant seeks instinctively for its mother's breast, never doubting that sweet nourishment awaits it, so we confidently thirst for that ultimate Life that we sense is the source of all our being.

The joy of holding to such an assurance was described by Plato's mentor, **Socrates** (469-399 BC). Just after the judges had condemned him to drink the fatal hemlock, Socrates resisted the pleas of those who were begging him to appeal the sentence. He explained to his friends why he was able to face death so calmly, even gladly, and what boons he expected to gain from it –

> *This thing that has happened to me must be a blessing, and we who think that death is an evil are surely mistaken in our belief. I have received striking evidence of this, for it is impossible that the divine sign should not have opposed me, unless I am going to fare well.*
>
> *Again, look at the matter in this light, too, and we discover high hopes for believing that death is a blessing. There are just two alternatives with regard to death: either the dead man has lost all power of perception, and wholly ceased to be; or else, as tradition has it, the soul at death changes its habitation, moving from its home here to its home yonder ...*

> *If ... death is a journey to another world, and if the traditional belief is true that all the dead are there, what blessing could be greater than this, O my judges? If, on arriving in the underworld, one is free from these pretended judges here, and finds the true judges who are said to sit in judgment there ... wouldn't that be a journey worth taking?*
>
> *Again, to associate with (the gods) – what would you not give for that privilege! For my part, I am ready to die over and over again if these beliefs are true; for I should find wondrous pleasure in life over there, meeting with Palamedes and Ajax, the son of Telamon, or any of the other men of old who met their death through an unjust judgment ... What inconceivable happiness to be with them, to converse with them ... One thing at least is certain: they do not put a man to death over there for asking questions!* (101)

Socrates may have had some knowledge of the Jewish scriptures, but he certainly knew nothing about Christ. Nonetheless, his thoughts, though coloured by Greek mythology, echo some of the great ideas of the later gospel. They show how deeply embedded in the spirit of mankind, both ancient and modern, is the sense of immortality, future justice, and heavenly happiness for the righteous.

Those beliefs can be traced back more than five thousand years in ancient Egypt –

---

(101) From <u>Preface to Philosophy</u>: *A Book of Readings*; ed. R. E. Hoople, R. F. Piper, W. P. Tolley; Macmillan Co; 1947; pg 25, 26, "Socrates Defence of Himself," by Plato.

> *The notion that the dead must be cared for and protected in their afterlife began in very ancient times. Even at the beginning of the predynastic era (c. 3500 B.C.) the provision of mats, food, and drink in even the humblest graves shows that there was a strong belief in life after death ...*
>
> *The downfall of the living god that was Pharaoh at the end of the Old Kingdom (c. 2000 B.C.) caused the people of Egypt to reconsider their own position. During the Eleventh and Twelfth Dynasties those people who could afford it were buried in brightly painted rectangular wooden coffins.*
>
> *Although the walls of their burial chambers were left bare, spells were written on the inner walls of the coffins. These Coffin Texts offer protection against eternal hunger, thirst, and the fierce heat of the sun, and for the first time, speak of the perilous journey the soul of the deceased individual must undertake to reach the land where it can live eternally.* (102)

What a flimsy foundation the ancients had for their belief in immortality! Yet still they clung to it with marvellous tenacity. Any absurdity was preferable to the total annihilation of conscious existence. By contrast, our hope is not based upon speculation, nor superstition, but upon the solid historical fact of Jesus' empty tomb. The risen Christ has for ever answered in the affirmative the cry: *"If a man dies, will he live again?"* (Jb 14:14)

---

(102)   Hobson, op. cit. pg 168, 169.

THE ARGUMENT FROM THE NATURE OF LOVE

Tennyson declared, *"Life is brief, but love is long!"* And Paul expressed the same idea, *"Love remaineth."*

Love possesses a quality that precludes us from thinking it ephemeral like a flower, blooming today but vanished tomorrow. It has a reality that goes beyond flesh and blood; it contains heights and depths that defy ordinary measurement. Love, we feel, is not defeated by the grave; it reaches beyond time and space, and cannot be restricted to the material realm.

Can love be explained merely in terms of chemistry and physics? How foolish! It is a mystery that defies analysis. To love is to touch eternity. We sense its imperishable character, and that its true fulfilment lies ahead, in a dimension we have not yet entered. More than just poetry compels lovers to express their devotion in undying terms: *"I will love you for ever ... Nothing can destroy my love for you ... For all eternity I am yours!"* We use such language because anything less seems inadequate. We have this deep innate *sense* that not all the raging waters of troubled time are sufficient to quench the bright flame of our love –

> *Love is as strong as death,*
> *Its passion unyielding as the grave.*
> *It burns like blazing fire,*
> *Like a mighty flame.*
> *Many waters cannot quench love;*
> *Rivers cannot wash it away.* (Ca 8:6-7).

Those who truly love, especially with the love of God, have already plunged into the stream of eternity!

We see, then, that human *reason* can provide grounds for belief in immortality. But since every argument can produce its counter, we turn to a safer refuge: the *revelation* of scripture.

THE WITNESS OF THE OLD TESTAMENT

The Hebrews held a complex set of ideas about the grave and the afterlife –

VARIOUS WORDS FOR THE "GRAVE"

The OT uses various words that simply refer to the grave as a place of burial, a cemetery, without any sense of continuing consciousness –

- *bei* (Jb 30:24; used only here)
- *geburah* (Ge 35:20; etc)
- *geber* (Ge 50:5; etc)
- *shachath*, the place of corruption (of the body) (Jb 17:14; Ps 16:10; 49:9; etc)
- *beer*, a pit, a well (Ps 55:23, *"pit of destruction"* is *beer shachath*; 69:15; etc)
- *bor*, a pit, a well (Ps 28:1; Is 49:19; etc. This word is also used to signify a prison; hence, as well as speaking about the grave as being a pit in the ground, it may refer symbolically to the prison of death.

None of those words conveys any definite thought of life after death; they speak primarily of the *place* where the dead are buried, more or less equivalent to our words *cemetery, burial place, graveyard, necropolis, tomb, crypt,* and so on.

However, the Hebrews used another word, *sheol*, to depict the *state* of the dead. *Sheol* means literally, *"the unseen state, the underworld"*.

In Hebrew thought, *sheol* originally signified only a kind of magnified grave, the place where all the dead were sent, and there lay in silence, without any true consciousness (cp. Jb 30:23; Ps 6:5; 88:10; Ec 9:10).

That was a very primitive concept, yet it still shows that *death was not extinction*; and it clearly discriminated between putting the *body* in the grave and the entrance of the *person* into the "underworld (sheol)" where all the dead were gathered.

Thus when Jacob lamented for his son, and cried, *"I shall go down to Sheol to my son, mourning"* (Ge 37:35), he was not saying that he expected to be buried in the same grave as Joseph, but that he expected to join his son, beyond the grave, in *sheol*.

Other references also, which speak of God entering *sheol*, show it to be a place distinct from the grave (De 32:22; Jb 11:8; Ps 139:8). That remains true, even though *sheol* was sometimes used as a synonym for death (Nu 16:33; 2 Sa 22:6; 1 Kg 2:6; etc.)

So the Hebrews taught that at death the *body* remained on earth (in the grave); the *soul* (*nephesh*) passed into *sheol* (Is 38:17; Ps 16:10; 86:13); but the *breath* or *spirit* (*ruach*) returned to God (Ec 12:7).

Several times, too, the word *rephaim* is connected with *sheol*. *Rephaim* means the *shades*; that is, what we might call "the departed spirits", the "ghosts" of the dead. It is distinct from the Hebrew word for a corpse (*muth* – and cp. the use of *muth* in Ge 23:4; Ex 14:30; etc). What the grave is to the body, so is *sheol* to the *repha* (the shade, soul, ghost). Hence *rephaim* and *sheol* are often linked to provide a description of the state of the departed dead in the nether world –

- The **shades** below tremble ... **sheol** is naked before God (Jb 26:5-6)

- The **shades** are there ... in the depths of **sheol** (Pr 9:18)

- **Sheol** is stirred ... it rouses the **shades** to greet you (Is 14:9)

- and cp. also Ec 12:5-7; 1 Sa 28:11.

So death is seen not as mere cessation of life, but rather as a change of state. From the soul-body unity of this life, the person passes into a state where the body lies in the grave, while the soul (shade) continues to have a separate life in *sheol*. However, in earlier times, this existence was thought to be mostly inert, dark, hardly viable. The *shades* were exactly that: "shadowy"; at best barely conscious, perhaps asleep.

That original concept of *sheol* was gradually enlarged by the Hebrews until it embraced the following ideas –

- The shades in *sheol* were no longer thought of as lying more or less comatose, but were now understood to be conscious and able to communicate with each other (Is 14:9-10).
- While all the people, wise and foolish, good and bad, would alike be shepherded into *sheol* by death, the upright would go down into *sheol* only until the *"morning"* – that is, the day would come when God would redeem their souls from *sheol* and receive them into his presence (Ps 49:10, 14-15).

Note that while the righteous will escape *sheol*, of the wicked it is said, *"their graves are their home for ever ... their form shall waste away;* sheol *shall be their home"* (vs. 11, 14).

- Thus *sheol* came to be thought of especially as a place of punishment for the wicked (Ps 19:17; 31:17; Pr 9:18; etc). But the righteous, although death and *sheol* will seize them because of their sins, will nonetheless escape *sheol's* grip (Ps 16:10; Pr 15:24; 23:13-14; etc).
- *Sheol* was divided into two sections: the place where the righteous abide, awaiting the day of release; and the "depths of *sheol*", reserved for the wicked (Pr 9:18).

However, those ideas all remained vague during OT days. *Sheol* was always thought of as a place of darkness, silence, and forgetfulness, where life remained at best restricted and shadowy. Even when the concept of *sheol* was later extended to include consciousness, activity, memory, the dead were still reckoned to subsist rather than truly live (Jb 10:21, 22; Ps 115:17; etc). And there were some Jewish teachers who denied any sort of individual immortality –

> *No one can talk about you among the dead; no one can praise you in Sheol* ... Who will be able to praise the Most High in the grave; away from the living, who will be able to offer him worship? When people are dead, and exist no longer, all gratitude must die with them. ... The dead lie in their graves, and all breath is gone from them. They cannot sing the Lord's praise, nor admire his justice – only living men can speak the praises of God (Ps 6:5; Sir 17:27-28; Baruch 2:17-18).

The main emphasis in the OT remained always on *family* or *national* survival, rather than on *individual* salvation. Devout Israelites found immortality mostly in the preservation of their tribe and family, and in the continuing glory of the nation –

> *When a father dies, he is not dead, for he has left behind him someone like himself. While he is still alive, he rejoices in the son who will survive him; and when he is about to die, he will not grieve. He is leaving behind him a son who will both avenge him against his enemies and repay the kindness of his friends.*

> *Children ... establish a man's name ... Guard the honour of your name, since it will last longer than a thousand warehouses full of gold.*

> *You can number the days of a man's life, but the days of Israel are beyond counting.*

> *People put their confidence in a man who shows himself truly wise, and his name will live for ever. The days of even the most noble life are numbered, but a good name endures for ever.*
>
> *Our forefathers were loyal men whose good deeds will never be forgotten (because) their prosperity will continue on with their descendants, and their inheritance will pass to their children's children ... Their posterity will never die out, and their renown will never be blotted out. Their bodies were buried in peace, but their names live on for ever.* (103)

Yet not everyone shared Sirach's enthusiasm about finding unending glory in one's children. The psalmist, for example, expressed poignant regret that his voice would be silenced in the grave, and he yearned for a further opportunity to praise God. Therefore some, as we shall see, reached toward a vision of personal immortality.

This process was heightened by two influences. *First*, the Persians, during their 200-year domination of the Middle East, brought with them their ideas on resurrection and Paradise (104), which were absorbed into Jewish thinking. *Second*, belief in the resurrection was enhanced by the bewilderment the people felt after their return from exile. The nation was now purged of all idolatry, yet still found itself under a foreign yoke. They had returned to Palestine fully expecting that God would deliver and prosper them. But their oppression continued. They found refuge and comfort in the growing realisation that this life is not the end of everything, but only preliminary to a greater life beyond the grave.

---

(103)　Sir 30:4-6; 37:25; 40:19; 41:12-13; 44:10-15.

(104)　The word "paradise" itself is based on an old Persian word for a "park", a "garden", come down to us via Greek, Latin, and French.

So, probably no later than a century before the time of Jesus, the people in general had come to believe in a picture of *sheol* like that described in the parable of *Dives and Lazarus* (Lu 16:19-31): the righteous after death enjoy bliss in paradise; the wicked suffer the flames of *gehenna*. Thus the anonymous author of *The Wisdom of Solomon* declared –

> *To know you, O Lord, is to embrace true righteousness, and to recognise your power is to discover immortality! (15:3)*

Some Jews (e.g. the Sadducees) did continue to reject the whole idea of life beyond the grave, but they were a minority. In popular opinion, the suggestions contained in the OT had firmed into a vivid picture of *sheol* as a place of sharp consciousness and activity, a place of pleasure for the godly and of pain for the ungodly.

This popular opinion was reinforced by a few OT indications of a coming day of *resurrection*, in which the wicked would suffer retribution, but reward would come to the righteous. But once that idea is accepted, it is an easy step to belief in the continued existence of the soul between the time of death and the resurrection.

The OT indications of the resurrection are of two kinds –

REFERENCES TO COMING JUDGMENT AND REWARD

These passages do presuppose a resurrection. The psalms and the prophets contain many references to the great day of judgment. They predict the wrath of God that will fall upon the wicked, and the eternal happiness of the righteous.

However, such oracles present a problem. It is sometimes difficult to ascertain whether their visions refer to the distant future, or to more or less contemporary events. It is also difficult to be sure whether or not the prophets were speaking about earthly or heavenly actions.

But even if they *were* talking mainly about contemporary and/or earthly events, the language they used, the style of expression, is so rich with hyperbole it is difficult to escape the conclusion that the local event was only a type of a greater day of judgment still to occur in the heavens. But such a day is impossible without a prior rising of the dead.

REFERENCES THAT SHOW A CLEAR EXPECTATION OF A FUTURE LIFE

There are several such passages, especially dealing with the righteous – Ge 5:24; Ex 3:6 (cp. Mk 12:26-27); 6:2-4 (cp. He 11:13-16); Nu 23:10; 1 Ch 9:20 (lit. *"may the Lord be with him"*); Jb 14:13-15; 19:23-27; Ps 16:9-11; 17:15; 23:6; 49:15; 71:20; 73:23-24; Pr 14:32; Is 24:22; 25:8 (cp. 1 Co 15:54); 26:19-21 (which shows the disembodied soul being reunited with the body in a resurrection that will take place when the Lord appears in glory); Ez 37:7-14; Da 12:2; Ho 13:14 (cp. 1 Co 15:55).

The passage from Isaiah (26:19-21) is particularly interesting, for it seems to show the prophet as one of the first men ever to realise that God has ordained a reversal of the death process: he links the *shade* and the *body* together in the resurrection.

Other suggestions of the soul's conquest over death shine out of the *translations* into heaven of Enoch, Moses, and Elijah.

Yet after considering all that the OT says about the ultimate destiny of man, whether righteous or unrighteous, the scene remains vague. The OT gives no specific detail, except to imply the torment of the ungodly (Is 66:23-24), and the bliss of the righteous in the presence of the Lord (Ps 16:11). There are hints of a bodily resurrection, but they never consolidate into a sure doctrine. Hope of immortality was primarily focussed on continuance of the family or tribe. Only during the intervening 400 years between *Malachi* and the birth of Christ did large segments of the population become convinced that all the dead will one day be called out of their graves to face the Judgment of God.

Eleven

HADES

During the centuries between Malachi and Christ, when the books of the *Apocrypha* were written, the hope of immortality became further clarified, and the Jews linked that hope with a more clearly formulated doctrine of the resurrection.

During the early part of this period, death was still generally thought of as the end of all conscious existence –

> *Who will sing praises to the Most High in* hades? *Who will give thanks to him, as do those who are alive? From the dead, as from someone who has never existed, thanksgiving has ceased; only those who are alive and well can sing the Lord's praises ...*

> *Many things lie beyond human grasp, since no human is immortal ... O death, how bitter is the thought of you to someone who is living peacefully, surrounded by luxury ... Whether life endures for ten years, or a hundred, or a thousand, no one will be asking questions about it in* hades. (105)

As I have already mentioned, Sirach preferred the idea that Israel's hope of immortality was national rather than personal. The death of an individual meant the end of life and consciousness –

> *When the dead are at rest, let their memory also come to an end. As soon as their spirits have*

---

(105)   Sir 17:28-30; 41:1-4.

> *departed, accept comfort from those who offer it (38:23).*

For him, children were the prime source of the continuity of life for each family and generation (30:4-6; 41:11-13). That is shown in one striking passage, which at first sight (until Sirach dramatically changes direction) seems to show faith in a physical resurrection –

> *May the memory (of the righteous judges) be glorious, may their bones stir with life where they lie; and may the name of those who have been honoured live again in their sons! (46:12)*

Just when you think the dead are about to be raised (*"their bones are stirring in the grave"*), Sirach shows he is using a metaphor. The honoured judges actually can hope for immortality only in their sons.

Nonetheless, even Sirach (who flourished 200 years before Christ) was beginning to move toward some idea of punishment beyond the grave. He may have been ambivalent on the matter, but he could not resist saying in one place –

> The way of sinners is paved with smooth stones, but at its end is the Pit of Hades (21:10)

THE PIT OF HADES

Elsewhere, as we have seen, *hades* was simply the abode of all the dead, good and evil alike. But when Sirach wanted to depict the end of the wicked, he could not bring himself to put them with the righteous; he felt obliged to consign them to the *Pit* of *Hades* – its deepest, darkest, most awful depository. Thus even the urbane rabbi, perhaps against his will, was being drawn unavoidably along a pathway toward full recognition of punishment and reward in the afterlife.

Within 50 years of Sirach, Jewish belief in the resurrection and in the distribution of honours and disgrace in a future judgment had come to full flower. This rapid change, as I have already suggested, was probably wrought by the impact of the persecution and conflicts suffered by the people during the Maccabaean period. The awful cruelty of Antiochus created the setting for some of the most stirring pre-Christian testimonies of faith in the resurrection. When the nation lay crushed under the tyrant's boot, the temple profaned, the priesthood corrupted, the devout mercilessly tortured to death, nothing remained except to locate faith beyond the grave, in a future indestructible kingdom of God.

That is why Eleazar, under threat of the lash, declared –

> *Send me quickly to my grave ... If I were to lie just to gain a few more brief moments of life ... I might escape the threat of human punishment, but <u>alive or dead, I shall never escape from the hand of the Almighty</u> (2 Mc 6:24-27).*

The same unshakeable confidence was expressed by seven brothers who were savagely mutilated by Antiochus –

> *... he in turn underwent the torture. With his last breath he said: "Foul demon though you are, you can do more than set us free from this present life, but ... the King of the universe will raise us up to an everlasting life, a life eternally made new" ... they tortured the fourth in the same brutal way ... (but) he said to the king: "I am not afraid to be killed by men, for I hold firmly to God's promise to raise us from death, but there will be no resurrection to life for you!" ... Their mother ... encouraged each (of her seven sons) in turn ... "The Creator of the universe is the one who shaped you when you were born ... In his great mercy, therefore, <u>he will restore life and breath to you</u>" (see 2 Mc ch 7).*

Notice the young man's reference to *"God's promise to raise us from death."* It shows that the Jews had at last begun to grasp the full significance of the various OT intimations of immortality.

Later in the same book there is an account of Judas Maccabaeus sending a contribution of 2,000 silver drachmas to Jerusalem for a sin-offering. The comment is added –

> *(This was) the right thing for him to do, for it showed how much he valued the resurrection. If he had not been expecting those who had fallen in battle to rise again, it would have been senseless and wasteful to pray for the dead. But since he had in mind the wonderful reward reserved for those who die a godly death, his purpose was a holy and pious one (2 Mc 12:43-45).*

THE WISDOM OF SOLOMON

The *Wisdom of Solomon*, probably written about the time of Christ, adds its testimony –

> *God created man for immortality (2:23-24) ... The souls of the just are in God's hands, and torment will not touch them ... they have a sure hope of immortality (3:1-10) ... The righteous will live forever, and their reward is in the Lord's keeping. The Most High will keep them in his care (5:14-16; 16:13-14) ... To know you (O Lord) is to discover righteousness, and to acknowledge your power is the root of immortality (15:3).*

And although he lived in the NT era, the writer to the Hebrews describes the godly of the OT as having a sure hope of the resurrection –

> *Some were tortured, refusing to accept release, for they wanted to rise again to a better life (11:35).*

The apostle was probably referring to the martyrs who died

during the Antiochan persecutions. Indeed, that terrible period in Jewish history saw something new happening on the earth – people, for the first time in history, were tortured and slain solely because of religion. The Maccabees were the first true religious martyrs. What a frightful river of blood has flowed since then! But religious persecution began with Antiochus Epiphanes, and out of the fiery trial of his brave victims was forged the first unequivocal statement of glorious life beyond the grave.

The issue of life after death was also addressed in *2 Esdras*, a composite Jewish/Christian work, composed probably just before or just after the time of Christ –

> *Then I said: "If I have won your favour, my lord, make this plain to me: at death, when every one of us gives back his soul, shall we be kept at rest until the time when you begin to create your new world, or does our torment begin at once?" "I will tell you that also," he replied. "But do not include yourself among those who are to be tormented. For you have a treasure of good works stored up with the Most High ... But now, to speak of death: when the Most High has given final sentence for a man to die, the spirit leaves the body to return to the One who gave it, and its first task is to adore the glory of the Most High. But as for those who have rejected the ways of the Most High and despised his law, and who hate all that fear God, their spirits enter no settled abode, but roam henceforward in torment, grief, and sorrow.* (106)

---

(106) 7:75-80. Then follows a further description of the misery of the damned, and a long, and beautiful, description of the bliss of the righteous (vs. 88-99), plus much other esoteric material about life beyond the grave.

THE WITNESS OF THE NEW TESTAMENT

JESUS' ARGUMENT WITH THE SADDUCEES

See *Mark 12:18-27*. The Sadducees mocked the idea of a resurrection, but Christ retorted: *"You know neither the scriptures nor the power of God."* According to Jesus, there are two proofs of the resurrection –

THE SCRIPTURES

"You don't know the scriptures!"

His statement is interesting, because it shows that Christ found sufficient proof in the OT to justify strong confidence in the resurrection. Given all that I have said above, that may seem surprising. The apparent lack of biblical data was the very reason why the Sadducees scoffed at those who believed in the resurrection. How was Jesus so confident?

> *The presuppositions from which belief in immortality springs have been present (in scripture) from the patriarchal period. The God of Abraham, Isaac, and Jacob is the God of the living, which includes the 'dead' patriarchs. God called them into fellowship with himself; therefore they were dear to him, hence he could not possibly leave them in the dust. That is, Christ based belief in immortality upon God's faithfulness.* [107]

THE POWER OF GOD

"You don't know the power of God."

Once the existence of God is accepted, and that he created the

---

(107)   Thompson, op. cit.

universe out of nothing, no inherent difficulty remains in the way of belief in the resurrection. If God by wisdom and the spoken word alone could call the world into existence, it cannot be thought impossible for him to call the dead back to life again. The simple fact is this: he can do whatever he chooses to do!

THE PLACE OF THE DEAD

Like Hebrew, Greek had separate words to describe the *"grave"* (the place where dead bodies lie) and the *"underworld"* (the abode of disembodied souls). The latter word in Hebrew is *sheol*, and the Greek equivalent is *hades*, which was used in the NT in the following ways –

- *"Hades"* must be understood in the light of the meaning it had throughout the ancient Greek world; which was *"the place beyond the grave into which the shades of the dead entered."*

The writers of the NT were aware of that commonly accepted meaning; if they had disagreed with it they would have taken care to give a corrected definition. Since they did not do so, we infer that the NT endorses the usual sense of *hades*, which is: the grave holds the body, but the soul/shade/spirit goes past the grave into the abode of the dead, that is *hades*. The Apocalypse clearly shows this distinction between *hades* and the *grave* (Re 1:18; 20:13-14).

- The NT asserts that all the dead enter *hades*, but they do not all share the same fate.

Just as the Hebrews spoke about the *"depths"* of sheol, so the Greeks held that *hades* contained various sections – the wicked were in one part, in torment; but the righteous in another, in *"paradise"*. You can see that paradise is part of *hades* by comparing Lu 23:43 with Ac 2:27, 31. Jesus said that on his death he would enter *paradise*; but the Acts passage claims that in fact he entered *hades*. Thus if paradise is part of *hades*, so also is the place of punishment (see Mt 11:23).

- In the parable of *Dives and Lazarus* (Lu 6:19-31), Christ plainly refers to the fully developed Hebrew concept of *sheol's* division into separate sections for the wicked and the righteous, and he identifies this with *hades*.

To some extent in this parable, Jesus may have been talking in terms of popular imagery, without intending to endorse each idea fully; some aspects of the parable, e.g. *"Abraham's bosom"*, seem hardly relevant to a Christian. However, the fact that he told the story at all seems to provide a general endorsement of the ideas embodied in the popular use of *hades*.

- All the dead will eventually rise from *hades*, and the condition of death will cease to exist.

As a result, *hades*, the place of the dead, will itself disappear. *Death* and *hades* are both doomed to destruction in the last judgment (Re 20:13-14; and cp. 1 Co 15:54).

The NT is emphatic that death is not annihilation, for death itself is to be destroyed (1 Co 15:22, 26; Re 21:4) and the prisoners will be released from death's dungeon (Re 1:18). Hence death is only a temporary power that has fastened itself onto human life. One day every man and woman, whether or not they wish to do so, will escape its confines and be called to stand before the bar of God.

THE INTERMEDIATE STATE

Once again, death cannot be annihilation, for death itself will be destroyed, which inevitably means the release of those who are imprisoned by death. But a prisoner who has ceased existing cannot be released; hence the prisoners of death must have a continuing existence. Death is their captor, but not their destroyer. The key to death's dungeon will one day be turned by Christ, and the captives will go free (Re 1:18).

The following references strongly indicate, if they do not absolutely declare, that conscious existence continues beyond the grave –

- **_Matthew 17:2-3_**. Were Moses and Elijah actually present on that day? Or were they just apparitions?

The story itself seems to affirm plainly enough that they were really there. If so, then their existence as conscious persons was not terminated by death.

- **_Matthew 10:28-33_**. If men cannot kill the soul, then the soul is not affected by physical death.

Note also, the agent God uses to *"destroy"* the soul is not death, but *"Gehenna"*. But such language would be absurd if "gehenna" and "death" were synonymous. Plainly, "gehenna" is a place that lies beyond the grave.

- **_Luke 23:42-43_**. The promise Jesus gave to the thief was emphatic: he would be with Christ in Paradise that very day.

Unless we are to suppose that "Paradise" is nothing more than the "grave", which is hardly reasonable, the dying Jesus affirmed that death did not end consciousness.

- **_Philippians 1:23_**. Could Paul have preferred death to ministry unless he expected to enter immediately into a state of conscious delight in Paradise with Christ?

If death meant annihilation, or at best unconsciousness, it would seem a poor choice, even allowing for the hope of the resurrection. It makes more sense to accept that the intermediate state will be spent in joyful and active fellowship with Christ.

- **_2 Peter 1:13-14_**. Peter implies that his real self had an existence independent of his body.

He could put off his mortal body like a man discarding an old tent, and then find dwelling in a new and eternal body (cp. also 2 Co 5:1-8).

However, there is no place where the NT speaks with any clarity about the intermediate state. The real vision and hope of the apostles was upon the return of Christ, which they expected would soon happen. Even in 1 Th 4:13, which specifically mentions the departed saints, Paul says nothing about their present state, but fixes his eye upon the Second Advent.

When Paul does touch on the intermediate state, he does not always feel the same way about it. He gives quite different descriptions of the resurrection in 1 Co 15 and 2 Co 5. Notice also how, in Ph 1:23, he seems to be leaping toward death; but in 2 Co 5:1-8 he fears death as a state of *"nakedness"* and hopes Christ will first return.

CONCLUSION

The scriptures are not free from ambiguity when they talk about the state of the dead and about *sheol* and *hades*. Usually, the biblical authors speak with cautious reserve, and they certainly avoid curious speculation. Nonetheless, it does seem possible to affirm the following –

- All the dead are in a conscious state; they are not permanently *"sleeping"*, they have not been obliterated.

- The ungodly are already undergoing some kind of restraint, even punishment, as they await the day of final judgment; they are like prisoners being held in "remand", waiting for the day of their trial and sentencing (cp. 2 Pe 2:9).

- The godly are in paradise, in the presence of the Lord, but waiting for the day of resurrection and their final splendid reward (Re 6:9-11).

Much mystery surrounds all ideas about the state of the dead, and there is no place for rigid dogmatism. The best attitude is the one scripture itself maintains, caution, matched with firm optimism! With that same divine hope, we may comfort ourselves in the presence of death.

Twelve

TOMORROW

When you get down to basics, very little separates us from the animals around us – we arrive in and leave this world in the same way; we have mostly the same physical needs; and we organise ourselves into similar social patterns. Yet there are a few things that mark us as standing well apart from all other creatures –

- our capacity for humour and laughter.

No animal can appreciate a joke; in fact, it is doubtful if even angels have a sense of humour. They can certainly rejoice and be happy, but tell them a joke, which you might find hilarious, and they will probably looked puzzled, wondering what it is all about. But God laughs (Ps 2:4; 37:13; 59:8); therefore, we who are made in his image laugh also.

- our sense of beauty.

No other creature, on earth or in heaven, can emulate, say, Keats, and write a rapturous *Ode to a Grecian Urn*. Or compose Beethoven's *Ninth symphony*; or paint Constable's *Salisbury Cathedral*; or build the *Taj Mahal;* or perform any of the other actions that reflect our human capacity to recognise, copy, interpret, and create beauty in a thousand ways. It marks us as being, alone in God's creation, made in the divine image.

- our moral and ethical culpability.

Angels do share this with us, at least in some manner, but no other creature possesses the innate sense of right and wrong that marks the human race. We alone have an absolute freedom, and the capacity, to choose a path of holiness or of iniquity, to serve God or to rebel against him.

But perhaps the thing that most separates us from the animal world around us is

- our sense of time.

That is, our ability to look toward tomorrow, to think about the future, to handle the knowledge that we must die (cp. Ec 3:11; 2 Es 4:64-67).

No human being can live without making a decision about the future; this is an issue that no one can evade. People may indeed decide that there is no future, that the grave will end it all; yet still they must decide.

How foolish then, to treat such a vital matter carelessly – which is a point made by Blaise Pascal (1623-1662), the French mathematical genius and thinker, in his famous "wager".

Noting the difficulty of trying to prove God's existence by logical reasoning alone, for all the so-called "proofs" of God ultimately fail, he tried a different approach. He pondered the question: *is it worth one's while, in terms of the mathematics of probability, to gamble on religious faith?* Addressed to his sceptical and freethinking friends, some of whom were enthusiastic gamblers, *Pascal's Wager* (as it has come to be known) answers that question –

> *The conditions are that one is already involved in the wager.*
>
> *To believe or not believe in God's existence is actually to wager that he exists or does not exist. If we believe he exists, and he does, the reward is eternal happiness. If we believe God exists, and he doesn't, nothing is really lost; and the same is true if we disbelieve and he doesn't exist. However, if we disbelieve he exists and he does, we are damned for eternity. Thus we have everything to gain and nothing to lose by wagering God exists. On the mathematics of*

probability alone every gambler should find the wager irresistible.

This does not imply that Pascal approves the calculating attitude involved in the wager. After the way is cleared, the gambler must learn to abase himself, to "stupefy" himself, establishing a way of life making appropriate the gift of divine grace, should God will it. The God who is hidden to fallen man is present in the power of grace. This is the God of Abraham, Isaac, and Jacob, not the God of the philosophers. [108]

Does God exist? Then there is indeed a future, a destiny to be faced beyond the grave. To gamble on the non-existence of God, and of this destiny, said Pascal, is to take an unconscionable risk, especially when there is nothing to gain from it.

As for us, we have no doubt about it. We know that we are

A PEOPLE OF DESTINY

I intend this chapter to be a kind of summary of what we have so far considered. Here are some of the principles that should guide our thinking about the future, and particularly about the return of Christ –

AN INCALCULABLE AEON

An Uncertain Date

Two aspects of the Lord's return are prone to be embarrassing –

---

(108) I have adapted this explanation of the "Wager" from <u>The Dictionary of Philosophy and Religion</u>, edited by W. L. Reese; Humanities Press, New Jersey, 1980; pg. 414, 415.

- **_unquenchable soothsayers_** – see again the list below, in *Part Two, Oracles Galore!*, and other similar examples of the countless unfulfilled predictions of Christ's return that have been made across the centuries. During the latter part of the last century, 1953, 1965, 1975, 1982, 1985, 1988, 1992, and, of course, 2000, were all vainly declared in advance to be key terminal points in prophecy. The predicted years came and went, without any sign of the Second Advent occurring.

- **_unconvinced skeptics_** – that is, people who mock the promise of Christ's return, either through unbelief, or because it has been so long delayed.

Such problems are not new. The early church faced those same two perplexing issues; that is –

- those who reject the promise because of its presumed failure; and

- those who reject the promise because of its presumed impossibility.

The result was a great falling away from the early church, especially after the death of the apostle John. The modern church has also suffered, and may still be suffering, a falling away because there have been so many bold and popular predictions that these are "the very last of the last days". Indeed, some millions of Christians were sadly disillusioned when the 21st century arrived without any divine fanfare, and began to unroll as every century before it has done.

What went wrong for the early church, and for many in our own time? Is the promise false? Or rather, is the common interpretation of the promise mistaken? I have already explored several answers to those questions; here I am content to note once again that all attempts to predict the time of Christ's return must be false. The Father alone knows the time of Saviour's coming! (Mt 24:36)

A VERY CERTAIN FAITH

But this still leaves us with a seemingly unconscionable delay in the fulfilment of the promise? How shall we solve this problem?

When we turn back to scripture, we learn that *time* was created by God, who inhabits eternity, and that *time* is the vehicle that carries us irresistibly on into the purpose of God. Therefore, in the economy of God there is neither delay nor haste. What may seem premature to us, is delayed to God; what seems delayed to us, is premature to God – except that, in reality, with God everything is simply right on time! (2 Pe 3:8-9). Hence we are called to steadfast patience (He 10:35-39).

In that latter text, note the conflict between *"he is coming soon"* and *"you must be patient"*; the first is spoken from God's perspective, and the second from ours. It means simply, Christ will come at the time appointed by the Father.

AN INDEFINABLE PARAMETER

See *Daniel 12:5-13*. What do those peculiar time sequences mean – the *"time, times, and half a time"*, that is, 1260 days, and the 1290 days, and the 1333 days?

A LONG TIME

There have been many interpretations and connections with many different dates. Daniel's oracle has been applied to Antiochus IV Epiphanes in 2nd century BC, also to numerous other events and persons throughout history, all the way to the supposed Great Tribulation at the end of the age. For example, vs. 11 (*"from the time the sacrifice is taken away"*) has been linked with

- the tyrant Antiochus IV (cp. 1 Mc 1:20-21, 44-49, 54-61);

- the Fall of Jerusalem (70 A.D.);
- the profanation of the Temple Mount by Islam and others; and with
- the future Antichrist; but we are no closer today than were our forefathers to unanimity on the matter.

Does the prophecy then have no meaning?

It certainly does not permit us to calculate dates, which not even Jesus was able to do, nor the angels (Mk 13:32-33). The scriptures show how *God* will determine the time, but they do not allow *us* to do so (vs. 34-36).

WHAT ABOUT THE "SIGNS OF THE TIMES"?

Well, as we have seen, despite popular opinion, Jesus made it clear that there are no unmistakable signs of the day when Christ will return (cp. Lu 17:20). Therefore he warned his disciples not to take any notice even of the things that most people still read as signs of the end (Lu 21:8-11; Mk 13:6-8; Mt 24:4-8).

So we can say with certainty, only that the *1260, 1290, & 1335 days* at least show a long delay! Just how long the delay was going to be, no one could have guessed! Certainly, the apostles would have been astonished, had they been told! (1 Co 1:7-8; Ja 5:7-9; etc.)

Nonetheless, although the delay has been far longer than anyone ever expected, the number sequences given by Daniel show quite definitely that it will be

A LIMITED TIME

The day is fixed by God! (cp. Ac 1:6-7). That being so, there are three things we should all do –

Wait

See again *James 5:7*. So, if Jesus does not come this year, or next, or even when the latest popular paperback on Bible prophecy predicts, we ought not to despair!

Work

See *1 Corinthians 7:29-31; Ephesians 5:14b-18*.

Watch

Not the newspaper, but yourself; for the purpose of prophecy is not to satisfy curiosity, but to inspire holiness and witness (Lu 21:34-36; 2 Pe 3:11-14; Ac 1:6-8).

And here is a good principle to remember – in all God's dealings, we need to realise that he

- ***sets his own agenda***: see *Hebrews 10:35-38*, which shows that we cannot know ***when*** the Lord will fulfil his promise; therefore faith is willing to wait patiently; and

- ***follows his own method***: see *Isaiah 55:8-11*, which shows that we cannot know ***how*** the Lord will fulfil his promise; therefore faith is willing to allow God to do his work in his own way.

Nonetheless, we remain certain that nothing can prevent the eventual fulfilment of every word God has spoken.

AN INDESTRUCTIBLE CHURCH

We looked earlier at *Matthew 24:14*, an oracle that may be (as many think it is) close to fulfilment; but uncertainty remains, because Jesus did not sufficiently define his terms. So while we must accept that it will never lie in our power to calculate when the time has come, nonetheless, the words of Jesus do reveal two powerful things, and I do not hesitate to remind you of them –

- the **_security of the church_**: for until the very last day the church will keep on proclaiming the good news of the kingdom! Not even the *Gates of Hell* can prevent the church from fulfilling its worldwide missionary mandate (Mt 16:18). Nothing has ever been or ever will be able to destroy the church that Jesus is building. He is coming back for his invincible church, which is a guarantee that the church will still be flourishing when he comes!

- the **_certainty of the mandate_**: for until the very last day the church will keep on carrying the gospel into every nation on earth! For Jesus commanded his church to go to all the world, and he insisted that the gospel *will* be preached in every nation (Mt 24:14; 28:19; Mk 16:15), and will continue to be preached until he comes again.

AN IRRESISTIBLE JUDGMENT

See *Matthew 24:27-28,* where Jesus used a familiar Jewish proverb of inevitability, of which examples can be found in every culture:

- Turkey: "Death is a black camel that kneels at every door."

- Rumania: "The sun will rise, whether or not the cock crows."

- England: "When death chooses to come, it will brook no denial."

The Jews also had such a proverb. They said that some things were as inevitable as "vultures falling upon a rotting carcass".

Jesus applied this proverb to

JERUSALEM

It had a terrible and literal fulfilment in AD 70, when the Roman soldiers carried their "Eagle" [109] into battle against the Jews. They saw the Roman "Eagle" as being "alive", inhabited by a divine spirit, which Josephus describes thus –

> *Now the Romans . . . brought their ensigns into the temple, and set them alongside its eastern gate, and there they offered sacrifices to (the "Eagles"), and proclaimed Titus as the emperor, with loud and joyful acclamations. And the soldiers collected such vast quantities of plunder that in Syria a pound of gold now fetched only half of its former value.* [110]

THE WORLD

See vs. 36-39a, which we may expect to be fulfilled as surely as was the oracle applied to Jerusalem in A.D. 70. That is, judgment has been decreed upon the nations by God, and nothing can prevent that inevitable day from arriving.

AN IRREVERSIBLE DESTINY

Only a Jew could have asked the question in vs.3, for no other people in those days saw time in linear terms. As we explored earlier, time was usually viewed by the Greeks and the Romans as an endlessly repeating cycle. Alone in the ancient world, the Jews, taught by scripture, viewed time as having a definite starting point, and also a final end – and all of it governed by divine decree. That linear view of time, with a beginning and an end, is now universal in the modern world, despite a few

---

(109) In Greek, the word for "eagle" and "vulture" is the same.
(110) Jewish Wars 6:6.

groups who still cling to a cyclic view. (111)

Yet despite the wide acceptance of the biblical idea that we are relentlessly moving toward a specific end, the great folly of our time is the failure of people to have any sense of the future. People live as if there were only today. If they think of the future, they see it only as a misty haze. They live without any goal; they have no clear picture of where they will be ten, twenty, thirty years or more from now.

Yet we can be truly alive only as we live with a vision of

HEAVEN

How wonderful are the promises of God (Re 2:26-29; 3:5-6, 11-13, 21-22; etc). But *now,* not on a death-bed, is the time to prepare for these things!

In April 1914, Robert Service was sitting alone in a Paris cafe, penniless, meditating on the strangeness of life: "I have no illusions about myself. I am not fool enough to think I am a poet, but I have a knack of rhyme and I love to make verses. Mine is a tootling, tin-whistle music … (Tonight) I am at the end of my tether. I wish I knew where tomorrow's breakfast was coming from. Well, since rhyming's been my ruin, let me rhyme to the bitter end – " Then he composed a poem whose title has now entered into common speech: *It is Later Than You Think.*

He describes the passing parade – a band of merry students; a

---

(111) Not so many years ago, many cosmologists believed that after the Big Bang the universe would expand for some billions of years, and then begin to contract right back down to an infinitesimal point, only to explode again in another Big Bang, and so on in endless cycles. Now the scientific consensus, in the simplest terms, is that the universe is not only expanding in all directions but will continue to do so for ever. The actual definition of that "expansion" is more complex than the common idea, but I cannot pursue that here.

willing young blonde; a successful playwright; a beggar destroyed by alcohol. He warns them all of approaching doom. Then finally turns to his readers –

> Lastly, you who read; aye, you
> Who this very line may scan;
> Think of all you planned to do ...
> Have you done the best you can?
> See! the tavern lights are low,
> Black's the night, and how you shrink!
> God! and is it time to go?
> Ah! the clock is always slow;
> It is later than you think;
> Sadly later than you think;
> *Far, far later than you think.* (112)

HELL

See *2 Thessalonians 1:7-10a; Revelation 19:11-16; 20:11-13*; etc.

But the biblical threat of damnation need not be gloomy news; rather, for a Christian, it can be the greatest word you will ever hear – there will be *requitement*! The God of Heaven is just, and he will see that justice is done, both in rewarding the innocent and condemning the guilty.

More of what that means can be found below, in the *Addendum on Hell* that follows the chapter titled *Judgment*.

AN INEXCUSABLE FOLLY

See *Matthew 24:37-41; Luke 17:26-30*. Why such pitiless destruction? Jesus did not accuse them of foul, barbaric, bestial behaviour; rather he listed eight things that are no more than

---

(112) Ballads of a Bohemian Bk. One, "Spring"; T. Fisher Unwin Ltd., London, 1921; pg. 29, last stanza.

the stuff of ordinary life – *"eating and drinking, marrying and giving in marriage, buying and selling, planting and building."*

If those things incur heaven's unyielding fury, then we are all undone!

The problem was not that they were doing such ordinary things but that they were doing nothing else! They lived for their bellies alone (Ph 3:18-19), having no care for anything beyond material needs and no yearning for anything more than physical pleasures. They gave no thought to matters of the spirit, had no interest in God, offered him no worship, ignored both heaven and hell, and were utterly indifferent to the warnings spoken by Noah. But much the same could be said of any goat grazing in a paddock, any pig rutting in a stall, any dog craving a bone, or of any cat chasing a mouse. More, much more, is expected from us!

So Jesus spoke the awful indictment – *"they did not know"* (vs. 39a). But they *should* have known, because Noah had been warning them for 100 years! And thus it will be on the Last Day, when sudden destruction will fall upon those who are living unaware, careless, godless and rebellious. Supposing themselves safe, they will be overwhelmed in a day (1 Th 5:3).

So the setting for the final judgment is not one of universal wickedness, but rather of universal indifference. The only way to escape that doom of God is to discover the will of God, and do it!

AN IRREVOCABLE LOVE

In a world full of violence, war, starvation, rape, injustice, the cries of the tortured, and the like, it is sometimes hard to believe that God is love. The cry goes up, *"Why do you delay? How long, O Lord?"* (Re 6:10); but then came the answer from heaven (vs. 11; and cp. 2 Pe 3:9).

We notice at once that God is not motivated by a principle of haste but of delay (2 Esd 4:33-37, esp. vs. 34), which is based upon

THE HEART OF A FATHER FOR HIS CHILDREN

See Ep 2:18, 19; and mark the wondrous discovery each new parent makes, that the capacity to love one's children is in no way diminished by their number, but the last is as much adored as the first!

THE HEART OF A KING FOR HIS KINGDOM

The glory of a king is bound up with the number of his people (Pr 14:28); so our King desires to keep on increasing his kingdom until it will be no longer possible to do so.

But the day will come when divine love can no longer hope to win more into the kingdom than are being lost from it, then the end will come.

AN INELUCTABLE GLORY

> *They will see the Son of Man coming in the clouds of heaven with power and great glory, and all the holy angels will be with him!* (Mt 24:30; 25:31; Lu 9:26;

Who can imagine the splendour of that hour! But why does he use the lesser title, *"Son of Man"*? Perhaps to identify himself with us, and us with him, for his glory on that day will also be our glory (1 Jn 3:2; and cp. Re 1:13-17a).

A PEOPLE OF ETERNITY

We are a people in the presence of eternity, carried along toward a meeting with God. Where is your eye fixed: on earth, or heaven; on today, or tomorrow?

One of the greatest English poets was Robert Browning (1812-1899), who was also a devout Christian. In one of his poems he contrasts a butcher who was an artist, a baker who was a poet, and a candle maker who was a musician, with a dismal man who lived only for his shop –

>   Because a man has shop to mind
>   In time and place, since flesh must live,
>   Needs spirit lack all life behind,
>   All stray thoughts, fancies fugitive,
>   All loves except what trade can give?
>
>   I want to know a butcher paints,
>   A baker rhymes for his pursuit,
>   Candlestick-maker much acquaints
>   His soul with song, or, haply mute,
>   Blows out his brains upon the flute!
>
>   But – *shop* each day and all day long?
>   Friend, your good angel slept, your star
>   Suffered eclipse, fate did you wrong!
>   From where those sorts of treasures are,
>   There should our hearts be – Christ, how far!

Thirteen

BEMA

Thomas Fuller tells about two English judges, one from the 15th century, and the other from the 17th. Fuller admired both judges for their high integrity –

> *It happened that Sir Thomas Cooke, late lord mayor of London, one of vast wealth, was ... arraigned for lending money to Margaret, the wife of King Henry the Sixth: this he denied, and the single testimony of one Hawkins, tortured on the rack, was produced against him.*
>
> *(The judge, Sir John Markham,) directed the jury (as it was his place, and no partiality in point of law to do) to find it only misprision of treason;* [113] *whereby Sir Thomas saved his lands though heavily fined, and life, though long imprisoned. The king was highly displeased at (the judge), and vowed he should never sit on the Bench any more. And here I hope it will not trespass on the grave character of this judge, to*

---

(113) "Misprision of treason" is still a federal offence in the UK, the USA, Australia, New Zealand, and other countries. It is defined as knowing that another person intends to commit treason, but failing to inform the relevant authority of it within a reasonable time, or failing to exert other reasonable efforts to prevent the commission of the crime. The penalty is usually imprisonment. Sir John was released from prison, retired to his country estate, and died there peacefully in 1479.

> insert a modern and pleasant passage, being privy myself to the truth thereof.
>
> A lady would traverse a suit of law against the will of her husband, who was content to buy his quiet by giving her her will therein, though otherwise persuaded in his judgment the case would go against her.
>
> This lady ... invited the judge to dinner, and (though thrifty enough of herself) treated him with sumptuous entertainment. Dinner being done, and the cause being called, the judge clearly gave it against her: and when in passion she vowed never to invite any judge again: "Nay, wife," said he, "vow never to invite a just judge any more." (114)

In many parts of the earth a just judge, who cannot be bribed or bullied, is rare indeed. But we have an assurance that when we are called before the bar of heaven – as we all must be – we will face a Judge whose justice is utterly incorruptible, whose sentence will be scrupulously fair (Ge 18:25; and cp. Lu 18:1-8).

This chapter, and the next, explore the great theme of the *Last Judgment*, beginning with –

THE JUDGMENT SEAT OF CHRIST

Immediately after the rapture, the resurrected saints will be made to stand before *the Judgment Seat of Christ*; the scripture will then be fulfilled, which says that *"judgment must begin with the household of God"* (1 Pe 4:17).

This special judgment of the church is twice affirmed by Paul –

> We shall all stand before the judgment seat of

---

(114) Op. cit. pg. 304, 305.

> God; for it is written, "As I live, says the Lord, every knee shall bow to me, and every tongue shall give praise to God" ... So each of us shall give account of himself to God (Ro 14:10; 2 Co 5:10).

In each of those places Paul uses the Greek word *"bema"*, which means *"an elevated place ascended by steps"* – hence, a throne or a tribunal. It conveys a picture of Christ sitting upon an awesome throne (his *"judgment seat"*) and calling each of his people before him for judgment.

That picture, of course, is probably figurative, but the solemn judgment it portrays will be real enough.

So let us ask some questions about this ***"bema"*** –

WHEN WILL IT BE?

You will realise by now (if you were not already aware of it) that scholars are divided in their answers to that question. There are two main views –

Those who hold to a <u>*pre-tribulation*</u> *rapture* believe the *bema* will occur

- ***<u>before</u>*** the tribulation
- immediately after the secret rapture
- in heaven
- prior to Christ's visible return
- during the period called *Daniel's 70th Week*
- and that only "church saints" will appear at the *bema* (the saints of the OT, and people converted after the rapture and during the "70th Week" are not reckoned as part of the church).

Those who hold to a *post-tribulation rapture* believe the *bema* will occur

- ***after*** the tribulation
- immediately after the rapture
- after the visible return of Christ
- in heaven
- and that it will include all of the people of God, from Adam to the end of the age (in this view, the church consists of all the redeemed of all ages).

The common factors in both views are

- the *bema* will occur ***after*** the rapture of the church
- the *entire* church will be present (although the church is defined differently).

So, to speak generally, the *bema* judgment will take place at the end of the age, at the time of Christ's return, immediately after the rapture of the church, and it will involve all who are part of the church. This great day is called –

- *"the day of Christ"* (1 Co 1:8; 5:5; 2 Co 1:14; Ph 1:6, 10; 2:12); and
- *"that day"* (2 Ti 4:8; 1:12).

It will be the day when the Lord will both *recompense* and *requite* his people –

- *recompensing* those who served him well (Lu 14:14)
- *requiting* those who served him ill (Lu 12:47)

WHERE WILL IT BE?

A *bema* was a seat built upon a raised platform, and such places were set up in prominent locations in every city and major town of the Roman Empire, and in every arena. They were used both as judicial benches, and by those who were judging events taking place in an arena – so they were places both of *punishment* and of *reward*.

See Mt 27:19; (115) Jn 19:13; Ac 12:21; 18:12, 16, 17; 25:6, 10, 17.

From those references we glean a picture of Christ sitting in royal apparel, with sovereign authority, assessing the spiritual development and stewardship of each saint, and granting reward or loss of reward, or even punishment (cp. Lu 12:48) based upon that assessment.

Presumably this will be a *spiritual* judgment, occurring in heaven immediately after the rapture of the church, and probably instantaneous for the whole church, while remaining intensely personal for each saint. It is difficult to imagine anything other than an instantaneous judgment. Any kind of sequential judgment, even allowing only a few moments for each saint, would presumably require an absurdly long time (Re 7:9).

Yet, since this judgment occurs in a new dimension, where one thousand is interchangeable with one (2 Pe 3:8), it may perhaps remain sequential.

WHO WILL BE THE JUDGE?

Ever since *Magna Carta*, (116) Anglo-Saxon jurisprudence has been built around trial by a jury of *"peers"*, as demanded in the following excerpts –

---

(115) Pontius Pilate was long ago canonised by the Abyssinian Church, and he may well have become a Christian. If so, the bema of Christ will represent an ironic twist!

(116) Or, "The Great Charter." Drawn up and signed at Runnymeade in 1215 by King John, under compulsion by the barons, Magna Carta protected the peerage, the church, established town customs, various individual liberties from royal tyranny, and trial by one's peers.

[21] Earls and barons shall not be amerced (117) *except by their peers, and only in accordance with the degree of the offence.*

[39] No free man shall be arrested or imprisoned or disseised (118) *or outlawed or exiled or in any way victimised, neither will we attack him or send anyone to attack him,* except by the lawful judgment of his peers *or by the law of the land.*

[52] If anyone has been disseised of or kept out of his lands, castles, franchises or his right by us without the legal judgment of his peers, *we will immediately restore them to him . . . and if a dispute arises over this, then let it be decided by the judgment of the twenty-five barons who are mentioned below in the clause for securing the peace . . .*

[56] If we have disseised or kept out Welshmen from lands or liberties or other things without the legal judgment of their peers *in England or in Wales, they shall be immediately restored to them; and if a dispute arises over this, then let it be decided . . .* by the judgment of their peers. (119)

That legal rule of trial by one's peers means that a commoner could object to a jury of royal dukes, or an educated person to a jury of illiterates, or a civilian to a military jury, or a citizen to a company of foreigners – or indeed, against any company of jurors whom the accused person could show were not truly of

---

(117)   Amerced = liable for punishment.
(118)   Disseised = wrongfully dispossessed.
(119)   The emphasis in the segments above is mine.

equal standing with him. (120)

This rule of judgment by one's peers is apparently honoured also by God, for he has handed our judgment over to Christ. He recognises that you could rightly object against the unfairness of being judged by the Father, and even more of being judged by Satan. But no one has grounds to protest against the One whom God *has* appointed – *Christ*! He alone is wholly fitted for the task (Jn 5:22; 2 Ti 4:8), for he lived among us for 33 years, and during that time suffered under the siege of temptation, yet he remained without sin (He 4:15).

Indeed, he is the fit Judge of all manner of people in every walk of life, and in every circumstance, for if Christ has not shared their actual experience, his perfect knowledge of human nature yet enables him to enter fully into all their pleasure and all their pain, their prosperity and their ruin, their sickness and their health, and into every imaginable circumstance and feeling (He 2:17; 5:2).

In fact, Christ is the *only* one fit to judge me; yet he refuses to do so! (see Ro 8:33-34). (121)

WHO WILL BE JUDGED?

THE ENTIRE CHURCH WILL BE THERE

The Bible speaks of a preliminary and selective resurrection, which will call the saints out of their graves prior to the raising of the rest of the dead. Thus we read of a resurrection *"from*

---

(120) In practice, courts in Australia, the USA, New Zealand, and some other democracies, tend to hold to the legal fiction that every citizen is a peer to all other citizens. But where there is some manifest discrepancy, even now judges sometimes uphold an appeal against an unfair jury, or against any jurors who may be deemed unfit to judge the accused.

(121) This idea, that Christ, as our true "peer" is therefore a fit judge, is taken up again, in more detail, in the next chapter.

among the dead" (Lu 20:35, lit); and, very emphatically, "_out from among_ the dead" (Ph 3:11).

Paul shows even more clearly the order of the resurrection in 1 Co 15:22-24, where he declares that the resurrection

- began when Christ arose from the dead
- will enter its second stage with the rapture of the church
- and will continue with the final raising of the rest of the dead.

The _bema_ belongs to that second stage, and to the church, not to the remaining dead.

Some have argued for a partial rapture that will include only "_overcomers_"; hence they claim that the _bema_ will be a place of reward only, not of censure. But against that partial rapture view, I would argue –

- Christ taught a general resurrection of all who believe in him (Jn 5:24-25; 6:39-40; Mt 16:27; Lu 14:4).
- The apostles included the entire church in their statements about the rapture, and about the gain or loss that different Christians will experience at that time.
- See Ro 14:9-12; 1 Co 4:5; 2 Co 4:13-14; 5:9-11; 1 Th 4:16-17; 2 Ti 4:1; 1 Pe 1:17; Re 22:12.

Notice the all-inclusive "_we_" that occurs several times in those references, which is an impossible usage if the apostles had thought that some of the saints would be excluded. Notice also the lack of any differentiation between victorious or defeated Christians. Indeed, those references show that the apostles used this very truth (that every Christian, whether living an overcoming life or not, will be made to stand before Christ at the _bema_) to exhort them _all_ to live righteously.

Paul stated clearly that all who are Christ's at his coming will rise to meet the Lord in the air (1 Co 15:23); and notice again the *"we"* in vs. 51-52. Remember also how many carnal and schismatic people there were in the church at Corinth! But Paul excluded none of them.

The partial rapture theory breaks the unity of the *"body"* of Christ (1 Co 12:12-13), and of his spotless *"bride"* (Ep 5:25-30; 2 Co 11:2), and of his *"holy temple"* (Ep 2:19-22). Can his *"body"* be dismembered, his *"bride"* disfigured, his *"temple"* made incomplete?

THREE JUDGMENTS FOR THE CHRISTIAN

Each Christian faces three judgments, that cover his *past*, his *present*, and his *future*; note them carefully –

- ***past*** judgment: as <u>sinners</u> (Jn 5:24; He 10:17-18); so that the sin question can never again be raised against us

- ***present*** judgment: as <u>sons</u> (He 12:6-9; etc)

- ***future*** judgment: as <u>servants</u>; which will occur at the *bema*

The issue at that third judgment, the *bema*, will not be one of eternal life, nor of entering heaven. The believers' salvation is not at stake. Nor will they be questioned about their faith in Christ. All who stand at the *bema* will already have an irrevocable claim upon a cluster of brilliant benefits, which by the grace of God alone fully belong to them in Christ. The promise of *Hebrews 10:17* is an indestructible refuge for every believer: *"their sins and their iniquities I will remember no more!"*

The sole matter to be determined at the *bema* will be the success or failure of our stewardship – what we have done with the gifts and opportunities made available by the Father during this present life, what motives controlled us, what obedience we gave, how far we allowed the character of Christ to be formed within us.

The condition of the church, and the differences between Christians demand this judgment, or at least one like it. Many Christians stand in dread of it; yet the Lord gives us all ample opportunity to look forward to it with inexpressible joy, expecting unbounded blessing.

WHAT WILL BE THE STANDARD OF JUDGMENT?

A PERSONAL RECKONING (RO 14:12)

"Each one of us must give an account of himself to God."

The word translated "account" is the Greek word *logos*, which had a variety of meanings, including the one it holds here: to render an account, whether of goods, money, or services. Jesus used *logos* in the same way –

- **Mt 12:36**: "on the day of judgment you will render an account for every careless word you utter."

What is the tenor of your speech? Is your daily conversation idle and unprofitable, or does it produce things of value to God? The accumulative effect of the words we speak, and the way we speak them, will be infallibly displayed on that day. Stripped of all polite disguise, we will be seen for what we really are.

Day by day your speech is shaping you, forming you, predetermining the kind of person you will be when you stand at the bema. Words that are continually sweet and godly, kind and winsome, true and righteous, will form a character of beauty and glory. Words that are perpetually carnal will form an opposite, shameful, and ugly image.

- **Mt 18:23-25**: "the kingdom of heaven may be compared to a king who wanted to settle accounts with his servants."

The criterion here is our *attitude* toward each other. Will you come before the *bema* still bearing a grudge, resentful, unforgiving? Have you held a vengeful spirit, or been cruelly critical, or pitilessly harsh? Have you placed uncrossable barriers between you and your fellow Christian (cp. Ro 14:10, 13). Rather let us walk together in gentle love (Ga 5:22-23).

- **Mt 25:19**: "now after a long time the master of those servants came and settled accounts with them."

The man who received five talents, and the man who had received two, both gained the same reward, and an identical commendation from their lord. They had both brought the same return upon their investment, 100%.

We too will be assessed, not on our accomplishments so much as our faithfulness in the opportunity we were given. (122) So we may say that this reckoning will be based upon *faithfulness* in our

- *calling* (2 Th 1:11; 2 Pe 1:10-11; Mt 18:23-25; 25:19; Lu 16:2)
- *conduct* (Ph 1:27; Ja 3:13; 1 Pe 1:15)
- *character* (Mt 12:36; Ph 2:1-5, 12-13)
- *consecration* (Ro 12:1; Ph 3:7; 1 Th 5:23; 2 Ti 2:2)
- *charity* (Ro 14:13; 15:1; Ga 6:1; 1 Pe 4:8)
- *confession* (Mt 10:32; Lu 12:32; 2 Ti 1:8; He 10:23)
- *commission* (Mt 10:27; 28:19-20; 1 Co 4:2; 2 Ti 4:1-2)

---

(122) Notice also: the position of this parable, between the parable of "the ten virgins" and the parable of "the sheep and the goats", suggests the time of the "bema": after the rapture of the church; but before the great judgment of the nations.

The *bema* will also lay bare our inner motives (He 4:12-13, the expression refers to a pagan priest searching through the entrails of a sacrificial victim, in order to find a hidden truth; 1 Co 4:3-5). Everything will be exposed; nothing can be hidden. What we hide now will be revealed then; what we reveal now will be hidden then (Mt 10:26; Lu 12:2-3; 1 Co 11:31; 1 Jn 1:8-9).

God allows no pretence; if we do not willingly open our hearts to his gaze now, we shall be unwillingly compelled to do so then.

At the *bema, omission* will count as much as *commission*; for not only will the judgment reveal what we *have* done as the servants of Christ, but also what we have *not* done (Ja 4:17). Yet the Lord is not much concerned about statistics. His real purpose will be to examine

- our aims more than our accomplishments (Ph 3:12-14)
- our character more than our conduct (1 Co 13:1-3)
- our hearts more than our hands (1 Sa 2:3-4)
- the worker more than the work (1 Sa 16:7)
- not so much *what* we have done as *why* we have done it, and what we have done *with* it (1 Pe 4:8-10)
- every hidden part, every impulse, motive, desire, measuring the centre not the circumstance, searching for the pith not the bark.

Especially, those who were shepherds of the flock will have to give an account for the souls committed to their care (He 13:7). And for all of us, the *bema* will examine the true nature of our *faith*: that is, the extent to which we have believed the promises of God and have entered into his "rest", or have hardened our hearts and so have fallen short of the promise through unbelief (cp. He 4:12 with vs. 11, and with 3:7-8, 17-19.)

ACCORDING TO WHAT WE HAVE DONE (2 CO 5:10)

We must ALL appear before the judgment seat of Christ, where EACH one will receive what they are due for the things they did while they were alive on earth, whether good or bad"

Paul used two important pronouns: *"all"*, which shows a collective judgment; and *"each"*, which shows an individual one. The entire church will be there; but each saint will be judged personally.

The basis of judgment will be whether our deeds were *"good"* or *"bad"*. The word translated "bad" means intrinsically worthless rather than morally corrupt; the actions described were not so much *wicked* as *wasted* – they are good for nothing, trash. The interest of the Judge will not be focussed upon whether these works are outwardly fine, or even whether they are obviously wretched. All attention is fixed upon the *character* of the worker. Those whose behaviour flows out of a debased character, or a selfish motive, no matter how noble the works may seem on the surface, will find those works scornfully dismissed and destroyed without remedy.

Works that may have been *"good"* can be made *"bad"* by the character of the worker.

BUILDING UPON THE FOUNDATION (1 CO 3:10-13)

The *bema* will examine the structure we have each built upon the Foundation that is laid within us, which is Christ. Paul uses a striking and fanciful illustration. He pictures a great city in which all the buildings begin with identical foundations, which presupposes a close similarity in the size, beauty, and splendour of the buildings. Instead, quite different superstructures are erected, some foolishly made of *"wood, hay, straw;"* others wisely made of *"gold, silver, precious gems."* Suddenly, a great fire sweeps through the city! What will be the result? Plainly, only the buildings made from non-flammable material will survive!

- ***The application is primarily to those who teach or preach***, and to the soundness or otherwise of their doctrines.

A heavy responsibility lies upon those who instruct others in the word of God, and a high penalty will be exacted from those who have wilfully or carelessly distorted the truth (cp. 1 Co 4:2-5; Ja 3:1).

- ***It is applicable also to those who have received and believed error***. Note –

We are each personally responsible for what we believe. God will certainly hold false teachers to account for the havoc their doctrines wreak upon the church; nonetheless, you cannot throw the blame upon them for the falsity of your own beliefs. God will no more heed such an avoidance of responsibility than he did Adam's attempt to blame Eve. Each of us is answerable to God for our beliefs. We each have a duty to ensure that we eschew heresy and hold only to sound doctrine (2 Ti 4:3; Ti 2:1).

Why is sound doctrine so important? Because improper doctrine leads to false development, unbalanced character, wrongful service, a failure truly to bring forth the character of Christ. People have grown careless about doctrine in our time; they become impatient when any discussion on doctrine arises; they little realise they are being lax about their own destruction. In the end, *nothing is so important as what you believe.* Doctrine shapes your life. Doctrine determines your destiny. Believe the wrong things, and an edifice of *wood, hay, and straw* must result. Believe the right things, and you will build with *gold, silver, and precious gems.*

Those things will all be made manifest through the fiery trial of the *bema*, leaving the person who has built only *"straw* with nothing but basic salvation. In both sanctification and service, *"straw"* doctrines produce a distorted Christianity that will be purged at the judgment seat of Christ.

- ***It is applicable to any aspect of our "work"***.

To some, the fire of the *bema* will come as a wrathful expression of God's judgment upon their carnal lives. To others, the same fire will be a brilliant light, guiding them into the splendours of their Lord's reward.

To those whose lives produced only dross, that fire will be a dreadful devouring thing (He 12:28-29). But to those whose hearts were already ablaze in the Spirit (Ro 12:11), the flames of the *bema* will be only a more glorious experience of the element in which they rejoiced during their earthly pilgrimage!

WHAT FORM WILL IT TAKE?

Please read again *1 Corinthians 3:10-13*.

We have seen that the *"foundation"* represents Christ, and that the *"work"* represents sound doctrine, faithful stewardship, and the development of true Christian character. But what about the *"fire"*? What does that mean?

- ***It is a symbol of God's presence and majesty***, devouring all that is antagonistic to his purpose (Ps 50:3-6).
- ***It is a symbol of the purifying of the saints***, so that they will be perfected to minister before the throne of God (Ma 3:2-3; Mt 3:11-12).
- ***It is a symbol of the divine jealousy*** that will expose all that we have loved more than we ought, and will purge out of us such spiritual betrayal (De 4:24).
- ***It is a symbol of the Lord's acceptance*** of all that we have wrought that is pleasing in his sight (Le 9:24; 2 Ch 7:1).
- ***It is a symbol of the ruthless destruction*** of all that we have wrought by our own hands, independently of God, so that only what Christ himself has built into us

and through us will remain (Jn 15:1-6; He 12:27-29; and cp. also 10:30-31).

The *"gold, silver, and precious gems"* are symbols of those things in us that are the work and gift of God; while the *"wood, hay, and straw"* speak of the products of unaided human labour. The former were done to please God; the latter, to please people. The former will abide the fire – indeed, will be purified and enhanced by it; but the latter will vanish without a trace.

Notice also that gems are a gift of God, which men can only dig up; but timber and hay are cultivated by human hands. The first are rare, the second bountiful; the first signify works done by faith, the second, the produce of toil and sweat.

It may be summarised as

- the fire that *reveals* (He 4:13; Re 1:14; 2:18, 23)
- the fire that *purifies* (Ma 3:2; 1 Pe 1:7; Ps 12:6; Ez 22:18-22; Zc 13:9)

The real character of each Christian's life and service will be swiftly and irresistibly revealed. One simple test will suffice– works that are *"good"* will be non-flammable; works that are *"bad"* will be at once consumed. Thus the destructibility or indestructibility of each person's work will instantly reveal its true worth, or its worthlessness.

How will it be for you? Will you be among those whose life-work, consumed to ashes, will cause the *bema* to be for them a place of humiliation? Or will you face it with eager joy?

The scriptures give fair warning –

> *The Lord will judge his people. It is a fearful thing to fall into the hands of the living God* (He 10:30-31).

> *"Knowing the fear of the Lord,"* said Paul, *"we*

> *persuade men"* (2 Co 5:11).
>
> *Look to yourselves, otherwise you may lose what you have worked for; instead, you should strive to win a full reward* (2 Jn 8).
>
> *Dear friends, abide in Christ, so that when he appears you will be able to greet him confidently and not shrink away from him in shame when he* comes (1 Jn 2:28).

What a tragic scene! A Christian shrinking away from Christ, ashamed, fearful, miserable! Yet the day of the Saviour's coming should be for every saint a day of unequalled joy and infinite delight.

But not all will be ashamed. Those who abide in Christ, says John, will meet their Lord with unalloyed happiness. His coming will usher them into his full and magnificent reward.

WHAT WILL BE THE OUTCOME?

The issue to be determined at the *bema* is whether the raptured saints will receive a full or partial reward (2 Jn 8); and, whether they will have a rich or poor entrance into the kingdom (2 Pe 1:10-12).

WHAT REWARDS CAN BE GAINED?

Some people are offended by the idea of serving God for a reward. They feel it is more worthy to serve the Lord simply because he is lord, without any thought of personal gain.

Who will deny that God should be served just because he is God? Nonetheless, to refuse the idea of rewards is to become more pious than the Bible, which often emphasises the prizes set before us, and urges us to strive for the fullest possible reward.

However, a distinction must be made between *faith* and *faithfulness* – *faith* gains an irrevocable salvation for every believer; but the degree of honour each person will have in the kingdom is dependent upon the measure of each person's *faithfulness*. As *sons* of God by *faith* we are all given an equal measure of Christ's *righteousness*; but only as *servants* of God by *faithfulness* can we seize his full *reward*!

Many scriptures promise a reward for faithful service e– Ps 58:11; Pr 11:18-19; Is 40:10-11; 62:10-11; Mt 5:11-12; 1 Co 3:8; He 6:10; 10:35; 11:26; Re 11:18; etc. And in more detail –

- to be ministered to by the Lord himself, perhaps the most marvellous promise in the entire Bible (Lu 12:37)
- to be a ruler over many (Mt 25:21-23)
- to gain a glorious inheritance (Cl 3:24-25; Ro 8:16-17; 1 Pe 1:3-4)
- to reign as kings and priests (Re 5:10; 20:4)
- to share in the judgment (1 Co 6:2-3; Re 20:4)
- to have dominion in the kingdom (Lu 19:17-19)
- to gain a crown –
    - of *life*, for courage and steadfastness (Re 2:10)
    - of *joy*, for successful soul-winning (1 Th 2:19)
    - of *righteousness*, for faithfulness and loyalty (2 Ti 4:7-8)
    - of *glory*, for shepherding the flock (1 Pe 5:1-4)
    - of *fame*, for running the race (1 Co 9:25; He 12:1-3)
- to receive the "overcomer's" prize (Re 2:7, with 22:1-2; 2:11, 17, 26-28; 3:5, 12, 31).
- to be "great" in the kingdom of God (Mt 5:19; and cp. the *"small"* and the *"great"* in Re 19:5).

WHAT LOSS CAN BE SUFFERED?

Note once again – it will not be a loss of eternal life, for the rapture has for ever secured the salvation of those who are standing before the *bema*. They are children of God, and all of them must gain at least some measure of the glory of God.

But some of them will suffer

- a degree of shame (2 Jn 8)
- a lessening of glory (1 Co 15:41-42)
- a diminishing of capacity (2 Ti 2:19-21; Ro 9:21; Is 22:24)
- a time of exclusion from the chief splendours of the newly inaugurated kingdom (Mt 22:13-14; 25:30).

Finally, remember that any reward we receive will in the end be an act of divine grace. We have no cause to commend ourselves, for even when we have done all that we should, we must still say, *"I am an unprofitable servant!"* (Lu 17:7-10). Thus God's rewards are also God's gifts, actually unmerited by us, but an expression of his loving-kindness. In the end God will apportion each reward, not as we demand, nor even as we may think we deserve, but only as it seems good to him (Mt 20:1-16).

Fourteen

JUDGMENT

On the day after the Naming of the Buddhas the screens with the paintings of Hell were carried into the Empress' apartments for her to see. They were terrifying beyond words.

"Look!" said Her Majesty. But I replied that I had no desire to see them; I was so frightened that I went and lay down in my room next door where I could hide myself from the screens.

It was raining very hard. Since the Emperor declared that he was bored, some of the senior courtiers were summoned to the Empress' apartments for a concert. Michikata, the Minor Counselor, played splendidly on the lute, Lord Narimasa played the thirteen-string zither, Yukinari the ordinary flute, and Captain Tsunefusa the thirteen-pipe flute. They gave a delightful performance of one piece; then, after the sound of the flute had stopped, His Excellency the Major Counselor, Korechika, chanted the line,

"The music stops, but the player will not speak her name."

While all this was going on, I lay out of sight in my room; but now I got up and went into the Empress' apartments. "Whatever guilt this may bring upon me," I said as I entered, "I cannot resist such a charming recitation." Hearing this, the gentlemen all burst out laughing.

> *I recall that there was nothing very remarkable about the Major Counselor's voice; yet it seemed to have been made especially for the occasion.* (123)

What a contrast with the sophisticated indifference of our time! Terror gripped the noble lady when she glimpsed just a *painting* of Hell! The cosmopolitan citizens of our land would probably find such screens merely ludicrous. Which shows their shallow folly and the lady's wisdom.

In the end, though, she was not much different from people today. She hoped to escape guilty fear by hiding herself in her room. How foolish. Yet people will still be doing the same thing on the last day –

> *Then the kings of the earth, the princes, the generals, the rich, the mighty, and every slave and every free man hid in caves and among the rocks of the mountains. They called to the mountains and the rocks, "Fall upon us and hide us from the face of him who sits upon the throne and from the wrath of the Lamb! For the great day of their wrath has come, and who can stand?" (Re 6:15-17)*.

How awesome are those lines! How irresistible the dread call, *"Come away to judgment!"* Where will *you* be on that day? What will be the outcome for those who will be judged?

The scriptures show three ways in which God judges sin –

- **<u>Sin is judged in *Christ*</u>**, at Calvary, and those who submit to the judgment of the cross need have no fear of any further retribution.

---

(123) From <u>The Pillow Book of Sei Shonagon</u>; tr. by Ivan Morris; Penguin Classics, 1967; page 87; selection # 50. Sei Shonagon was a lady-in-waiting at the imperial court of 10th century Japan.

- **Sin is judged in this *present life*** – by the gnawing pangs of conscience; by various temporal punishments (such as sickness, poverty, and the like); by punishment administered through human courts of law; by exclusion from the church; by prevention of repentance; and the like (Mt 12:31; He 12:16-17).

Of course, not every sorrow or pain in this life should be identified as a direct punishment for sin; but such things *may* be agents of divine justice, and they are all at least an indirect consequence of our mortal and corruptible state (1 Co 15:54).

- **Sin will be judged at the *Last Judgment*,** which will involve every person who was not present at the *bema*, and will determine their eternal destiny.

Many people refuse to accept the idea of the *Last Judgment*. They are deeply offended by the idea that many of those who are judged there will be consigned to *"the lake of fire"*. Derision and anger accompany an impatient refusal even to consider the idea. "Hell" to them may be a convenient invective, a piece of street slang, or perhaps an expression of present misery; but they scorn the thought of hell as a real place of supernatural and eternal punishment.

"Hell," they say, *"is a ghoulish invention of the Middle Ages, designed to terrify people into submission to the authority of the church and of the state; it has no place in modern society."*

They claim that the idea of judgment, and of punishment in hell, is absent from the best parts of the Bible, and especially from the teaching of Christ. They could hardly be more wrong! See how much scripture has to about the matter –

- ***in the OT***, Jb 21:30; Ps 50:3-6; 96:13; Ec 3:17; 12:14; Da 7:9, 10; 12:1, 2; and cp. also Is 66:22-24
- ***in the gospels***, Mt 3:12; 7:22-23; 11:22; 13:30, 40-43, 49-50; 18:8-9, 34-35; 22:13; 25:29-30, 41, 46; Mk 9:43-

47; Lu 3:17; 10:14-15; 12:2-5; 16:23, 24, 26; 20:45-47; etc

- **_in the letters_**, 2 Th 1:9; He 6:2; He 6:2; 9:27; 10:27; 1 Pe 4:5; 2 Pe 2:4, 9; Ju 6, 14, 15, 24; Re 6:15-17; 9:1-2; 14:10-11; 19:20; 20:10-15; 21:8; etc.

The above list is not exhaustive; it deals mainly with the *Last Judgment*, but there are scores of additional general references, which show that judgment is an integral and inescapable part of God's universal justice. The concept of judgment is a major biblical doctrine, and it cannot be ignored. Calvary itself is a revelation of both the necessity and the horror of the Day of Judgment, for there we see the implacable anger of God against sin; there God judged sin in Christ, and demonstrated both the terror of the judgment and the greatness of his love.

Concerning the *Last Judgment* notice –

THE LAST JUDGMENT

THE JUDGMENT BY FIRE

The first stage of the final judgment will be a time of world-wide chaos that will accompany the return of Christ and the rapture of the church –

- see Is 2:10-22; 66:15-16; Jl 2:1-2, 11, 31; Zp 1:14-18; Ma 4:1; 2 Th 1:6-9; 2 Pe 3:10-12; Re 6:12-17; etc.

Some of those references, and others like them, probably refer primarily to various contemporary events; but the language used seems to presuppose a larger world-wide fulfilment at the time of the Second Advent – see also Ps 46:6-9; Ez 38:19-39:6; Zc 13:8-9; He 12:26-29.

This act of judgment will not entail the destruction of all the wicked, for the ruin will primarily be *physical* and *natural*. It will be an awesome display of the wrath of God against all ungodliness, and of his irresistible might. The *Antichrist* will be overthrown, *Armageddon* will be terminated, and all the earth brought into subjection to the will of God. It will prepare the way for the final act at the *Great White Throne*.

Apparently this judgment by fire will begin just prior to the day of Christ's return, with initial tremors and startling signs in the earth and sky. These natural upheavals will increase in severity until they are climaxed by the coming of the Lord with his saints and all the holy angels (Jl 2:30-32; Mt 24:29-30; Mk 13:24-26; Lu 21:25-28).

The duration of this judgment may be suggested in Re 3:10,

> *Because you have kept my word of patient endurance, I will keep you from the hour of trial that is coming upon the whole world, to try those who dwell upon the earth.*

Robert Orr says –

> *This promise was primarily for (the church at) Philadelphia alone, and was probably fulfilled in the persecutions of Domitian toward the close of the century. Yet a wider fulfilment is also in view, involving the whole earth at the time of the end, as indicated by our Lord's words immediately following:* "I am coming soon" *(vs. 11) ... In this second and larger view, the trials which are to come upon* "those who dwell upon the earth" *(that is, the ungodly) are those judgments represented in chapters 15 & 16 as* "bowls of wrath". *At his advent, all true Christians will be gathered together to the Lord*

> *Jesus, while his wrath will be poured upon the rebellious world.* (124)

Some argue that *"the <u>hour</u> of trial"* means only the *period* of trial, with no indication of its actual length. But it seems better to interpret *"hour"* to mean a trial of brief, but still indeterminate, duration. Thus it is linked with the swift fiery trial that will accompany the return of Christ.

There has been much argument about the meaning of the word *"from"* – *"I will keep you <u>from</u> the hour of trial."*

In the case of the church at Philadelphia, the promise can only mean *"I will bring you <u>safely through</u> the time of persecution;"* and the references to *"the whole world"* and *"the earth"* must be localised to mean the Roman Empire (in those days the empire was commonly thought of as embracing the world).

Does it mean the same for the whole church at the last day? Some say "yes", and argue that the church will go through the tribulation. Some say "no" and argue that the church will not go through the tribulation.

I prefer to ignore the whole tribulation quarrel, and simply relate the passage, first, to the ancient Philadelphian church; then, second, to the church of the last days. In the latter case, the preposition probably means *"to rescue right out of"*. The Greek construction of Re 3:10 will carry either the sense of *"going safely through"*, or of *"escaping safely from"*. Both readings seem to be necessary; the first for Philadelphia; the second for the latter-day church. Notice that the Lord said, not that the church would be delivered merely from the *"trouble"*, but rather from the *"time"* of the trouble. Also, this judgment is actually designed to fall upon *"the whole world"*, and upon *"those who dwell upon the earth"*. Those descriptions belong to

---

(124) <u>Victory Pageant</u>; by Robert Orr; Pickering & Inglis, London, 1972; pg 48.

the ungodly, not to the saints; they make a distinction between the world and the church.

So the church will not be on earth during the judgment by fire. Which raises the question –

Where will the church be during this fiery outpouring of divine wrath? The answer: in position with Christ as the actual executors of the justice of heaven!

- See 2 Th 1:6-10; Re 2:26-27; 3:10, 21-22.

THE TWO RESURRECTIONS

The Bible divides the resurrection into two parts: the resurrection of the *just*; and the resurrection of the *unjust* – Da 12:2; Jn 5:28-29; Ac 24:15.

Commentators differ as to whether those are two separate events, or two parts of the same event; but in any case, they may be designated *"the first resurrection"* and *"the second resurrection"* –

THE FIRST RESURRECTION

See *Revelation 20:4-6*. Does this describe the present victory of the church over sin and Satan? Or does it refer to a future literal resurrection of the dead in Christ, along with the translation of living believers?

In the former view, the first resurrection and the rapture are *separate* events; in the latter, they are *identical.* However, both views generally agree that the *"blessed and holy"* people who share in the first resurrection comprise the total membership of the church – that is, all the redeemed of all ages, from Adam to the return of Christ. [125]

---

(125) Note also that those who believe in a pre-tribulation rapture also believe the rapture is merely the first stage of the first resurrection.
Continued on next page ....

Notice that these people have *"come alive"*, they shall *"reign with Christ"*, they are *"blessed and holy"*, they are *"priests of God"*, and *"the second death has no power over them"*. For them the Last Judgment at the *Great White Throne* holds neither promise nor peril. We know this, because John widely separates those who participate in the *first* resurrection from the *"rest of the dead"* who will not rise until the time of the final judgment (vs. 12-15). That second and immense multitude are participants in

THE SECOND RESURRECTION

The people raised *"after the thousand years are ended"* (vs. 5) are divided into two groups –

Those whose names are not in the "Book of Life"

That is, the ungodly, the unbelievers, the unsaved of all time.

Those whose names are in the "Book of Life"

These people cannot be the *church*, which has already been raised, judged, and rewarded at the *bema*. Who then are they? There are three suggestions –

Despite what I have just said, some argue that the *Book of Life* really *is* nothing more than a register of the names of all who are members of the *church*, who were raptured at the Second Advent, and who have already passed before the *bema*. The argument here is that only the *unrighteous* will be judged at the *Great White Throne*; the *Book of Life* is said to be simply a record of the names of all who were previously saved, and the unrighteous are condemned because their names are not found

---

The final stage will take place at the moment of Christ's visible return (with the previously raptured church), after the tribulation. It is clear from Re 20:4 that the first resurrection does include the "tribulation" saints.

there. Therefore, it is claimed, there will be no *saved* people in the second resurrection, only the *unsaved*.

However, that argument seems to do some violence to a natural reading of the passage, so it is also suggested that

They are *millennial saints,* and/or *tribulation saints.* However, that argument is acceptable only if one accepts the idea of a pre-tribulation rapture of the church, and/or a premillennial return of Christ – propositions that numerous scholars reject. So a third alternative is offered –

They are people who cannot be an original part of the church, because they lack the new birth that results from earthly faith in Christ, yet because of their goodness and sincerity, righteousness has been credited to them. Note how it is twice said that these people *"will be judged according to what they have <u>done</u>"* (vs. 12, 13). A similar idea is suggested in Ac 10:34-35; Ro 2:6-16; 4:3; Je 17:10, which all imply that salvation can be conferred upon those whose hearts (within the limits of their knowledge) are humble before God.

Historical examples of such people can be seen in

- ***Abraham***

Because of his link with the covenant people of God we know that Abraham will rise with the saints in the *first* resurrection. He is part of the church. By faith he was able to look ahead (just as we look back) to Christ (Jn 8:56).

But there may have been thousands of other men and women of every generation just like Abraham. Although they had no contact with the Bible, Israel, or the church, they were stirred in their consciences to forsake sin and idolatry and to worship the one true God. They saw indistinctly, they worshiped him imperfectly, their knowledge of him was distorted, but they were true to the light they were given. Perhaps their faith has been accounted to them for righteousness and their names added to the Lamb's *Book of Life.*

Archaeology has provided an interesting confirmation that Abraham may not have been alone in his monotheistic beliefs. There are indications that other people at Ur may have come to the same faith as Abraham. A. H. Sayce writes –

> *In the pre-semitic days of Chaldea, a monotheistic school had flourished, which resolved the various deities of the Sumerian belief into manifestations of one supreme god, Anu; and old hymns exist in which reference is made to "the one god". But this school never seems to have numbered many adherents, and it eventually died out. Its existence, however, reminds us of the fact that Abraham was born in "Ur of the Chaldees"."* (126)

- ### *Egypt*

An interesting example of this principle is found in ancient Egypt. For the first thousand years or so of its civilised history Egypt (according to some authorities) followed a form of monotheism. The idolatry of Bible days was a later introduction. An attempt to restore that early monotheism was made by the Pharaoh Akhenaten, of the 14th century B.C. He apparently revolted against idolatry, and tried to call the nation (or at least the royal family and nobility) back to the worship of one God, whom he represented by the sun (the *Aten*). He was an astonishing religious innovator, a man centuries before his time in his abandonment of polytheism and his embrace of a vigorous monotheism. He discarded the rigid artistic conventions of the past, and encouraged artists and his sculptors to portray him and his family naturally. Few of the art

---

(126) Assyria, Its Princes and People; The Religious Tract Society, London, 1926; pg 72-73. The few adherents to this monotheistic school may show that true religion was no more popular in ancient Ur than it is in modern society!

works from his reign have survived, but they do include the stunning bust of his obviously lovely wife Nefertiti.

Unhappily, immediately after his death, the idolatrous priests restored themselves to power, and the faith of Akhenaten was rapidly obliterated. But some fragments of his teaching remain, including almost the entire text of an astonishing psalm composed by the Pharaoh. Archaeologists found this striking work carved on a wall of the tomb of Akhenaten's uncle and close confidant, Ay. You will find a large part of this psalm in my book *"The Bible"*, but here again are some of its lines –

> *Creator of the germ in woman,*
> *Maker of the seed in man,*
> *Giving life to the son in the womb of his mother,*
> *Soothing him that he may not weep,*
> *Nursing him even while he is in the womb,*
> *Giver of breath to animate every one you create! ...*
> *How manifold are all your works!*
> *They are hidden from our sight and knowledge,*
> *O sole God, whose powers no other possesses.*
> *You created the earth according to your own purpose,*
> *While you were quite alone ...*
> *You dwell in my heart,*
> *For there is no other who knows you*
> *Except your son* (the Pharaoh).
> *You have taught him well*
> *To know your might and your purpose ...*
> *Your hand brought the whole world into being;*
> *Everything exists according to your plan ...* (127)

---

(127) Various translations of Akhenaton's hymn are available. I have two or three in my own library. Unfortunately, I have lost the source of the translation given above, which is barely a quarter of the entire hymn. Wikipedia has a fine article on the Pharaoh himself, and for the hymn, see http://en.wikipedia.org/wiki/Great_Hymn_to_the_Aten .

Akhenaten had no Bible to guide him, no prophet to teach him, he was not a member of the covenant race. How did he come so close to the truth about God? We must suppose that he was driven by his own conscience, by some inner grasp of spiritual reality, which enabled him to see what is plain to all who have eyes. Paul wrote about it one and a half millennia later –

> *Everything that can be known about God by men lies plainly in front of their eyes. Indeed, God himself has revealed it to them. Ever since the world began the invisible attributes of God have been open to the eye of reason. His everlasting power and deity are amply disclosed through the physical creation all around us. Therefore, there is no possible excuse for their behaviour* (Ro 1:19-21).

Did Akhenaten's discovery of God's *"eternal power and deity"* secure him a place in the Lamb's *Book of Life*? Only God knows. But the king did say of his god, *"You dwell in my heart."* Perhaps he truly was a fellow pilgrim with Abraham, and with all whose faith has been turned by God's grace into righteousness.

- ### ***Assyria and Babylonia***

Akhenaten was not alone. As I have already mentioned, there were other monotheists among Abraham's neighbours in ancient Chaldea. They were apparently never wholly stifled, for centuries later, among the Assyrians and Babylonians, monotheistic ideas continued to appear –

> *As among the Israelites, (Assyrian) offerings were of two kinds, sacrifices and meal offerings. The sacrifices consisted of an animal, more usually a bullock, part of whose flesh was burnt upon the altar, while the rest was handed over to the priests or retained by the offerer. There is no trace of human sacrifice among the*

> *Assyrians, which is the more singular when we remember how common they were among the Canaanites ... On the other hand, the idea of vicarious sacrifice was not unknown. There are evidences, moreover, of a monotheistic school among the priests which resolved the manifold deities of the pantheon into forms of Anu and his counterpart Anat; but the school had few adherents ... (In Assyria) there was a strong tendency to monotheism. The supreme god, Assur, is often spoken of in language which at first sight seems monotheistic: to him the Assyrian monarchs ascribed their victories, and in his name they make war against the unbeliever ... (Thus the) higher minds of the nation struggled now and again towards the conception of one supreme God, and of a purer form of faith, but the dead weight of polytheistic beliefs and practices prevented them from ever really reaching it ...* (128)

Archaeology has shown that around the time of the Assyrian monarch Adad-Nirari III (810-783 B.C.) there was a strong movement toward monotheism in Assyria. Adad-Nirari himself worshiped a single god. This was shortly before the time of the prophet Jonah in Israel, and may explain the extraordinary response the people of Nineveh gave to Jonah's preaching –

> *When the news reached the king of Nineveh, he rose from his throne, took off his royal robes, covered himself with sackcloth and sat down in the dust. Then he issued a proclamation in Nineveh –*

---

(128) Ibid. pg 92, 94, 103, 105.

> "By the decree of the king and his nobles: ... Let everyone call urgently upon God ... Who knows? God may yet relent and with compassion turn from his fierce anger so that we will not perish."
>
> When God saw what they did, and how they turned from their evil ways, he did have compassion and did not bring upon them the destruction he had threatened. (Jo 3:6-10).

Adad-Nirari was a powerful monarch who greatly enhanced Assyria's prestige during his reign. Much blood dripped from his sword. Is his name in the *Book of Life*? Probably not. Certainly, the Assyrian nation as a whole failed to attain to true religion, which finally brought upon them the judgment Jonah had pronounced. But underneath all the clatter of empire-building there may have been many ordinary people who did come to know the God of heaven, whose faith, though imperfect in many ways, secured for them the Father's favour.

- ### *The Greeks*

Many of the ancient philosophers in their best moments displayed a remarkable insight into the nature of God and of true worship. For example, the Greek Stoic philosopher Epictetus taught that

> a wise, divine Providence governs all things, so that what seem to be calamities are really parts of a divine plan that orders everything for the best ... Have courage to look up to God and say, "Deal with me as thou wilt from now on. I am as one with thee; I am thine; I flinch from nothing so long as thou dost think that it is good. Lead me where thou wilt, put on me what raiment thou wilt. Wouldst thou have me hold office or

eschew it, stay or flee, be rich or poor? For all this I will defend thee before men." (129)

Among the higher thinkers of ancient Greece and Rome there was a constant tendency to rationalise the numerous gods and goddesses of the mythical pantheon into expressions of the one great Creator and Governor. Would you say that not one of those serious and upright men and women ever came to an Abraham-like faith?

So from the most distant past until now, in every nation and generation, there have surely been some who reasoned well, who opened their eyes, who saw the glory of God in the world around them, who heeded the cry of conscience and the stirring of the Spirit within them, and whose faith has obtained for them a place in the kingdom of God. They cannot belong to the church this side of the resurrection, for they had no knowledge of Christ. But their names may be in the *Book of Life*, and the resurrection may bring them full revelation of the gospel and wondrous union with Christ. If so, their place will then truly be with the redeemed for ever.

THE FALLEN ANGELS

If judgment will fall heavily upon ungodly men and women, an even fiercer wrath of God is reserved for the fallen angels, who once stood around his throne –

THEIR JUDGMENT HAS ALREADY BEGUN

See *Jude 6; 2 Peter 2:4*.

- if the fallen angels are synonymous with demons, then *"the place of darkness"* must be the earth's atmosphere (cp. Ep 2:2 with Cl 1:13)

---

(129) I have lost the source of this quote.

- if the fallen angels are other than demons, then *"the place of darkness"* may be away from this planet.

THEY ARE DESTINED FOR "TARTARUS"

Hence they *"believe and tremble"* and are full of fury, knowing that their doom is sealed (Ja 2:19; Re 12:3-4, 7-9, 12; Mt 8:29; and see also Re 20:10). But what is *"tartarus"*?

One of the mythical heroes of ancient Troy was the warrior Aeneas. He escaped the ruin of his city, and after many adventures arrived in Italy, where his descendants Romulus and Remus founded mighty Rome. Among his exploits, says the myth, was a visit to the nether regions –

> *Aeneas would have lingered long with his Trojan friends, but the Sibyl hurried him away. They next came to a place where the road divided, the one leading to Elysium, the other to the regions of the condemned ... Before him was the gate of adamant that neither gods nor men can break through. An iron tower stood by the gate, on which Tsisiphone, the avenging Fury, kept guard. From the city were heard groans, and the sound of the scourge, the creaking of iron, and the clanking of chains. Aeneas, horror-struck, inquired of his guide what crimes were those whose punishments produced the sounds he heard? The Sibyl answered, "Here is the judgment hall of Rhadamanthus, who brings to light crimes done in life, which the perpetrator vainly thought impenetrably hid. Tsisiphone applies her whip of scorpions, and delivers the offender over to her sister Furies." At this moment with a clang the brazen gates unfolded, and Aeneas saw a Hydra with fifty heads guarding the entrance. The Sibyl told him that the gulf of Tartarus descended deep, so that its recesses were as far beneath their feet as heaven*

> *was high above their heads. In the bottom of this pit, the Titan race, who warred against the gods, lie prostrate; Salmoneus also, who presumed to vie with Jupiter ... (until Jupiter) taught him the difference between mortal weapons and divine ...* (130)

"Tartarus", then, was seen by the Greeks as a subterranean prison, as far *below* even Hades as heaven is *above* Hades. It was peculiarly a place of terrible confinement and punishment for those who had presumed to war against heaven, or to usurp divine prerogatives. Peter seized that aspect of *Tartarus* and used it as an apt symbol of the doom awaiting the angels who, puffed up with pride, thought they could capture the throne of God.

There was no hell lower than *Tartarus*, no pains more awful than those inflicted there. A fit place indeed for angels who, though they had seen with their own eyes the glory of the Lord, preferred the darkness of their own tortured ambitions.

"Happiness," says an old proverb, *"ends where ambition begins."* Be warned by the fallen angels!

THEY WILL BE CONDEMNED

Jude (vs. 6) tells us that their just punishment will be decreed on *"the great Day"*, which Re 20:10 implies will occur just prior to the *setting up of the Great White Throne*.

THEY WILL BE JUDGED BY THE SAINTS

See 1 Co 6:3; and who better than the saints to act as the judges of their former tormentors? Those who remember the sin, the afflictions, the persecutions, that Satan thrust upon them will

---

(130) From <u>Bullfinch's Mythology</u>, by Thomas Bullfinch; undated reprint by The Modern Library, New York; pg 215, 216.

now have opportunity to sentence their foe to the wrath of God. Paul encouraged the church with this great thought –

> *The God of peace will shortly bruise Satan under your feet!* (Ro 16:20).

The word *"bruise"* is *"suntribo"*, and it means to "make utterly helpless ... to crush into pieces." That will be the dominion of the saints and the destruction of Satan on that glorious day!

THEY ARE ALREADY PRONOUNCED GUILTY

The condemnation of the Fallen Angels is assured because –

- they *"sinned"* (2 Pe 2:4)
- they *"did not keep their own position"* (Ju 6)
- they *"left their proper dwelling"* (Ju 6)
- and their fate is an example, for

> *if God did not spare the angels when they sinned ... and if he rescued righteous Lot ... then ... the Lord knows how to rescue the godly ... and to keep the unrighteous under punishment until the day of judgment"* (2 Pe 2:4-9).

THE GREAT WHITE THRONE

> Lo! He comes with clouds descending,
> Once for favored sinners slain;
> Thousand thousand saints attending,
> Swell the triumph of his train!
> Hallelujah!
> Jesus comes, and comes to reign.
>
> When the solemn trump has sounded,
> Heav'n and earth shall flee away;
> All who hate him must, confounded,
> Hear the summons of that day –

Come to Judgment!
Come to Judgment, come away! (131)

What awesome words! How chilling the dread call: *"Come to judgment! Come away!"* Yet nothing is more certain than that coming day. Only a fool wilfully chooses to remain ignorant of it. We prefer to be wise and to learn as much as we can –

LOCATION

The Last Judgment will take place before the *Great White Throne*, which will be situated neither on the earth, nor in the sky, but in some intermediate position (Re 20:11).

DESCRIPTION

It is *"**great**"*, because

- divine omnipotence will be displayed when the dead are called out of their graves and compelled to stand in judgment; and because

- this will be the greatest act of judgment in all time; and because

- the sentence it imposes will be eternal.

It is *"**white**"* because its judgment will be absolutely impartial (Ro 2:11), based upon the standard of holiness established by Christ when he lived among us.

It is a *"**throne**"* because the Judge seated there will be the King of kings, and Lord of lords (Jn 5:22; Ac 17:31).

Christ is eminently suited to be the Judge of every man and woman because

- he is wholly just (Ac 17:31)

---

(131)   Charles Wesley.

- he has perfect knowledge of every person (Jn 2:24-25)
- he has all power (Re 1:8)
- he is eternally righteous (Ps 45:6; He 1:8)
- he is closely related to the human family.

Jesus delighted to call himself *"the Son of man"* (Mt 16:13; plus about 70 other places). We are prone to think of him rather as *"the Son of God"*. Both identities are essential. As *"Son of God"* he has the *power* to judge mankind; but as the *"Son of man"* he has the *right* to do so.

I have already mentioned that were God himself to sit upon the throne of judgment, people could rightly complain that a principle of justice was being violated. We accept it as axiomatic that an accused person has a right to be tried by his peers. We disqualify those who hold a social status significantly higher or lower than that of the accused. How then could the Almighty be our Judge? What kinship does he have with us? None. But stay! The Son will be our Judge, not the Father; and Christ has truly established a peer relationship with every person. And, as their peer, he is worthy to judge all people for

- to the **poor** he says, *"Foxes have holes, and birds have nests, but the Son of man had nowhere to lay his head!"* (Mt 8:20)
- to the ***rich*** he shows all the kingdoms of the world and their glory, and tells how they could all have been his. But he remained impervious to their enticing corruption (Mt 4:8-9; and cp. 14:19-20).
- to the ***labourer*** he holds out his own hands, toil-worn from many years toiling at his step-father's bench. Yet he was neither envious nor bitter when he encountered those who had great wealth (Mk 6:3).
- to the ***servant*** he says that despite his preeminent

glory he was willing to be a servant to all mankind (Mk 10:45), and indeed, took on the very nature of a servant (Ph 2:7).

- to the *lonely* he tells how he too had endured isolation and abandonment, yet without complaint, finding solace in communion with his Father (Mt 14:23; Jn 16:32; Mt 26:56).

- to the *popular* he reports the huge crowds who constantly clamoured for his attention, who even laid palm branches and their garments on the road before him (Lu 5:15; Jn 12:13; Mt 21:8).

- to the *physician* he points to the multitudes who clamoured for his healing ministry (Mk 6:56), so that he could find no time to rest (Mt 9:35-36; Mk 3:20; 6:31).

- To the *psychiatrist* he displays his perfect knowledge of the human heart, the human mind, the human condition, yet he himself remained humble and full of empathy (Jn 2:24; 16:30; He 4:13).

- to the *scholar* he recounts the story of his experience in the temple, at 12 years of age, when the doctors were astonished by his questions and answers. Yet he was never arrogant, but always gracious toward those whose understanding was simple (Lu 2:46-47; Cl 2:3).

- to the *teacher* he presents the acclaim he had as an instructor, and how the crowds hung upon his every word (Mt 7:28; 13:54; Jn 7:46; 13:13;

- to the *meek* he says, *"I am gentle and lowly in heart; I did not wrangle nor cry aloud in the streets; and as a sheep before its shearers is dumb, so was I"* (Mt 11:29; 12:19; Ac 8:32). But he remained strong, refusing to surrender to cowardice, passivity, or weakness.

- to the *ruler* he reveals the awesome authority that

enabled him to hush the stormy sea, ride the wild colt, and call the dead from their graves. Yet he scorned the idea of using his might to protect himself or to harm others (Jn 13:13).

- to the **military** commander, he arrays the twelve legions of angels that were always at his command, along with the entire host of heaven that would have leaped to do his bidding (Mt 26:53). But how then would the Father's will have been done? He came not to build his own kingdom, but the kingdom of God.

- to the **tempted** he says, *"I suffered, for I was tempted in every way, just as you are, yet I stayed outside of sin"* (He 2:8; 4:15)

- to the **weak** he shows his forty days in the wilderness, fasting and praying, until he was at the point of death (Lu 4:2). Yet when the devil came to him, he resisted every beguilement, and cast the Evil One aside.

- to the **tortured** he exposes the marks of the spikes in his hands and feet, and the scars of the lash, and of the crown of thorns (Mk 15:15-25)

- to **every man, every woman**, who has ever been assaulted by *"the lust of the flesh, the lust of the eye, and the pride of life"* he will say, "I too felt all the force of all those temptations, yet overcame them all" (He 7:26).

Therefore the Father has rightly appointed Jesus of Nazareth the fit Judge of every person who has ever lived (Ac 10:42; 2 Ti 4:8; 1 Pe 4:5). No one standing accused before his throne on the great day will have any legal ground upon which to dispute his right to pass sentence. He is truly the Peer of each one of us and worthy to pass sentence upon us all.

So, again, the Last Judgment will be an actual event, occurring at a definite point in the future (Ac 24:25; He 10:26-27). The resurrection is preparatory for the judgment and will be as unavoidable as the judgment itself, for which the ungodly in particular are reserved (Jn 5:29; He 9:27; 2 Pe 2:4, 9).

PURPOSE

AN ACT OF REVELATION

The purpose of the Last Judgment at the *Great White Throne* will be, not to **ascertain** each person's character or deeds, but simply to **reveal** to all witnesses what is already known to God, and so to vindicate the justice of the divine verdict (Ro 2:5-6; 1 Ti 5:24-25).

AN ACT OF DAMNATION

For the ungodly, the result of the Last Judgment will be *"eternal damnation"* (Mt 25:41, 46 with Re 19:20 and 20:10), which includes the idea of a fiery torment in *"Gehenna"* (Mt 5:22, 29, 30; 10:28; 18:9; 23:15, 33; Mk 9:43, 45, 47; Lu 12:5; Ja 3:6).

"Gehenna" is the Greek form of the Hebrew noun *"Hinnom"*, which was the name of a valley outside of Jerusalem. The Jews once burnt their children alive there, as a sacrifice to Molech (2 Ch 28:3; 33:6; Je 7:31-32). By the time of Jesus it had become a vast incinerator for the city's refuse, and by an analogy that referred both to its history and to its contemporary use, it had become a symbol of the place of punishment for the wicked.

"Gehenna" is probably synonymous with *"the lake of fire"* (Re 20:10, 14, 15), and with such expressions as *"the furnace of fire"* (Mt 13:41-43, 49-50), *"the smoke of their torment"* (Re 14:9-11); etc.

Many have reacted against that orthodox view, and have suggested certain alternatives –

Universalism

- every soul, even the fallen angels, will eventually be restored to God; therefore the *"lake of fire"* will be a place of <u>reformation</u> rather than of <u>retribution</u>.

Conditional Immortality

- initially, death means total obliteration for every person, but in the resurrection the righteous will be restored to life; the unrighteous, however, will *never* be restored, but will simply remain perished in the grave for ever.

Annihilationism

- after the judgment, the righteous will be given eternal life, but the wicked will be annihilated.

None of those views are fair to the biblical data; but the orthodox view also has some shortcomings –

- ***<u>In favour of the orthodox view it may be said that</u>***

Punishment, in the legal sense, is not **_reformative_**, but retributive; in other words, punishment, to be just, must be deserved (cp. Ga 6:7); it is immoral to inflict pain upon a man just to improve him.

Universalism relies upon a human concept of love when it tries to determine in advance what would or would not be a proper action for the love of God; but measuring divine love by the criterion of human love is a risky enterprise. How can we tell what is or is not a proper expression of the love of God? How do we know what choices will be in the best interest of each individual and of God's entire creation?

Universalism also assumes that the damned will repent when they find themselves in hell; therefore they will be held there against their will, which would be an act of arbitrary cruelty.

But remember *Dives* (Lu 16:19-31), and *Judas*. They both showed remorse, but not repentance. As Jesus said about Dives, if the love of God expressed in the preaching of the gospel does not persuade people to repentance, then neither will the wrath of God expressed in the judgment. They may hate their torment; but they will hate holiness even more. Far from compelling them to repentance, their punishment will itself provide proof of its justice. Their very reaction to their misery will show how much their pain is deserved. Not now, nor in eternity, will this fact change: if men and women refuse to repent and believe, they cannot be saved (Jn 3:36; Ro 1:16; 3:26; He 11:6; 1 Jn 5:11-12).

Annihilationism cannot stand before the kinds of statements quoted above about *"Gehenna"* and the *Lake of Fire"*. the terminology used plainly describes continuing punishment. See also Re 19:20; 20:10, which show that after *"1000 years"* of torment the beast and the False Prophet will still be alive. Remember also, *"the fire that shall never be quenched"* (Mk 9:43, 45); *"their worm does not die"* (vs. 44, 46, 48); *"(in the furnace of fire) there will be weeping and gnashing of teeth"* (Mt 13:42, 50), *"for ever and ever"* (Re 14:11).

Jesus also distinguishes between *"death"* (as a mere extinction of physical life) and the power of God to punish an offender in *"hell"* (Lu 12:4-5). How can that passage mean anything less than the continuing conscious existence of the soul beyond death? Death kills the body, but not the soul. After death, God still has power to cast the soul into *"hell"*.

If you still feel that such awful dooms have no place in a gospel of love, remember that the most dreadful warnings about *"hell"* were spoken by Jesus himself. More than any other biblical figure, he used such expressions as *"unquenchable fire ... undying worm ... wailing ... gnashing of teeth ... punishment ... furnace of fire;"* and he also spoke about being *"cut in sunder"* (Lu 12:46); *"beaten with many stripes"* (vs. 47); *"in torments"* (16:23); *"damnation"* (Jn 5:29); *"dying in sin"* (8:21); *"damnation of hell"* (Mt 23:33); etc.

The idea of continuing punishment (as distinct from annihilation) also occurs in 2 Th 1:9 (*"They shall suffer the punishment of eternal destruction and of exclusion from the presence of the Lord"*); see also He 6:2; Re 21:8; 22:15; Ro 2:8-9; Mt 8:12; 22:13; 25:30; etc.

- ### *Against the orthodox view it may be said that*

There are several passages which suggest an ultimate, universal reconciliation between God and the entire creation, or that everyone will eventually be saved (Ac 3:21; Ro 5:18-19; 8:21; 1 Co 15:22; 2 Co 5:19; Ep 1:9-10; Cl 1:20; 2 Pe 3:9; 1 Jn 2:2; Re 21:5; plus a number of other similar references). It is reasonable to think that God can scarcely claim to have defeated Satan if the majority of the human race, far from being saved, is condemned to a pitiless eternity of pain, forever in the thrall of sin and its penalty. Surely, to demonstrate that he has indeed triumphed over sin, death, and all the powers of darkness, God must find a way to bring, if not all people, at least nearly all into eternal life? And there are many scriptures that tell how Christ died for all and for the whole world (Jn 1:9, 29; 4:42; 12:47; Ph 2:10; He 1:2; 2:9)

Surely also, justice demands varying degrees of punishment for varying degrees of sin? See *Luke 12:47-48*, which seems to preclude a common penalty for all sin, whether that penalty is annihilation or eternal damnation. Surely some variance in both the severity and duration of punishment is required? If every sinner, regardless of degree of fault, is condemned to the same doom, how can heaven's justice be called impartial?

The Greek word for "eternal/everlasting" is *"aion"*, which does not necessarily mean "eternal" in an absolute sense – indeed, the Greeks had no word exactly equivalent to our "eternal", for they did not think of time as an unbroken linear sequence (as we do), but rather as a series of repeated cycles (or "ages").

Let us explore this further, not from a universalist viewpoint, but as a statement of fact –

DURATION

Aion signified any period of time whose limit, at least in one direction was either not fixed or not known; thus it was often used in a limited sense (Mt 13:22; Jn 9:32; Ac 15:18; Mk 11:14; 1 Co 8:13; and see also 1 Co 2:7; 2 Ti 1:9; Tit 1:2.) Thus it could describe the duration of this planet, or the lifetime of a tree or of a man, or the span of years since creation, and the like.

That limited sense did not prevent the Greeks from using *aion* in a setting (especially when it was applied to God) more or less equivalent to our idea of *"eternal"* (Ro 16:26; He 9:14; Jn 8:35; Ro 1:25; etc). But in that setting, *aion* gains its idea of "eternal", not from its own intrinsic meaning, but from the nouns with which it is associated.

Generally, however, the idea of an everlasting state is absent from *aion*. Usually, it contains some suggestion of a limit, it allows the possibility of change, unless the context in which it is used denies that possibility. It is more open-ended, more flexible in meaning, than is our word "eternal". It leaves the final outcome indeterminate; or, at least, the outcome cannot be determined by the meaning of *aion* itself, but must be settled by other means.

So *aion* may be said also to be a *qualitative* more than a *quantitative* term; it describes the *nature* rather than the *duration* of the "life" or "damnation" of which it speaks. That is, "eternal" (*aionic*) life is not so much *endless* life as it is that kind, or quality, of life that is proper to the eternity in which God dwells. Likewise, "eternal" (*aionic*) damnation is not so much *endless* torment, as it is that kind, or quality, of punishment that will be characteristic of the age to come.

Note also that "eternity" in scripture is never just endless time, but rather a sphere of existence that lies right outside the realm of time; it is that realm in which God dwells (Is 57:15). Time is inseparable from the physical universe, and will cease to exist when the universe perishes (He 1:10-12; Re 21:1). Eternity will then be the only remaining dimension. There is a quality of *life* that belongs to the eternal realm, and it will be imparted to the saints. There is a quality of *punishment* that belongs to the eternal realm, and it will be imposed upon the wicked. What the ultimate outcome of that life and that punishment will be is left unstated in scripture.

I am not suggesting that the saints may lose heaven, nor that sinners will necessarily be able to escape hell. I am not teaching the ultimate salvation of every soul ("universal reconciliation"). Those propositions can hardly be said to be clearly taught in scripture, despite certain allusions. But then, neither is eternal (in the sense of endless) damnation so clear that it cannot be questioned. I am simply saying that the language of the Greek text is not so emphatic as many of our English translations imply.

Note too, that scripture is silent about God's activity prior to the creation, and equally silent about his actions after the completion of the new creation. Caution should therefore be exercised about stating too firmly just what the outcome will be for humanity in the coming ages. Neither heaven nor hell (as we presently understand them) may represent God's final goals. We can be certain only about this: at the point where the biblical record ends, the saints are in heaven, the sinners are in hell; the former are enjoying bliss, the latter, torment. What lies beyond, during the everlasting ages to come, we are not told; we do not know God's ultimate purpose.

CONCLUSION

Judgment, just as much as salvation, results from Calvary. The holiness of God, his goodness, his love, will be as fully displayed in hell as in heaven. The damned will demonstrate his kindness as richly as the redeemed. Heaven, to the unsaved, would be a worse hell than the most scalding lake of fire. For the unholy, no anguish could be compared with dwelling in the presence of the Holy. By his mercy they are *"cast into outer darkness."*

The act of raising the unjust, and of punishing them, will be just as much a result of the resurrection of Jesus as the act of raising and rewarding the just. The same degree of omnipotent might will be exercised. The cross will be equally present in both dimensions, heaven and hell, bringing redemption to the one and condemnation to the other. Neither of them would be possible without the dying and rising of Jesus. So God will gather as much glory from hell as he will from heaven, and in both realms his majesty and power will be equally manifest.

Here then is the awful tragedy. Gaze into hell. There you will see the wisdom, grace, love, mercy, and redemption of the Almighty. Gaze into heaven. There you will see the wisdom, grace, love, mercy, and redemption of the Almighty. Why is one heaven and the other hell? The difference is solely one of *relationship* – a relationship established in this life, based on belief in or rejection of the gospel.

You and I establish that relationship now, by our own choice.

May your choice be to believe, and become a child of heaven.

Addendum – on Hell

Doleful Dungeons of Darkness!

I hope that you will enjoy good health, happiness, and prosperity, for that is the general will of God for his people. Yet in the end, that is not the main function of the church, which is not to solve problems nor make life smooth, but rather to get people out of **hell** and into **heaven**. If hell and heaven are real, then no cost is too great to escape the one and gain the other. Even if the price is abject poverty, or a maimed body (Mk 9:43-48), you would be insane if you did not pay it cheerfully!

But what do we mean by hell?

THE DOMINANT *POPULAR* IMAGE

FIRE

The common view of hell is that of a place of dreadful torment. Consider this passage from *"A Puritan Catechism"* (17th cent American) –

Q. What is the misery of that state whereunto man fell?

A. All mankind, by their fall, lost communion with God (Ge 3:8, 24), are under his wrath and curse (Ep 2:3; Ga 3:10), and so made liable to all the miseries in this life, to death itself, and to the pains of hell for ever (Ro 6:23; Mt 25:41).

PURGING

However, it is better to see the imagery of "fire" as a symbol of God purging iniquity from his creation. This is obviously the basic idea behind the use of "Gehenna" (note also the use of *"refiner"*, Je 9:7; Ma 3:2-3). Thus the angels will *"purge"* iniquity from the world on the Day of Judgment (Mt 13:40-43). So let us turn from the lurid and sensational to

THE DOMINANT *BIBLICAL* IMAGE

In 1889 two NZ poets described a Kiwi's reaction to a tour of Australia –

> It was when in Australia making a stay
> That I happened to hear an Australian say,
> With a patriot's pride, that his country was one
> Boasting all the advantages under the sun;
> That it offered no drawbacks, or at least very few,
> And he swore that they only amounted to two,
> And so small, by their absence that no one was vexed;
> Want of water the first, good society next:
> Then I ventured my friend most politely to tell
> That the same disadvantages happen in hell! [132]

Blackness, _Loneliness_, _Thirst_, and _Pain_, which the poet suggested describe Australia, in the Bible are the essence of hell. Thus Jesus taught (Mt 25:30; Mk 9:47-48; Lu 16:24)

BLACKNESS – LACKING ALL SPLENDOUR

- "*cast into outer darkness*" (Mt 8:12; 22:13; 25:30)

- not only outward, but also inner darkness; total blackness of environment, mind, and soul

- a total absence of anything that might be called "light"

I once stood with a small group of people in the solitary confinement cell of the 19th century "Model Prison" at Port Arthur, in Tasmania. Our guide switched out the light, and total, utter blackness surrounded us, tangible, suffocating,

---

(132) George Williams & William Reeves, Colonial Couplets: Being Poems in Partnership, "*A Globe-Trotter's Views on New Zealand.*"

almost unbearable. It was impossible to see anything at all, except that enclosing blackness. After barely a minute or less, some of the people began to demand that the light be turned on, which the guide swiftly did. Indeed, he told us that he had to stand with his hand actually on the switch, for some people found the darkness so terrible that they were prone to panic or faint.

The guide also told us that many prisoners locked into that terrible cell (where no chink of light was ever allowed to penetrate, not even when food and water were pushed through a small trap door) completely lost their minds, and had to be transferred to a nearby insane asylum.

That blackness, awful though it was, is but a pale reflection of the outer darkness that Jesus said would be the fate of those whose names are not written in the Lamb's Book of Life. Indeed, this state of impenetrable darkness is probably a stronger image of the place of punishment than the common idea of a Lake of Fire.

LONELINESS – LACKING ALL SOLACE

This answers the question, *"How many will there be in hell?"* The answer: *hell has a population of* – <u>one</u>. That is, there are as many hells as there are sinners, all isolated from each other, for *separation* is the ultimate consequence of sin – but see *Ephesians 2:12-13*

Hell, we may say, is like an enormous prison with each felon in solitary confinement.

- The torment of the *"worm"* is the gnawing pain of regret, of remorse that cannot be eased (Mk 9:48).

- The torment of the *"fire"* is the burning hunger of a relentless yearning for heaven and for God, a loneliness of soul too terrible to tell.

Note how in the parable of *Dives and Lazarus* (Lu 16:19-31) the rich man was alone in the flames of Gehenna (there is no mention of any other sufferer), which mocks the foolish claim of the ungodly when they scoff at hell, saying, "Why should I care? My mates will be there with me!" Yes, they may be there, but none will ever know, for each condemned person is *alone*, for as long as their sentence lasts.

THIRST – LACKING ALL SATISFACTION

Mark the chief torment of Dives – *"thirst"*.

Nearly every summer the Australian media report a pitiful story about someone who perished from thirst in the harsh Australian desert. Who can imagine the misery those people suffered? Yet their torment did eventually find an end. But in that place of *"outer darkness"*, for so long as the wrath of God endures, there will be an unquenchable thirst for –

HOLINESS

- a need to be "clean" is one of the most insistent demands in life; yet the condemned will be locked into a squalor of their own making

- how wondrous is the sweet and joyous holiness we have found in Christ!

LOVE

- who can live with an absence of all love; lacking even one creature to love or to be loved by?

- but the condemned will be locked into total rejection and self-loathing

- only from Christ can the mystery and treasure of love fully come to us.

BEAUTY

- not even those who are most repulsive morally find joy in outer ugliness; even the worst criminals love to build and dwell in a beautiful mansion filled with priceless art and other treasures

- but the condemned in hell will suffer a deprivation of all beauty, both inward and outward (1 Co 15:42-44)

- to the church however is promised the rapture of unsullied beauty for ever.

JOY

- even the worst of people crave laughter

- but the condemned, said Jesus, will be abandoned to a long night of weeping, wailing, and gnashing of teeth.

- but our lot, says God, will be one of unfailing and eternal joy in the heavenlies.

SUCCESS

- all people yearn to succeed in their endeavours, whatever their goals may be

- but the condemned will be enclosed within a sense of utter failure

- how great the contrast with our never-ending triumph in Christ!

IS HELL A PLACE OF PAIN?

In 1832 the NZ painter and writer Augustus Earle described the Maori reaction to the preaching of a missionary five years earlier –

> *The missionary began to expatiate on the torments of hell, at which some of them seemed horrified, but others said, "they were quite sure such a place could only be made for the white faces, for they had no men half wicked enough in New Zealand to be sent there"; but when the reverend gentleman added with vehemence that "all men" would be condemned, the savages all burst into a loud laugh, declaring that "they would have nothing to do with a God who delighted in such cruelties"; and then (as a matter of right) hoped that the missionary would give them a blanket each for having taken the trouble of listening to him so patiently.* (133)

My sympathies are all with those Maoris! The missionary was a fool – although, sadly, he still has many kin. However, we should be careful about taking too literally the description of hell as a place of fiery torment, because –

- Statements like those in *Revelation 20:14-15* must be read metaphorically, for *"Death and Hades"* themselves will be *"thrown into the lake of fire"*.

- The statements by Jesus about *"unquenchable flames"* are linked with Gehenna (or the Valley of Hinnom, often translated as "hell"), which was a perpetually burning rubbish dump outside the walls of Jerusalem, and obviously he was speaking in a metaphor.

- The dominant image among the Jews in the time of Christ was one of exclusion from the presence of God – an exclusion that was based, not upon divine vengeance, but upon the sinner's own choice (cp. Wis. 17:21, *"Over*

---

(133) Earl, Augustus. <u>Narrative of a Residence in New Zealand</u>. Oxford University Press, London, UK; 1966; pg. 133.

the people of Egypt alone heavy night was spread, an image of the darkness that was destined to receive them; but still heavier than darkness <u>were they to themselves</u>.")

- Nonetheless, it cannot be denied that *"consuming pain"* (albeit spiritual rather than physical) must be an inescapable condition of a soul that has become morally and spiritually awakened, only to find itself irrevocably cut off from God.

Still, one must admit that many mysteries surround the processes and consequences of divine judgment, and too much curiosity is unwise (cp. 2 Esd 9:9-13, esp. vs. 13, *"You must not be too curious about how the ungodly will be punished, and when. Rather, focus on how the righteous will be saved, to whom the world belongs, and for whom the world is created."*

One of those mysteries lies in the Greek word (*aion*) commonly translated "eternal" in our English Bibles. Neither the Greeks, Romans, nor Jews had any concept of eternity as meaning endless time. Rather, the common idea was one of repeating cycles of time. An "aion" to the Greeks meant a period whose beginning was known, but whose end was unknown; but it did not, and could not, mean "eternal" in the sense of the modern English word.

The Bible is much more a book about this age (*aion*) than about the next. Concerning the ultimate destiny of all things, including the souls in "hell", a little humble agnosticism is a sensible attitude.

"But if we don't preach a terrible and eternal hell, no one will get saved!" So the cry goes. But I like the comment made by the President of Vision International University, Dr Stan DeKoven –

> *My perspective is that it is difficult to see how God can be called just while condemning to a dread hell multitudes of people (both before and*

after Calvary) who never had the slightest opportunity to learn about Christ. So, on the strength of various biblical hints, if not plain statements, I have long assumed that in every nation people of good conscience and devout hearts will find themselves redeemed because of the work of Christ (Ac 10:34). Or, to put it differently, God knows the inner soul of every person, and he knows those who, had they heard the gospel, would have received it gladly. So I take it that the atonement includes not only those who knowingly believe in Christ, but also those who would and will believe when they see Christ on the day of his coming. I would agree that the saying "God is just" requires that he be Just. I would think God would be more justified in condemning the lukewarm believer than a well-meaning and open-hearted Muslim ... Hindu ... even pantheist.

Nonetheless, I would see a distinction between such people and those who have consciously embraced Christ. The latter are members of both the "body" and "bride" of Christ, with inestimable privileges; the former (presumably) cannot be part of the "body", nor share in the "wedding feast" of the Lamb, but will nonetheless be part of the Kingdom. I have always believed that those of us "in Christ" have innumerable benefits, here and now, which include the clear knowledge of our eternal destiny and the peace that passes understanding we can now experience. To know the love of God in Christ is with question not to be traded for anything this world has, and motivates me to want all men (and women of course) to experience his love, grace, forgiveness, acceptance, etc. At least, this will, I think, be the state of things when "the new heavens and the new earth" are inaugurated. What the eventual outcome will be, only God knows. I for one have a hope that ultimately even the worst of sinners will be rescued and transformed. It would seem a sad defeat for the majority of God's creatures to be consigned for ever to a fiery hell.

The judgment is real, and the punishment to follow will be equally real, and terrible; but I find it hard to believe that it will be eternal. Such a punishment would seem to be out of all proportion to the crime.

If the orthodox evangelical view of an eternal hell is true, then it would surely place upon a righteous and compassionate God an absolute demand to show himself and the coming judgment so clearly that no one could possibly hold to any doubt. The consequences of allowing the possibility of doubt would be too terrible to allow any valid argument for heaven's silence.

The one qualification to that belief is that I can accept that some people are so resolutely committed to iniquity, so possessed by hatred of God, that even in "outer darkness" and while "gnashing their teeth" in anguish, they would still despise righteousness and reject the offer of salvation. In other words, there may be people (like the devil and his hordes) who will prefer to suffer rather than end their rebellion and yield their hearts and will to the Lord God. Also a position I have held, is that in mercy, hell would

> *be merciful for some who so despise the very thought of a loving God.* (134)

CONCLUSION

Darkness and light can be known only as they are contrasted with each other – a light that shines in a dark night will irresistibly draw every eye!

Thus these two things are necessary for true life: a vision of both hell and heaven – to have one without the other is to be deficient in both sight and faith

Indeed, for that very reason, I would preach on hell (as Jesus did), not to unbelievers, but only to those who claim to be Christians.

One final question remains: how to escape the one and be sure of the other? For the answer, see *Revelation 20:11-15*.

---

(134) From a personal email he sent me several years ago.

Fifteen

ETERNITY

What lies beyond the return of Christ, beyond the *Great White Throne*, beyond the inaugurating of the eternal Kingdom of God? What activity will fill the everlasting ages to come?

The answer to such questions is not easy to find, for while the Bible paints a marvellous picture of the future, the colours it uses are broad splashes rather than carefully drawn lines. The scenes are general, rather than detailed. An exciting impression, more than specific description, is given. And the language used is so symbolic, so rich with imagery, that it is difficult to know what is sober fact and what is poetry soaring on the wings of spiritual ecstasy.

Remember, too, that the Bible is primarily a record of God's dealings with the human race from the time of Adam to the Last Judgment. It begins with the *Flaming Sword* and ends with the *Great White Throne*. It tells of Paradise Lost and Paradise Regained. Its opening pages describe the first couple's expulsion from the *Tree of Life*; its closing pages show the restoration of the covenant people to that same Tree.

But then the record closes. A veil of mystery surrounds the eternal ages that lie beyond the dissolution of the present heavens and earth. A new revelation for the new creation will then be given to God's new race of redeemed humanity. Exactly what occupations will fill the new Paradise with endless joy and satisfaction are not at present revealed to us.

However, it is impossible to believe that God has planned an eternity of idleness, nor even one of endless worship (fingering a harp on a fleecy cloud, as popular mythology supposes.) What then does lie ahead?

THE AGES AFTER CHRIST'S RETURN

THE MILLENNIUM

The beasts of the field and forest, said Aesop, the teller of fables, had a Lion as their king. He was neither wrathful, cruel, nor tyrannical, but just and gentle as a king could be. During his reign he made a royal proclamation for a general assembly of all the birds and beasts, and drew up conditions for a universal league, in which the Wolf and the Lamb, the Panther and the Kid, the Tiger and the Stag, the Dog and the Hare, should live together in perfect peace and amity. The Hare said, "Oh, how I have longed to see this day, in which the weak shall take their place with impunity by the side of the strong." And after the Hare said this, he ran for his life. Moral: Even when there is a just ruler, the weak cannot trust the strong.

How different that is from the picture drawn by many people of the millennial kingdom of Christ, which they expect lies ahead of us, right after the Second Advent. They develop from the scriptures a complex and rich picture of life on earth during that beautiful age of peace and prosperity. Under the sovereignty of Christ, war and crime will be utterly banished, and all will live together in perfect harmony. Christ will have Jerusalem as his capital, and, along with the glorified saints, he will reign over a restored Israeli empire. Every nation on earth will be brought under that benign, yet irresistible, dominion.

During that time, it is said, the earth will be lovely in every way, rich, flourishing, filled with laughter, dance, and song. Then the oracles will be fulfilled of astonishingly rich harvests (Ps 72; Am 9:13), of all creation dwelling together in joyful prosperity and safety (Is 11:6; 65:25), of weapons of war being turned into useful tools (Is 2:4), of universal longevity (Is 65:20), and of all hurt and destruction ceasing (11:9).

At the end of the thousand years, it is said, there will be a great rebellion of the nations against Christ's rule; but that rebellion will be swiftly crushed, the second resurrection will occur, and the final judgment will begin.

After that, the present creation will be replaced by the *"new heaven and new earth"* and the eternal ages will begin.

There is much to commend that view, and one can hardly help but wish it were surely true. It is based upon a fairly literal reading of many prophecies, and it has a hoary tradition, going right back to some of the church Fathers.

However, this millennial scheme has many opponents, who present various other scenarios, some more plausible than others. Nonetheless, this much is certain: following the return of Christ, the saints will enter into bliss and into their glorious inheritance.

Whether or not that endless bliss will begin with a millennial prelude on earth is in the end scarcely significant when measured against the vast ages to come! It is hard to see why some people get so excited about a paltry thousand years. What a small thing to generate so much heat and cause so much broken fellowship! In fact, one is constrained to observe that all too often in church life, the less important the doctrine, and the more flimsy its foundation, the more racket some teachers make about it!

In any case, we are assuredly promised a new heaven and a new earth, wherein righteousness will dwell, not for a millennium, but for ever (Is 65:17-19; 66:22; 2 Pe 3:13; Re 21:5).

THE GREAT BEYOND

As the new creation enters eternity, we shall come into full possession of all that has been promised us in Christ.

Those future ages will witness the ever-progressing growth of the saints into the likeness of their Lord (1 Jn 3:2-3; 1 Co 13:13). *"Hope,"* says Paul, *"will be eternal"* – so there will always be a glittering goal to be attained. Our position in the kingdom will not be static; there will always be room for choice, room to grow, and opportunity to be creative and fruitful.

The future will be one of service to God and to the Lamb (Re 22:3-5). Notice that the word *"reign"* implies a *"kingdom"*, which in turn implies an organised government, rulers, subjects, diverse activity, culture, creative achievement – all the varied life and accomplishment contained in the idea of a *kingdom*. Of the *"increase"* of this kingdom there shall be no end (Is 9:7).

The location of the kingdom will be *"the new heaven and the new earth"* (Is 65:17; 66:22-23; 2 Pe 3:13; Re 21:1). But what does that mean? Some say it refers to the present universe, which will be *restored* to its pristine state, unspoiled by sin. Others prefer the idea that the present universe will be *replaced* by a brand new creation. The argument is difficult to determine from scripture. Many references can be quoted to support both views.

Possibly the *"new heaven and the new earth"* will be neither a *restoration* nor a *replacement*, but a *"resurrection"*, so that the new will have the same kind of link with the old as our resurrection bodies will have with our present bodies. Perhaps that coming world will be like our *"spiritual bodies"* (1 Co 15:42-44), neither wholly physical nor wholly spiritual, but a kind of marvellous hybrid.

After the inauguration of the *new heaven and new earth*, God's plan for *"the fulness of time"* will then come into effect. That plan is nothing less than to bring the entire creation into *"the glorious liberty of the children of God"* (Ep 1:10; Ro 8:21; 1 Co 15:24-28).

The Eternal City will be a place of infinite joy, and even the memory of the former world will be obliterated (Is 65:17-18; Re

21:4, 10-21). Within the beautiful *City of God* there will be no sorrow, only infinite joy. Indeed, the very blessedness of the saints lies in their right of citizenship in the New Jerusalem (Re 22:14). Never again will the people of God be drawn away into disobedience (Re 21:27), and every saint will have open access to the tree and fountain of unending life (Re 22:1-2).

Eternity itself will be needed for the saints to possess fully the inheritance that is promised them in Christ (1 Pe 1:4; Ro 2:7; 2 Co 4:17). Presumably that inheritance will not be confined to the new earth but will embrace the entire far-flung universe, with its myriad stars and countless galaxies. Consider the thousands of years men and women have been on earth, yet we have hardly begun to explore the treasures and secrets that are locked within this one small planet. Think then of what it will mean when the full expanse of the new heavens and the new earth are made open to the saints in the eternal kingdom, for discovery, utilisation, artistry, and enjoyment.

But our chief bliss will be found in the endless delight of our bridal union with Christ and in our unending fellowship with the Father (Re 21:2, 3, 9).

CONCLUSION

And now let me conclude this part of my book with a passage from one of the very earliest documents of the church, dating from about the year 100. It is known as *The Didache*, which is an abbreviation of its Greek name, <u>The Teaching of the Twelve Apostles</u> –

> *Watch for your life's sake. Let not your lamps be quenched, nor your loins unloosed; but be ready, for you know not the hour in which our Lord will come. But come together often, seeking the things which are befitting to your souls: for the whole time of your faith will not profit you, if you are not made perfect in the last time. For in the last days false prophets and corrupters*

shall be multiplied, and the sheep shall be turned into wolves, and love shall be turned into hate; for when lawlessness increases, they shall hate and persecute and betray one another, and then shall appear the world-deceiver as Son of God, and shall do signs and wonders, and the earth shall be delivered into his hands, and he shall do iniquitous things which have never yet come to pass since the beginning. Then shall the creation of men come into the fire of trial, and many shall be made to stumble and shall perish; but those who endure in their faith shall be saved from under the curse itself. And then shall appear the signs of the truth: first, the sign of an outspreading in heaven, then the sign of the sound of the trumpet. And third, the resurrection of the dead – yet not of all, but as it is said: "The Lord shall come and all his saints with him." *Then shall the world see the Lord coming upon the clouds of heaven.* (135)

---

(135) From the final part of The Didache, Chapter 16. See http://www.earlychristianwritings.com/text/didache-roberts.html.

Addendum

THE "SEVENTY WEEKS" PROPHECY

See *Daniel 9:1-4, 20-27*.

Since the time of the Fathers, Daniel's prophecy about the *"Seventy Weeks"* has been a source of controversy. The argument has stormed back and forth, with some insisting that the *"Seventy Weeks"* came to their fruition in Christ and the early church, while others are equally adamant that at least the *"70th week"* is still future.

There is no possibility of the quarrel being solved by this *Addendum*! But perhaps I can present you with some guidelines for thoughtful consideration.

Even a casual check of the literature will show a multitude of interpretations of the *"Seventy Weeks"* oracle, which is hardly surprising, since even *translators* are baffled by obscurities in the Hebrew text of Daniel. No one is sure what Daniel *wrote*, let alone what he *meant* ! [136] Such diversity and uncertainty should surely make us cautious about

- any fixed interpretation of either the meaning or historical fulfilment of the prophecy; and about
- any system of eschatology that depends upon a particular interpretation of this one prophecy.

This seems to me to be one of the chief problems with the pre-tribulation rapture view-point. It relies too heavily upon the

---

(136) You will see what I mean if you compare several different translations, or check a textual commentary on the passage.

device of placing the *70th week* in the future. The doctrine of the pre-tribulation rapture may be correct; but this part of its foundation, if not actually suspect, is certainly susceptible to a different reading. A doctrine resting so much weight upon such shaky ground must be a risky refuge.

THE 70 WEEKS

Daniel's prophecy deals with *"70 weeks"*, which are usually taken to represent 490 years (70x7). Whether those "weeks" *do* represent "years", and whether those "years" should be taken literally or figuratively, are debatable issues. But for the purpose of this study I will accept the common reading: the *weeks* are "years", and the years are literal. If so, then those *weeks* will be divided into three groups, thus

- 7 weeks = 49 years
- 62 weeks = 434 years
- 1 week = 7 years.

The many different interpretations of Daniel's *70 Weeks Prophecy* can be grouped under four headings ...

FOUR MAIN SCHOOLS

THE CRITICAL

This school claims that the entire book of Daniel was written, not by the prophet Daniel, but by an unknown Jew in the second century BC. His purpose was to encourage the people to resist the tyranny of Antiochus Epiphanes IV, [137] and to encourage the Maccabean revolt against the Seleucids.

In this view, the book contains no real predictive element, and its images and "prophecies" were all based upon events that

---

(137)   The Greek ruler of the Seleucid Empire. He died 164 B.C.

had already happened, or were in the process of happening.

No one who is committed to a high view of scripture as the word of God could accept with any comfort such a "critical" and distorting reading of the oracles.

THE SYMBOLIC

According to this view, the *"70 Sevens"* are a symbol of the entire span of human history, from Daniel to the end of the present age.

Some say that the first *7 weeks* ended with the first advent of Christ; the next 62 cover the present age; and the final week will be the great tribulation just before the Second Advent of Christ.

The main objection to this view is that the *"70 weeks"* are plainly linked to the *"70 years"* predicted by Jeremiah (25:12; 29:10) for the Jews' captivity in Babylon, which suggests two things –

- the *"weeks"*, like the *"years"*, probably represent a specific period of time; and
- since Jeremiah's *"years"* were not exactly fulfilled, but were at least partly symbolic, so also may be the *"weeks"* – in other words, the best interpretation of the prophecy will probably mix a literal with a figurative reading of the *seventy weeks*. (138)

THE HISTORICIST

This view argues that the *"70 weeks"* were brought to fruition in the life, death, and resurrection of Christ, and that the *"70 weeks"* were to be followed by this present gospel age (of

---

(138) Note: no exact way of measuring the "70 years" of the captivity has yet been found. All the known dates either fall short of, or extend, the actual time predicted by Jeremiah.

indeterminate length), which is also the period of *"the great tribulation"* and of the manifestation of various *"antichrists"*.

More detail on this view is given below.

THE FUTURIST

This view argues that only the first *69 weeks* were brought to fruition in the time of Christ, and that the *70th week* is still *"future"*. Then it is claimed that during this future *"week"* the final Antichrist will appear, and the *Great Tribulation* will occur.

Opinions differ as to whether or not the church will remain upon the earth during this future *"70th week"*, that is, during the *Great Tribulation* (which, in this view, is seen as an event that follows the secret rapture of the church, prior to the visible return of Christ, with his church, to end the time of trouble and to inaugurate the Millennium).

This separation of the *"70th week"* from the 69 dates back at least to Hippolytus (c. 200), but it was not commonly followed by the Fathers.

More detail on this view is given below.

THE ACTUAL PROPHECY

ITS MAIN ELEMENTS

<u>The Jewish captivity in Babylon was to end</u> (vs. 1-23), and a command would be given for the people to return to Palestine, and to rebuild Jerusalem and the Temple (vs. 25).

<u>This restoration of Israel</u> was to take place during a period of "70 sevens" (= 490 years), which would begin with the issuing of a *"decree"* (vs. 25).

Many dates for that decree have been suggested; but the most common are linked with two announcements concerning the Jews, made by the Persian emperor Artaxerxes in the 7th and

20th years of his reign – namely, 457 BC (Ezr 7:7 ff); and 445 BC (Ne 2:1-8).

The purpose of the "70 weeks" was to achieve 6 things

(see vs. 24) –

- *"to finish transgression"*
- *"to put an end to sin"*
- *"to atone for wickedness"*
- *"to bring in everlasting righteousness"*
- *"to seal up the vision and prophecy"*
- *"to anoint the most holy".*

THE SIX PROMISES

Note that the Hebrew text in *verse 24*, and elsewhere in the prophecy, is not so precise as our English translations tend to indicate. So the meaning of the terms used is open to debate, and quite different translations of some phrases are possible. There are two main views –

THE HISTORICIST

This view (which is held generally by *a-millennialists, post-millennialists, praeterists*, and, of course, *historicists*) argues that the six promises have been fulfilled in Christ and the church. Here they are again, as historicists would apply them –

- *"to finish transgression" (Mt 23:32-26; Ac 3:14-15)*
- *"to put an end to sin" (He 9:26)*
- *"to atone for wickedness"*
- *"to bring in everlasting righteousness" (2 Co 5:21; Ro 3:21-22)*

- *"to seal up the vision and prophecy" (Mt 11:13; Ac 3:18; Ro 15:8)*
- *"to anoint the most holy" (Lu 1:35; 4:18; Ac 10:38).*

However, not all are agreed that they were adequately fulfilled in the church. So some argue that the promises relate to *Israel* (not the church). They draw attention to such expressions as *"your people"* and *"your holy city"*, which, they say, can refer only to Israel. Therefore many commentators choose to adopt another view, known as

THE FUTURIST

This view holds that the six promises will be fulfilled in the Jews, arguing that the *church* is nowhere suggested in the prophecy, and that the entire *"70 weeks"* were to be accomplished in three stages within national Israel. Since the third stage (that is, the *"70th week"*) has not yet had a *national* fulfilment (in the Jews), it must still be future.

To that opinion, *historicists* object that Israel's national appropriation of the promise must be distinguished from its actual fulfilment, which can take place apart from Israel's acceptance or rejection of it. For example, look at Je 31:31-34; Ro 15:8. According to the apostles, those, and many other promises made to Israel, have been fulfilled in the church. But they have not yet been appropriated by national Israel.

If it is asked, *"Where does the church fit into the '70 weeks'?"* futurists reply: this church age must be seen as a parenthesis in the program of God, lying between the 69th and 70th weeks, and unseen by the OT prophets (like a hidden valley between two mountain peaks).

To which, historicists object that –

- the real time sequence of the prophecy is quite destroyed by inserting a gap (now nearly 2000 years in length, four times longer than the original oracle) between the two final weeks; and that

- the Messiah was to be *"cut off"* <u>after</u> the *"69th week"*, which must mean <u>in</u> the *"70th week"* – how then can the *"70th week"* be future? And that

- the church cannot be a mere *"parenthesis"* in the divine plan; rather, the church was and is *central* in God's purpose.

CLAIMS AND COUNTER-CLAIMS

<u>Futurists</u> claim that the words *"unto Messiah the Prince"* (vs. 25) found their fulfilment on Palm Sunday, and therefore the Passion brought the *"69 weeks"* to an end.

By contrast, **<u>historicists</u>** argue that the *"69 weeks"* ended three years earlier, at the time of Christ's baptism (note the wording of Mk 1:14-15), and that the *"70th week"* began with Jesus' public ministry, ending 3½ years later, when he was *"cut off"* in the *"middle of the week"*, thus effectively causing *"sacrifice and offering to cease"* (Mt 27:51; He 8:13; 10:7-10).

<u>Futurists</u> agree that the first three promises do indeed relate to the redemptive work of Christ, and they were accomplished at Calvary (although not yet believed by Israel). But the second group of promises (they say) relates to the *reign* of Christ, so they cannot be fulfilled until after the Second Advent. [139] Yet all six promises must be fulfilled *within* the *"70 weeks"*, therefore the *"70th week"* is still future.

In this view, the expression *"the most holy"* is seen either as a reference to the millennial kingdom, or to the rebuilt temple in

---

(139) Remember that futurists look for Christ to come invisibly for a "secret" rapture of the church, after which the tribulation will break out. This, they say, is the 70th week, after which Christ will come visibly, with his church, to establish his millennial reign on earth.

Jerusalem.

This futurist view, of course, is linked with a strong commitment to a *pre-tribulation, pre-millennial* return of Christ.

THE MESSIAH

Daniel gave a magnificent prediction of the coming of the Messiah (vs. 25, 26a). His prophecy contains the following ideas –

- From the date of the decree to rebuild Jerusalem, 490 years would elapse until the time when the messiah would come and be *"cut off"*.

- During the first 49 years, the streets and walls of the city would be rebuilt, though the times would be *"troubled"* (see Ezra and Nehemiah).

- Following this, another *62 weeks* (= 434 years) would elapse before the appearance of the Messiah; which leads to the following calculations (among other possible variations) –
    - 457 BC + 483 solar years = 27 AD
    - 445 BC + 483 lunar years = 32 AD

Given the fact that authorities differ by as much as 10 years in the time when they reckon Christ began his public ministry, the above dates represent a miracle of accurate prophecy.

"After" the *"69th week"* (that is, after 481 years) the Messiah would be *"cut off, but not for himself"* – a vision of the cross.

THE WAR

The fifth element (140) in the prophecy concerns a great war that was to begin (vs. 26, 27b).

- **_Historicists_** claim that *"the prince"* was Titus, and that the prophecy was basically fulfilled in 70 AD, except that *"war"* and *"desolation"* were to continue until *"the end"* (of the age) (cp. Mt 24:15-16; Lu 21:20-24).

- **_Futurists_** claim that while the prophecy may have had an initial fulfilment in AD 70, its greater fulfilment awaits the coming of the *"70th week"* and of the Antichrist. They argue that the expression *"the end"* (which is repeated 3 times) is more reasonably a reference, not to the end of the age, but to the end of the *"70 weeks"*.

THE COVENANT

The final element in the prophecy is the covenant that was to be *"confirmed"* (vs. 27a).

- **_Futurists_** argue that *"he"* refers to *"the Prince who is to come"* (vs. 26b), and that the reference is therefore to the Antichrist, who will make a false covenant with the Jews at the beginning of the *"70th week"*.

As part of that covenant, he will rebuild the temple and reinstate the sacrifices. But then, in the middle of the week (after 3½ years) he will break the covenant and unleash a terrible persecution (*"the Great Tribulation"*).

---

(140) The four dealt with already above are: (1) the Jewish captivity would end; (2) Israel would be restored during a period of "70 weeks"; (3) the same "70 weeks" would bring the fulfilment of the six great promises; (4) at or after the 69th week, the Messiah would appear and be "cut off".

- **_Historicists_** argue that *"he"* must refer to the nearest preceding singular noun, which is *"the Anointed One"*, hence Christ.

They insist that *"he"* cannot refer to the "Prince", because "prince" is actually part of an adjectival phrase, linked to the plural noun *"the people"* (which would require the pronoun "they", not "he"). Historicists therefore argue that the same two persons are in fact mentioned in the two parallel verses (26 & 27), who are –

  - *"an Anointed One"* (vs. 26) and *"he"* (27); both referring to Christ; and
  - *"the people of the prince"* (26) and *"who makes desolate"* (27) both referring to Titus (and the Roman army).

- **_Historicists_** note also that the expression *"confirm"* requires the existence of a previous covenant, either one that had lapsed, or had not yet been implemented; but it cannot refer to a previously unknown covenant.

They see this, of course, as a reference to the gospel covenant predicted in the OT and implemented by Christ.

- **_Futurists_**, however, point out that *"sacrifice and offering"* continued for some 40 years after Christ's death, yet Daniel said that these were to stop *"in the middle of the week"*.

And as for the *"covenant"*, it is God's covenant with Israel, concerning their possession of the land, which the Antichrist will first *"confirm"* with the Jews, but the in the middle of the *"week"*, will break.

CONCLUSION

Note that both views are strong at some points and weak at others. In fact, a final solution to the mysteries of the *"70 *weeks"* would seem impossible.

However, both views eventually reach the same end –

- the time of the Messiah's appearing was amazingly predicted by Daniel, some 500 years before the event;
- Antichrist in all his manifestations will assuredly be destroyed;
- tribulation for both Israel and the church will one day come to an end;
- Israel will be restored;
- the church will be redeemed;
- an *"end"* has been decreed by God;
- Christ and his people will be stunningly triumphant!

With all parties agreeing that the end result is a magnificent oracle concerning the ultimate victory of Christ and the Church over every power of darkness, does anyone really care about differences in detail? I suppose some people do. But for myself, I cannot find such quarrels important. We win! That's enough for me!

PART TWO

ORACLES GALORE!

A survey of failed soothsayers across 20 centuries

SOOTHSAYERS EVERYWHERE!

Christian soothsayers are not easily discouraged!

For nearly twenty centuries, generation after generation, they have stood with parchment or newspaper in one hand, and the Bible in the other, crying out, "The prophecies are now fulfilled! The end of the age is upon us! Christ will soon return! Get ready to meet your God!"

Errors in past predictions have not in the least dismayed either former prophets or those of our own time. So through sermons and books, by radio and television, these modern foretellers are still insisting that ours is the *Last Generation*, that Christ will surely come back within our lifetime. "His coming," they cry, "can be delayed no longer!"

For proof they offer an assortment of current newspaper headlines and carefully selected biblical texts, to which they add the solemn assurance that the evidence of *"fulfilled prophecy"* is undeniable. Christ is coming soon!

I wonder if they have ever really listened to Jesus? –

> *The kingdom of God does not come with signs that can be observed* (Lu 17:20) . . . *When you see these things, do not be alarmed. They must all happen, <u>but they do not mean that the end is near</u>* (Mt 24:6) . . . *Of that day and hour <u>no-one knows</u>, not even the angels of heaven, nor the Son, but the Father only* (Mt 24:36).

It is surely astonishing to find that sundry events, which Jesus distinctly declares are <u>not</u> signs of the end, are so often taken to be proof that the end is near! And again, how more plainly could Christ have spoken when he said that *no one* except the Father knows when the Last Day will come?

Nevertheless, that uncertainty about the time of Christ's return has been a cause of much frustration. How zealously people have struggled to penetrate the veil and to gain some inside information on it! As a result, a great many absurd books have been written and sermons preached, confidently predicting that Jesus *must* come soon. So far, they have all been wrong! In the end, we can do no more than keep on looking for his appearing, and waiting for it patiently, while never allowing our confidence in the promise itself to waver –

> *You need to stay patient, and keep on doing God's will, so that you will be sure to receive what he has promised; for in just a short time he who is coming will come; he will not delay* (He 10:36-37).

Of course, our problem is that what God deems a "short time" has so far extended some twenty centuries! But, as Peter tells us in a similar context, a thousand years to God is no more than a day! (2 Pe 3:8) Hence he adds –

> *The Lord is not tardy in fulfilling his promise, as some people accuse him; rather, he is patient toward you, because he does not want anyone to perish. Instead, he desires that they should all turn away from their sin (vs.9).*

Daniel too declared that the *"Book"* will remain sealed until the *"end"* actually comes (12:9). And both Christ and the apostles averred that the Last Day would come as unexpectedly as *"a thief in the night"* (Mt 24:43; Lu 12:39; 1 Th 5:2-4; 2 Pe 3:10; Re 3:3; 16:15).

Furthermore, Christ says that life will continue normally right up to the very last minute, with no special warning of his coming (Mt 24:37-39; Lu 17:26-30).

Yet, despite all such statements in scripture, a great mass of material exists, spanning the centuries, which shows that Christians in every generation have believed they were living in *"the last days"*, and that the End of the World was at hand.

From the sources available to me I began (back in the 1960s) [141] to make a collection of predictions, covering the expression of this hope from the 2nd century to the 21st These present pages are a compilation made from that collection. My hope is that at least some readers, when they see how wrong the prognosticators have been in the past, will become more cautious about the soothsaying of modern prophets.

THE CHURCH FATHERS

THE SECOND CENTURY

- **_Papias_** (c. 60–c. 130); bishop of Hierapolis, in Phrygia (see also below, under **Jerome**, 4th cent.)

Only fragments of his writings survive, but enough to show that his views on the Millennium were very literal. He looked for an earthly paradise, and for the world to be supernaturally fruitful during the thousand-year rule of Christ. He is said to have been a disciple of the apostle John himself, and to have known the daughters of the evangelist Philip.

- **_"The Letter of Barnabas"_** (c.100) –

    It therefore behoves us, who enquire much concerning events at hand to search diligently

---

(141) Please note the date! It shows that some 60 years ago I abandoned all attempts to foretell when Jesus would come again, including predictions that the year 2,000 would surely see, if not the Last Day, then its near approach. Some people reproached me when I first put this list into print (in the 1960s), and some thought I was brave to do so. All were sure that the Second Advent was at hand. I hope it is! But it certainly hasn't happened yet!

> *into those things which are able to save us . . . The final stumbling-block (or source of danger) approaches, concerning which it is written . . . "For this end the Lord has cut short the times and the days, that his Beloved may hasten; and he will come to the inheritance." And the prophet also speaks thus: "Ten kingdoms shall reign upon the earth, and a little king shall rise after them, who shall subdue under one three kings." In like manner Daniel says concerning the same, "And I beheld the fourth beast, wicked and powerful, and more savage than all the beasts of the earth, and how from it sprang up ten horns, and out of them a little budding horn, and how it subdues under one three of the great horns." Ye ought therefore to understand.* (142)

Notice how 20 centuries ago Barnabus was quoting the same scriptures that modern prophecy buffs use to prove that Christ is coming soon!

From the same letter –

> *. . . God made in the six days the work of his hands, and made an end on the seventh day, and rested on it and sanctified it. Attend, my children, to the meaning of this expression, "he finished in six days." This implieth that the Lord will finish all things in six thousand years . . . Therefore my children, in six days, that is, in six*

---

(142) Chapter Four. The "stumbling block" he refers to is the Antichrist, whom the author thought was about to appear. The scripture quotations are loosely taken from Daniel 9:24-27; 8:24; 8:7-8. My source was The Ante-Nicene Fathers, reprinted by Eerdmans Publishing Company, Grand Rapids, Michigan, 1979, from the original 1885 edition, Volume One. Hereafter this work is abridged as ANF.

> *thousand years, all things will be finished. (Ch. 15).*

This is one of the earliest occurrences in Christian writings of the idea of the *"Cosmic Week"*, sometimes called *"God's Great Week"* – that is, the idea that the six days of creation show that the present time will last only six thousand years. This notion was popular among the Jewish rabbis, and it was taken up enthusiastically by the early Christians. Numerous references to it are scattered through patristic literature (some of which are below).

The Fathers, of course, usually managed to compute the end of the sixth millennium as being near to their own time. The same idea remains popular in some prophetic circles today, except that not so long ago the sixth millennium was supposed to end with the 20th century, climaxing in 2000 with the Second Advent, and the beginning of the 7th millennium.

From the same letter –

> *Let us take earnest heed in these last days . . . that the Black One may find no means of entrance . . . For the day is at hand on which all things shall perish with the evil one. The Lord is near, and his reward . . . And be ye taught of God, inquiring diligently what the Lord asks from you; and do it that ye may be safe in the day of judgment (Ch. 4 & 21).*

- ***Justin Martyr*** (c. 100–165); an important early Christian philosopher, apologist, and martyr, who wrote –

  > *. . . the times are now running on to their consummation; and he whom Daniel foretells will have dominion for a time, and times, and a half, is even already at the doors, about to speak blasphemous and daring things against the*

> *Most High . . . So short a time is left to you . . .*
> (143)

- **_Clement_** (fl. c. 90–100); bishop of Rome.

The *Letter to the Corinthians* by Clement was accorded almost biblical status by many early Christians, and in it he notes that some, because of the delay in Christ's return, had already lost faith. He rebukes them, and declares that the time is now at hand –

> *Wretched are they . . . who say, "These things we have heard even in the times of our fathers; but behold, we have grown old, and none of them has happened to us." Ye foolish ones! . . . Of a truth, soon and suddenly shall his will be accomplished, as the scripture also bears witness, saying, "Speedily will he come, and will not tarry;" and, "The Lord shall suddenly come to his temple, even the Holy One, for whom ye look."* (144)

- **_Irenaeus_** (fl. c. 175 – c. 195); renowned Christian apologist; bishop of Lyons.

He developed a detailed account of the appearance of the Antichrist, the approaching return of Christ, and the Millennium that would follow. (145) He based his confidence in the nearness of Christ's return on the prophecies of Daniel (as did many of the Fathers); but his discussion shows that even so early there were already many diverse opinions about how the prophecies should be interpreted. Irenaeus had no doubt that

---

(143)   Dialogue With Trypho, Ch. 28 & 32. ANF Vol. One, pg. 208, 210
(144)   Ch. 23; ANF Vol. One, pg. 11.
(145)   See his Against Heresies, Bk. 5, Ch. 25-36. Chapter 28 of the same writing, expresses Irenaeus' belief in "the Cosmic Week", and in the approaching end of the "sixth" week.

the Apocalypse was being fulfilled in his day.

- **_"The Shepherd of Hermas"_** (written c. 140).

Hermas was an emancipated slave, whose brother Pius was bishop of Rome (140–154). His writings were enormously popular in the early church, and for more than two centuries *The Shepherd* was counted by many as scripture. Even after it was excluded from the canon (c. 4th century), the book continued to be highly regarded for several more centuries. Hermas wrote –

> *Happy are ye who endure the great tribulation that is coming on (the earth) . . . (Ch. 2).*

According to Hermas, an aged woman presented to him a vision of the Church under the figure of a tower that was being built. He asked her if there were any signs of the End of the Age –

> *She cried with a loud voice, "Foolish man! Do you not see the tower yet building? When the tower is finished and built, then comes the End; and I assure you, it will soon be finished!" (Ch. 9).*

- **_Clement of Alexandria_** (c. 155–220)

Sometimes called "the first true Christian scholar", Clement was perhaps the most influential teacher and writer of his time. He made a series of elaborate calculations (based on scripture and history) that led him to conclude –

> *From Adam to the death of Commodus (192) was five thousand seven hundred and eighty-four years, two months, and twelve days.* [146]

---

(146) Miscellanies, Bk. 1, Ch. 21; see also ANF Vol. 2, Pg. 332 (a), 333 (a).

Clement's main purpose was to show the antiquity of the Jewish scriptures, and hence of the Christian faith; but it is usually accepted that he also held the notion of the "Cosmic Week". Like many others, he anticipated that the present world would come to its End with the termination of the sixth millennium – which, of course, was an event supposed by most to be near at hand.

- **_Montanus_** (fl. 150).

During the latter half of the 2nd century, a kind of charismatic renewal broke out under the leadership of Montanus. The renewal was marked by what was called "the new prophecy", in which predictions of the nearness of Christ's return were a prominent element. Montanus was convinced that Christ would return before his death, and even went so far as to urge all his followers to gather at a place in Phrygia, where they were to await the coming of Christ, and where the New Jerusalem would be established. (147)

One of his followers, a lady by the name of Maximilla, prophesied that Christ would appear, not in Jerusalem, but in an obscure village called Pepuza. She declared –

> *After me there is no more prophecy, but only the End of the World!*

Unhappily for her oracle, she died in 179 A.D! However, during her lifetime she was reckoned by no less a person than the bishop of Rome to be a true prophet –

> *(The) Bishop of Rome . . . acknowledged the prophetic gifts of . . . Maximilla, and, in consequence of the acknowledgment, . . .*

---

(147) Nicene and Post-Nicene Fathers: Second series; ed. Schaff & Wace; 1979 reprint of the original 1890 edition by Eerdmans Pub. Co., Grand Rapids; Vol. One; pg. 254, Footnote 2. This work is hereinafter referred to as PNF/2.

> *bestowed his peace on the churches of Asia and Phrygia . . .* (148)

Nonetheless, all who trusted her predictions died disappointed. Writing about the same period, Latourette says –

> *The belief in the early coming of Christ was not new, nor was it exclusively a tenet of the Montanists . . . Not far from the time of Montanus, at least two bishops, one in Pontus and one in Syria, were expecting the early return of Christ. The one declared that the judgment would come in two years, and those that believed him ceased to cultivate their fields and rid themselves of houses and goods. The other led his flock into the wilderness to meet Christ. Since the return of Christ and the last judgment were regarded as being so imminent, believers were urged to be strict in their living.* (149)

They all died disappointed. Christ did not come. The fault was not in the promise, but in the foolish manner in which the scriptures were understood. The same folly remains rampant in our time.

- **2 Esdras**; a composite work, a mixture of Jewish and Christian writings, composed between the 1st and 3rd centuries.

Perhaps around the middle of the 3rd century the first two and the last two chapters of *2 Esdras* were added to the Jewish part of the book by a Christian writer who evidently believed that

---

(148) Tertullian, <u>Against Praxeas</u> (c. 190); ANF Vol. III, pg. 597. The Bishop referred to was Victor.

(149) <u>A History of Christianity</u>, Vol. One, Pg. 128-129; Harper & Row, New York, 1975.

the end of the world was at hand —

> *Look forward to the coming of your Shepherd, for his coming is promised at the end of this age and now it is near at hand. He will give you everlasting peace, so be ready to receive the prize that will be yours in his kingdom (2:34).*

This belief in the nearness of the end of the world had certainly been shared by the Jewish author of the main body of the book, who composed it around 110 A.D. The angel Uriel is speaking to Esdras —

> *"If you live long enough, you will be amazed, for you will see the rapid passing away of this present age . . ."*
>
> *I asked: "Is (the earth) still young, or is she already growing old?"*
>
> *" . . . The creation is indeed growing old; it has lost the strength of its youth . . . The past far exceeds the future in length; what remains is but a few raindrops (after a great storm) and a little smoke (after a great fire) . . ."*
>
> *"My Lord," I replied, "you have now revealed to me the many signs which you are going to perform in the last days; but you have not told me when that will be."*
>
> *The angel answered: "Keep a careful count yourself; when you see that some of the signs predicted have already happened, then you will understand that the time has come when the Most High will judge the world he has created."*
>
> *" . . . The Most High has surveyed the periods he has fixed; they are now at an end, and his ages have reached their completion . . . The world has*

> *lost its youth, and time is growing old . . . Calamities are here, close at hand, and will not delay . . . In a very short time wickedness will be swept from the earth, and the reign of justice over us will begin . . . The kingdom is ready for you now; so be on the watch! . . . Look forward to the coming of your shepherd . . . for he who is to come at the end of the world is close at hand."* (150)

Despite bitter disappointment over the surprising delay in the Second Advent, the hope of the church did not die out. But the terminal date for the End of the World was constantly pushed further forward. Eventually it was tied to the continuation of the Roman Empire, which the Fathers widely identified with Daniel's *"Fourth Kingdom"*, the mighty "iron" empire. It seemed to them, from *Daniel 2:40, 44-45*, that no other empire could follow Rome, except the eternal kingdom of God, the *"stone kingdom"* (vs. 35). Thus the fall of Rome, which the Fathers confidently predicted, could only mean the rise of Antichrist, his swift destruction by God, and the Second Advent. No monarchy could follow that of *Caesar*, except that of *Christ*.

Once again they were wrong, and of course several empires bigger than Rome's have since come and gone, and still we await the coming of the Kingdom of God. That Kingdom will certainly come, but the uncertainty about *when* is highlighted by Jesus' own words in the prayer he taught us – *"Thy Kingdom come and thy will be done, in earth as it is in heaven"* (Mt 6:10, KJV). If the prayers of the church, or the lack of them, can hasten or delay the coming of the Last Day, then

---

(150) 2 Esdras 4:26, 44-52; 5:50-55; 6:34; 8:63-9:2; 11:43-44; 14:10-12; 16:35-36, 52; 2:10-14, 34-36. In another passage, Uriel interpreted Esdras' Eagle Vision as a symbol of the Roman Empire, which would soon be destroyed by the coming of the Messiah (12:10-35).

no one can predict when that day will dawn.

THE THIRD CENTURY

As persecution against the church increased in severity and extent, and as the empire began to show signs of collapse, so the hope of Christians that the End of the World was near waxed more fervent. Indeed Irenaeus, using the prophecies of Daniel, had already predicted that the collapse of the Roman Empire would open the way for the Antichrist and for the swiftly following consummation of all the prophecies. That theme was taken up with growing conviction by church leaders of the 3rd, 4th, and 5th centuries –

- **_Tertullian_** (c. 165–220); the renowned Montanist theologian and author, and the virtual creator of Latin Christianity.

He describes charismatic prophecies that had been given in the Montanist churches of his time, predicting the approaching manifestation on earth of the heavenly Jerusalem. (151) Then there is this graphic passage from his great "Apology" –

> *All that is taking place around you was fore-announced . . . The swallowing up of cities by the earth; the theft of islands by the sea; wars, bringing external and internal convulsions; the collision of kingdoms with kingdoms; famines and pestilences and local massacres, and widespread desolating mortalities . . . the decay of righteousness, the growth of sin . . . the very seasons and elements going out of their ordinary course . . . it was all foreseen and predicted before it came to pass. While we suffer*

---

(151) Against Marcion, Bk. 3, Ch. 25. ANF Vol. Three, Pg. 342 (b), 343 (a).

> *the calamities, we read of them in the scriptures. (Ch. 20)*
>
> *For two comings of Christ (have) been revealed to us: a first, which has been fulfilled in the lowliness of a human lot; a second, which impends over the world, now near its close, in all the majesty of the Deity unveiled . . .* [152]

Again Tertullian writes –

> *But what a spectacle is that fast-approaching advent of our Lord . . . How great the glory of the rising saints! How great the kingdom of the righteous that will follow!* [153] *. . . For so long as the world shall stand, for so long as that shall Rome continue."* [154]

Note the ambiguity of that last statement. It was meant to allay the suspicions of those who hated the church while actually declaring the church's belief that the world was soon to end.

> *How many there are who forsake virtuous living ... as the last days approach!* [155] *. . . There is another and greater need for us to pray for the emperor, and indeed for the whole estate of the empire, and the interests of Rome. For we know that the great upheaval which hangs over the whole earth, and the very End of all things . . . is only delayed by the respite granted to the Roman Empire . . .* [156]

---

(152) Ch. 21. ANF Vol. Three, Pg. 33, 35.
(153) <u>The Shows</u>, Ch. 30.
(154) <u>Scapula</u>, Ch. 2.
(155) <u>To the Nations</u>, Ch. 1.
(156) <u>Apology</u>, Ch. 32.

In that last passage, Tertullian refers to the common idea in his time that Rome was the *"restraining power"* mentioned in 2 Th. 2:6. It was reckoned that the collapse of the empire would open the way for Antichrist and the end of the world to come.

This belief became ever more common when Christ failed to return before the first generation of Christians had died. The date of his return was gradually pushed forward, until it was eventually tied to the fall of Rome and the subsequent rise of the Antichrist. These events in turn, as I have already shown, were identified with the fulfilment of Daniel's prophecy about *"the fourth empire"*, the kingdom of iron. That particular interpretation was worked out in detail by an immensely popular author –

- **Hippolytus** (died c. 236); a pastor, teacher, and commentator in the church at Rome.

He wrote various commentaries, including one on *Daniel*. The language is obscure in places, but as far as I can determine, he predicted that the fall of Rome would bring about the end of the succession of world empires, followed first by the rise of the Antichrist, and then quickly by the coming of Christ and the beginning of the eternal kingdom of God. All this, he said, must occur at the end of 6000 years from the day of Creation, for

> *six thousand years must be accomplished, in order that the sabbath may come, the rest, the holy day "on which God rested from his works". For the sabbath is the type and emblem of the future kingdom of the saints, when they shall "reign with Christ" when he comes from heaven . . .*

Hippolytus goes on to calculate that Christ was born in the year 5500; then he continues –

> *From the birth of Christ, then, we must reckon the 500 years that remain to make up the 6000, and thus the end shall be . . . (so) when the times*

> *are fulfilled (for Rome's collapse), and the ten horns spring from the beast in the last time, then Antichrist will appear from among them. When he makes war against the saints, and persecutes them, then may we expect the manifestation of the Lord from heaven.* (157)

Clearly, based on his revised version of the "Cosmic Week", Hippolytus expected the return of Christ to occur about the year 500 A.D. Some two hundred years after his death, when that date was approaching, the western empire was already reeling under the shock of barbarian invasions. For the first time, its final ruin seemed probable. Consequently the views of Hippolytus became very popular, his commentary was widely circulated, and spawned many imitations.

Peculiarly, he enjoyed another resurgence of popularity some 1300 years later, during the 19th century. His teaching that the *"ten toes"* Daniel saw in his vision of the Great Image were symbols of the "ten democracies" into which the Roman Empire would break up, became much admired. Europe seemed to be doing just that – the fragmented remnants of the empire were regathering themselves into roughly ten democratic states. That process is still continuing in our time, over a hundred years later. Is it a fulfilment of the things symbolised by the *"ten toes"* of Daniel's image? You will have to decide that for yourself!

Continuing with Hippolytus – he wrote an extended treatise, containing 67 paragraphs, <u>On Christ and Antichrist</u>. It is a generally cautious and commendable study, in which he avoids, and indeed condemns, the excesses of other apocalyptic writers. Nonetheless, he did not hesitate to apply the biblical prophecies to events in his own time, and he argued

---

(157) ANF Vol. 5, Pg. 178, 179. See also pg. 242 ff.

- that Antichrist would come out of the tribe of Dan;

- that Antichrist would rise when the Roman Empire had broken up into ten democratic states;

- that Christ would then come, to destroy Antichrist, and to establish his own everlasting kingdom.

- **_Commodianus_** (c. 240); a north African bishop who believed that Antichrist would soon appear, in the form of Nero come back from the grave.

That idea did not originate with him, but reflected a widespread superstition, known as *Nero Redivivus*, which in different ways was believed for centuries by both pagans and Christians.

Commodianus was also expecting Elijah to appear in the near future, and for Armageddon to break out. [158] He too linked the climax of the age with the predicted fall of Rome. [159]

- **_Bardesan_** (154–222); an eloquent and versatile scholar and poet.

He wrote a set of "synchronisms", in which he hoped to establish beyond doubt the principle of the *"Cosmic Week"*. They conclude with the words –

---

(158) See also the description of a poem of his, which gave a vivid portrayal of the approaching climax of the age, in ANF Vol. 4, Pg. 219.
(159) ANF Vol. 8, Pg. 734.

> *These things did Bardesan thus compute when desiring to show that this world would stand only six thousands of years.* (160)

I am not sure when Bardesan thought the sixth millennium would end, but I assume he shared the opinion of many of his contemporaries that it could not be far distant from their own time.

- **_Judas the Historian_** (202)

We know nothing about this man except that he wrote what was probably a commentary on *Daniel*, in which he attempted to show that the few unfulfilled oracles in *Daniel* would shortly be accomplished. He calculated that the *Seventy Weeks* prophecy (Da 9:24-27) would run its course by the tenth year of the reign of the emperor Severus (that is, c. 203), that Antichrist would then appear, and the end of the world would soon follow. (161)

- **_Cyprian_** (bishop of Carthage from 248 until his martyrdom in 258).

He shared the common view that the coming of Christ was imminent –

> *Nor let any of you, beloved brethren, be so terrified by the fear of future persecution, or the coming of the threatening Antichrist, as not to be found armed for all things . . . Antichrist is coming, but above him comes Christ also. The enemy goeth about and rageth, but immediately the Lord follows to avenge our suffering and our wounds . . . (The) devil so blinds (some) that, without considering the eternal punishments of*

---

(160) ANF Vol. 8, Pg. 734.
(161) See Eusebius, Ecclesiastical History Bk. 6, ch. 7.

> *Gehenna, they endeavour to imitate the coming of Antichrist, who is now approaching.* (162)

How wrong they all were! Is there any reason to suppose that modern soothsayers will do any better than their mistaken forefathers? Yet I say again, let no blame be laid at the feet of scripture; the fault lies rather in the foolish hermeneutic followed by all too many Bible commentators across the centuries.

THE NICENE FATHERS

THE FOURTH CENTURY

- ***Jerome***, (*circa* 347-420) the most renowned theologian and historian of the era. He translated the Bible into Latin, known today as the *Vulgate*.

He records that ***Victorinus*** (died 303) wrote a book on "The Second Coming of Our Lord, or the Millennium", in which he presented the same views as those held by ***Papias*** – that is, the nearness of the Second Advent, and that Christ, immediately after his return, would reign in power on the earth, for a thousand years. (163)

- ***Lactantius*** (c. 240–c. 320); an eminent teacher of rhetoric, historian, and instructor of the emperor Constantine's son.

In his "Divine Institutes", having described the terrible events of the last days, the expected fall of the Roman Empire, the rise of the Antichrist, the Second Advent, the resurrection and judgments, and the like, he then wrote –

---

(162) Letters #55, para. 7, and 54, para 19. ANF Vol. 5, Pg. 349, 346.
(163) See Jerome's Lives, #18.

> *Perhaps someone may now ask when these things of which we have spoken are about to come to pass? I have already shown above, that when six thousand years shall be completed (from the creation of Adam) this change must take place, and that the last day of the extreme conclusion is now drawing near.*

He then acknowledges that different writers had calculated different dates for the last day, but reckons that

> *all expectation does not exceed the limit of 200 years.* (that is, the end was expected before the year 500; then he continues) . . . *the fall and ruin of the world will shortly take place; except that while the city of Rome remains it appears that nothing of this kind is to be feared. But when that capital of the world shall have fallen . . . who can doubt that the end has now arrived to the affairs of men and of the whole world . . . and the God of heaven is to be entreated . . . lest, sooner than we think for, that detestable tyrant should come who will undertake so great a deed, and dig out that eye, by the destruction of which the world itself is about to fall.* (164)

The Roman Empire in the west came to an end in 476, when the German rebel Odoacer deposed the last emperor, the ineffective youth Romulus Augustulus, who reigned from A.D. 475-476. The deposed emperor was despatched to a villa near Naples with an annual pension of 6000 pieces of gold. His ultimate fate is unknown. Odoacer became the first barbarian king of Italy. That all took place less than 200 years after the death of Lactantius – so he was correct in estimating the date of Rome's collapse, but wrong in equating that event with the

---

(164)   Bk. 7, Ch. 25. ANF Vol. 7, Pg. 220.

return of Christ. The eastern empire, of course, now called the Byzantine Empire, continued to thrive for another thousand years. But even its collapse in the 15th century, which again was seen by many as a harbinger of Christ's return, failed to usher in the end of the world.

- **_Cyril_** (c. 310–386); bishop of Jerusalem.

He may not have been confident that the return of Christ was near, but he did believe it was possible that Christ could come in his lifetime –

> ... *already, as thou hast seen, many have begun to say, "I am Christ;" and "the abomination of desolation" is yet to come, assuming to himself the false title of Christ. But look thou for the true Christ, the only begotten Son of God, coming ... from heaven, appearing to all more bright than any lightning ... that he may judge both quick and dead, and reign in a heavenly, eternal kingdom ...* (165)

In a later lecture (#15) Cyril says –

> *As to the time (of Christ's return) let no one yet be curious ... Venture not to declare when these things shall be (para. 4).*

Yet he cannot resist pointing out the many *"signs"* that had already been fulfilled, and that surely the Second Advent must soon occur –

> *But since it was needful for us to know the signs of the End, and since we are looking for Christ ... observe thou, which of those signs (Mt. 24:2 ff.) have already come to pass, and which yet remain ... (Ibid).*

---

(165)　Catechetical Lectures #4.

Cyril then lists a number of signs that he reckoned were already fulfilled: *false Christs* (vs. 5); *wars* (vs. 6); *famine and pestilence* (vs. 7); *fearful heavenly prodigies and storms* (Lu 21:11); *betrayal in the church* (Mt 24:9-10); *falling away from Christ* (vs. 12); *the gospel preached throughout the world* (vs. 14); and so on. (Ibid, para. 4-9).

Cyril claimed that *"the falling away"* predicted in 2 Th 2:3-10 had been fulfilled in his time, and he said –

> *(Therefore) the enemy (Antichrist) is soon to be looked for (para. 9).*

But he does add –

> *Look therefore to thyself, O man, and make safe thy soul . . . (but whether these things) will happen in thy time we know not, or whether they will happen after thee we know not; but it is well, knowing these things, thou shouldest make thyself secure beforehand (Ibid).*

Yet he still expected that the delay, if any, would be short. Accordingly, he says later (para. 12) –

> *But this aforesaid Antichrist is to come when the times of the Roman Empire shall have been fulfilled, and the End of the World is now drawing near.*

Cyril adds that it had always been "the tradition of the church's interpreters" to identify Daniel's *"fourth monarchy"* with Rome (para. 13). [166]

It is impossible not to notice how Cyril called upon the same "signs of the times" that have been endlessly cited by preachers of Bible prophecy from the beginning until now. They were not

---

(166)   From PNF/2 Vol. Seven.

signs in his time. They are not signs now. Jesus expressly said, *"When you see them, do not be alarmed, for the end is not yet!"* (Mt 24:6). Why do people persist in the perverse folly of calling things signs of the end, which Jesus declared are *not* signs?

- **_Gregory_** (330–c. 395); bishop of Nyssa.

He expressed the prevalent attitude of the latter part of the 4th century (at least among bishops), when he poured scorn on the idea of a literal and future Millennial reign of Christ –

From the records available to me there seems to have been a general lessening, in the 4th century, and into the 5th, of hope in the nearness of Christ's return. There was certainly a loss of belief in the millenarian idea that Christ would eventually establish his throne in Jerusalem and reign on earth for a thousand years. This diminishing of chiliastic [167] fervour was undoubtedly caused by the conversion of the emperor **Constantine**, the cessation of persecution, and the renewal of the fortunes of the empire. The threat of the collapse of the empire receded, and a new, though temporary, era of peace and prosperity was granted to the Roman world.

Nonetheless, the very vehemence of Gregory's protest against chiliasm shows that there were still a significant number of prominent teachers proclaiming those early doctrines. Indeed, they have never ceased to proclaim them – although, in modern times as in the past, the popularity of Christian soothsayers has tended to wax and wane in parallel with fluctuations in society. In times of peace and plenty, millenarian hopes and predictions of the approaching End of the World have received scant attention; but in times of trouble

---

(167) "Chiliastic" comes from a Greek word meaning "one thousand". It is used to describe people who believe in the personal one thousand year reign of Christ upon the earth. Associated words are chiliasm, and chiliast. They mean much the same as millennialist, millennialism, millenarian, and the like.

they have found, and still find, an avid audience.

The excesses and errors of some of the 2nd and 3rd century chiliasts were another reason for the strong reaction against such views that arose in the latter part of the 3rd century, and especially in the fourth. Christ had not returned when expected, nor had the predicted End of the World occurred. People reacted by calling into question the method of handling scripture upon which those predictions had been based. Accordingly, chiliasm became

> *more and more widely regarded as heresy, and received its worst blow from Augustine, who framed in its stead the doctrine, which from his time on was commonly accepted in the church, that the Millennium is the present reign of Christ, which began with the resurrection.* (168)

That claim is partly correct and partly false. Certainly, among evangelical Protestants and most Pentecostals, chiliastic belief is as strong today as it has ever been.

During the early part of the 4th century, one of the most scathing opponents of chiliasm was –

- **_Eusebius of Caesarea_** (c. 265–c. 339); renowned as the "Father of Church History".

As mentioned above, **_Papias_**, a friend of the apostle John, was an early and enthusiastic chiliast, who described the Millennium in graphically literal terms. (169) Some 200 years after the death of Papias, Eusebius wrote concerning him –

> *(Papias) gives also other accounts which he says came to him through unwritten tradition . . . To these belong his statement that there will be a*

---

(168)   McGiffert; see next century, below.
(169)   ANF Vol. One, Pg. 153.

> *period of some thousand years after the resurrection of the dead, and that the kingdom of Christ will be set up in material form on this very earth. I suppose he got these ideas through a misunderstanding of the apostolic accounts, not perceiving that the things said by them were spoken mystically in figures . . . But it was due to him that so many of the Church Fathers after him adopted a like opinion.* (170)

Eusebius also records the views of

- **Dionysius the Great** (died c. 264); bishop of Alexandria.

He strongly opposed the chiliast teaching of **Nepos**, an Egyptian bishop of the same period. Eusebius says that Nepos

> *taught that the promises to the holy men in the Divine Scriptures should be understood in a more Jewish (that is, literal) manner, and that there would be a certain Millennium of bodily luxury upon this earth.* (171)

Dionysius in fact wrote a book against the views of Nepos (who was by then dead), in which he argued that the Millennial promises should be understood figuratively as applying to the church today. Eusebius quotes from that book, and in particular includes a description that Dionysius gave of a debate between himself and some chiliast leaders. The debate, it seems was conducted peacefully, with mutual respect, and with an amicable result. One could wish that the same sweet temper would prevail in modern disputes about the

---

(170) Church History, Bk 3, Ch. 39. PNF/2 Vol. One.
(171) Ibid, Bk. 7, Ch. 24.

interpretation of Bible prophecy! (172)

The point that comes out of Eusebius, however, is this – while the major part of the church in the 4th century had begun to discard belief in a speedy return of Christ, and had begun to adopt what would now be called an *"a-millennial"* position, belief in both a literal Millennium and in the nearness of Christ's return was plainly still held tenaciously by many people, including some bishops. They clung to those beliefs with an assurance and zeal quite equal to that displayed by chiliasts in the 1st and 2nd centuries, and, for that matter, in the 21st !

Among such men were the following –

- **_Ambrose_** (c. 339–397); bishop of Milan.

He apparently believed that the world would end in the year 1000. Using the legend of the Phoenix bird as an analogy, he wrote –

> *So to that bird the five-hundredth is the year of resurrection, but to us the thousandth.* (173)

- **_Sulpitius Severus_** (c. 363–420); a noble Roman presbyter and historian.

He recorded the life of the saintly **_Martin_** (c. 335–400), the bishop of Tours. Martin was greatly admired for his holiness, and for the prodigious miracles he was reputed to have performed. (174) According to Severus, Martin once warned the devil that

---

(172) Ibid, Ch. 24 & 25.
(173) On The Resurrection, para. 59. PNF/2 Vol. 10.
(174) Many of which were lovingly and vividly described by his friend Severus – see Life of St. Martin, PNF/2 Vol. 11, Pg. 3-17, plus other references in the Letters of Sulpitius Severus, and in his Dialogues, in the same volume.

> *the day of judgment is at hand.* (175)

– and a little later, Severus himself added,

> *We may infer . . . since false prophets of such kind have appeared, that the coming of Antichrist is at hand.* (176)

Despite his miracles, the saint's eschatology was evidently a little shaky –

> *When we questioned Martin concerning the End of the World, he said to us that Nero was to be destroyed by Antichrist, and that the whole world, and all nations, were to be reduced by the power of Antichrist, until that impious one should be overthrown by the coming of Christ. He tells us, too, that there was no doubt but that the Antichrist, having been conceived by an evil spirit, was already born, and had, by this time, reached the years of boyhood, and that he would assume power as soon as he reached the proper age. Now this is the eighth year since we heard those words from his lips: you may conjecture, then, how nearly about to happen are those things which are feared in the future.* (177)

Strangely, I can remember hearing a remarkably similar story when I was a youth – that Antichrist was already born, and would in my lifetime come to power. I was sceptical then. I am even more so now.

In his "Sacred History" (PNF/2 Vol. 11), Severus again mentions his confidence that the End of the World was near

---

(175) Life, Ch. 22.
(176) Ibid, Ch 24.
(177) Dialogue #2, Ch. 14.

(Ch. 33).

- ***Tyconius***; an influential layman and author who flourished during the last part of the 4th century.

He wrote a commentary on the Apocalypse, in which he expressed his firm conviction that the time of the End was near, and that Antichrist would soon rise to power. (178)

THE FIFTH CENTURY

This century, as shown by McGinn in the following passage, was a time of heightened expectations of the End of the age –

> *The six-thousand-year scheme of history as revised by Hippolytus, indicated that the End of the World would come in the year 500. Barbarian onslaughts, and the partial collapse of the Roman governmental structure . . . seemed to confirm this in the eyes of many writers of the late 4th and early 5th centuries. When Rome, "the restraining force", was dissolving before men's eyes, could the final enemy be far off?* (179)

However, the scene remained confused.

On the one hand, there were those who felt that the social and political chaos overtaking the west left no room for doubt that the Second Advent was about to happen.

On the other, there were those who thought it an act of disloyalty to talk about the coming fall of Rome, or who were disenchanted by the wild and unfulfilled predictions of the past. They refused to have anything to do with attempts to

---

(178) Visions of the End, by Bernard McGinn; Columbia University Press, New York, 1979; Pg. 27; hereafter referred to as McGinn.
(179) Ibid pg. 52.

apply the biblical prophecies to current events. Both viewpoints are represented in the following selections.

- **_Gennadius_** (died 496); a church historian.

He said that he desired to

> shut the mouths of those who, on some daring guess, idly philosophise concerning the advent of Antichrist, or of our Lord. (180)

His very desire, of course, shows that there were enough such speculators in the church to warrant complaint by those who refused to engage in date-setting.

- **_Augustine_** (354–430); the revered bishop of Hippo.

He reveals a similar situation. The following comment shows that among both leaders and lay people there were many who were still trying to predict the time of Christ's return –

> It is customary to ask, "When shall that be?" But this is quite unreasonable . . . (for the Master said), "It is not for you to know the times, which the Father hath put in his own power" . . . In vain, then, do we attempt to compute definitely the years that remain to this world . . . Yet some have said that four hundred, some five hundred, others a thousand years, may be completed from the ascension of the Lord up to his final coming. (181)

Surprisingly Augustine himself had once held chiliast views (stated in his _Sermon #259_). But in later life he repudiated that opinion and then

---

(180)   Lives #1.
(181)   City of God, Bk. 18, Ch. 53; see also his Sermon #47 on Mk. 13:32.

> *revolutionised the prevailing . . . view of the apocalyptic Millennium by understanding it of the <u>present</u> reign of Christ in the Church.* (182)

In *The City of God*, Augustine argues for a "spiritual" or "figurative" understanding of the Millennium. He prefers to treat the prophecies allegorically rather than literally – see 18:52-53; 20:7, 19, 30, from which the following is taken –

> *I do not imagine that we should rashly assert or believe the theory that some have entertained or still do entertain: that the church is not going to suffer any more persecutions until the time of Antichrist, beyond the number she has already endured, namely ten . . .*

> *(Those) who hold this theory have shown such highly-wrought ingenuity in comparing the details in each case – but they did this not so much by prophetic inspiration as by the speculation of the human mind . . .*

He then tells about those who tried to calculate the date of the Second Advent, and comments –

> *But to show how each of them supports his opinion would take too long; and in any case it is unnecessary, for they make use of human conjecture, and quote no decisive evidence from the authority of canonical scripture.*

Speaking about the "Cosmic Week" and belief in a literal earthly Millennium, Augustine says –

> *I also entertained this notion at one time . . . But this can only be believed by materialists; and those with spiritual interests give the name*

---

(182) PNF/1 Vol. 2, Pg. 426, footnote #5.

> *"Chiliasts" to believers in this picture, a term which we can translate by a word derived from the equivalent Latin, "Millenarians".*

Plainly, "chiliast" had become a derogatory term to Augustine and to those who shared his views on the matter, despite his former adherence to chiliast teaching.

On the meaning of 2 Th. 2:6-7, he writes –

> *Paul did not choose to speak explicitly, because, as he says, they already knew it. And that is why we who have not their knowledge, are anxious to arrive at the Apostle's meaning; but we find ourselves unable to do so, for all our efforts . . . I admit that the meaning of (Paul) completely escapes me. For all that, I shall not refrain from mentioning some guesses at the meaning which I have been able to hear or read . . .*

I cannot resist suggesting that Augustine's dubiety here is commendable, and that modern "guesses" about *"he who restrains"* are no more reliable than the ancient ones. [183]

Augustine systematised and perfected the rather loose *a-millennial* views that some other leaders had held before him. He tended to understand the Millennium as typifying the present triumph of the church, and he resisted the popular notion that 6000 years of human toil would soon be terminated by the return of Christ, who would grant his saints a thousand years of bliss on earth (the seventh "day" of God's "Great Week").

But Augustine did hold to a figurative, or symbolic, view of that "week" –

---

(183) The above citations are taken from Henry Bettenson's translation, Penguin Books, London, 1977; pg. 835, 838, 906, 932.

> ... *the sabbath of this world shall be, when six ages shall have passed away. The six days as it were of the world are passing away. One day hath passed away from Adam to Noah another day from the Deluge unto Abraham; the third from Abraham unto David; the fourth from David unto the carrying away into Babylon; the fifth from the carrying away into Babylon unto the advent of our Lord Jesus Christ. Now the sixth day is passing. We are in the sixth age, in the sixth day ...* (184)

Augustine, then, was unwilling to join some of his fellow bishops in trying to calculate just when the sixth millennium would end; yet he certainly would have been astonished to learn that it was going to endure (thus far) nearly 1600 years beyond the time when he preached that sermon! He did share the opinion of his contemporaries that the End was not too far distant –

> *The thousand years, as it seems to me ... may indicate that this event (the overthrow of Antichrist) happens in the last thousand years, that is, in the sixth millennium, the sixth day, as it were, <u>of which the latter stretches are now passing</u>, and a Sabbath is to follow that has no evening, the rest, that is to say, of the saints, which has no end.* (185)

Concerning the so called *"signs of the times"* (cp. Mt. 24:4-14) and their interpretation in the 5th century, there was an exchange of letters between Augustine and **Hesychius**, in which Hesychius argued that the wars, famines, disasters, that were everywhere occurring as the empire began to collapse,

---

(184) <u>Sermon</u> #75, on Jn. 5:2. PNF/1 Vol 6, Pg. 477.
(185) Bettenson, op. cit., Pg. 907, 908; emphasis mine.

were undeniable signs of the End of the World. Augustine replied that such things had been a part of human experience since time immemorial, and it was altogether arbitrary to assume that present troubles were greater than those that had been suffered before, or that present troubles were more a sign of the End than were those of the past. (186)

Augustine's arguments probably failed to convince Hesychius. They certainly failed to convince many later theologians, who have continued with passion from then until now to link the tragic events of each succeeding generation with those tantalising *"signs"*.

- ***John Chrysostom*** (c. 344–407); bishop of Constantinople, and one of the most gifted preachers of all time.

He wrote –

> *Let us . . . show forth repentance, for the judgment is surely at our doors. But even if it were further off, we ought not even so to be emboldened, for the term of each man's life is the End of the World virtually to him that is summoned. But that it is even at the doors, hear Paul saying,* "The night is far spent, the day is at hand" . . . *For the signs too are now complete, which announce that day.* (187)

In another place however, Chrysostom was more cautious –

> *Nothing, as it seems, is so curious, and so fondly prone to pry into things obscure and concealed, as the nature of men . . . Many things therefore*

---

(186) Letters #197, 198, 199.
(187) Homily #10, on Mt 3:1-2. See also #77, on Mt 24:332-33. PNF/1 Vol. 10.

> *our mind is in haste to learn already and to comprehend, but especially concerning the period of the consummation . . . (But) hear (Christ) saying to his apostles, "It is not for you to know the times or seasons, which the Father hath set within his own authority" (Ac 1:7). Why are you curious? . . . For tell me, what would be the advantage? Let us suppose that the End would be after twenty or thirty or a hundred years, what is this to us? Is not the end of his own life the consummation to every individual? Why art thou curious, and travailest about the general end? . . . Now what concern is that of yours? For if you make your own a good end, you will suffer no harm from the other, be it far off, or be it near. This is nothing to us.* (188)

Yet he did hold to the old view about Antichrist appearing when Rome falls –

> *. . . when the Roman Empire is taken out of the way (2 Th 2:6-7), then (Antichrist) shall come. And naturally, for as long as the fear of this empire lasts, no one will willingly exalt himself, but when that is dissolved, he will attack the anarchy, and endeavour to seize upon the government of man and of God . . . So will (the empire be destroyed) by the Antichrist, and he by Christ . . . And these things Daniel delivered to us with great clearness."* (189)

Chrysostom, you will note, followed the popular opinion that Rome was "*the one who restrains* (the Antichrist)."

---

(188) <u>Homily</u> #9, on 1 Th. 5:1-2.
(189) <u>Homily</u> #4, on 2 Th 2:6-9.

For that reason, Chrysostom could not escape saying in another place –

> . . . *no long time now remains until the consummation, but the world is hastening to its End – this the wars declare, this the afflictions, this the earthquakes, this the love which hath waxed cold . . . The End of the World (is) nigh and at the very doors, and therefore ten thousand woes are everywhere scattered abroad.* (190)

Notice again Chrysostom's citing of the familiar *"signs of the times"* from Jesus' Olivet Discourse. Those famous signs (*earthquakes, floods, famines, pestilence, wars, false prophets,* and the like) have been quoted by enthusiastic preachers with monotonous regularity in every generation from the 1st century until now. So forgive me for repeating – they were **not** signs of the End of the age then, nor are they today (take special note of the words of Jesus in Mt 24:6, 8, 23-26; Lu 17:20-21; 21:9). The passage just quoted, although it comes from one of Chrysostom's sermons on the gospel of *John,* is actually a discussion of Ph 4:5-6, *"The Lord is at hand,"* which the bishop says refers to the Second Advent. He adds –

> *If the Lord was "at hand" then, much more is he "at hand" now. If 300 years ago, when those words were used, Paul called that season "the fulness of time", much more would he have called the present so.* (191)

The mistake here is assuming that "at hand" must mean the near return of Christ; whereas, it more naturally means simply that the Lord is always near, that in a sense the Kingdom of

---

(190)   <u>Homily</u> #34, on Jn 4:28-29.
(191)   Ibid.

God is already with us, in us, around us (Lu 17:21).

- **_Quintus Julius Hilarianus_** (c. 400)

He wrote a book called "The Progress of Time", and said –

> *There remain 101 years to complete the six thousand (in the year 500) . . . When the Antichrist has been overcome and killed at the completion of the six thousand years, the resurrection of all the saints will take place . . . So when the six days, that is, the six thousand years of labour and pain for the saints have passed, the seventh day, the true Sabbath, will come for all of them who have existed from the beginning of the world.* (192)

- **_Quodvultdeus_** (died c. 453); a pupil of Augustine and later bishop of Carthage

He wrote –

> *Gog and Magog (Ez 38:1 ff.), as some say, are the Goths and the Moors . . . through whose savagery the devil himself already lays waste the church and will then persecute it more fully. . . For this reason the Lord warns: "I am coming quickly . . ."* (193)

Then in a "Sermon on the End of the World", an unknown author declared –

> *. . . we have already told you that the End of the World is near . . . Has not faith withered away among mankind? How many foolish things are seen among youths, how many crimes among*

---

(192)   McGinn, pg. 52-53.
(193)   McGinn, Pg. 54.

prelates, how many lies among priests, how many perjuries among deacons . . . (He continues the recital of woes, and then says) when the Roman Empire begins to be consumed by the sword, the coming of the Evil One is at hand. It is necessary that the world come to an end at the completion of the Roman Empire. (194)

THE SIXTH CENTURY

- <u>**Pope Gregory the Great**</u> (540–604); head of the western church during a time of terrifying upheaval and change.

The empire in the west had collapsed. Pestilence was raging almost everywhere. Barbarians were invading from all sides. Civilisation seemed to be in ruins. With good reason he wrote to a friend –

> *. . . there is a general smiting as the End of the World draws near.* (195)

And then to Ethelbert, king of the Angles (in Britain), he wrote –

> *The End of the present world is already close at hand, and the reign of the saints is coming, which can have no end. And, now that this End of the World is approaching, many things are at hand which previously have not been, to wit, changes of the air, terrors from heaven, and seasons contrary to accustomed order of times, wars, famines, pestilences, earthquakes in diverse places. Yet these things will not come in our days, but after our days they will all ensue.*

---

(194) McGinn, Pg. 61.
(195) <u>Letters</u> #123.

> *You, therefore, if you observe any of these things occurring in your land, by no means let your mind be troubled, since these signs of the End of the World are set beforehand for this purpose, that we should be solicitous about our souls . . .*
> (196)

Gregory's letters contain many other references to the perils of his time, and to the approaching End of the World, which, to the end of his life, he thought was near at hand. (197)

For the peoples of the 6th century in western Europe, the fall of Rome, and the heathen hordes who swept over once peaceful and prosperous lands, were an unspeakable horror. The invaders everywhere left a wake of rapine, desolation, disease, and terror. It was a tragedy as shattering as those that tore apart the world of the 20th century. Indeed, the social, political, cultural, and economic ruin that overwhelmed the 6th century was perhaps greater than anything the modern world has thus far experienced. Europe required centuries of struggle to regain the level of civilisation and prosperity it had known during the best days of the empire.

Nonetheless, despite the horrors they endured, it was not the End of the World. They cannot be blamed for fearing the worst, yet they were wrong. They made scripture say what it did not say. They were not the first to make that error, nor have they been the last. Surely, though, this succession of false alarms challenges us to find a better way of understanding the biblical prophecies – one that is not tied to the fluctuating fortunes of the secular world?

---

(196) *Letters* #66.
(197) See PNF/2 Vols. 12 & 13.

THE MIDDLE AGES

THE YEARS 600 - 1500

During the years 600–1500 the fortunes of Christian soothsayers waxed and waned. But no generation lacked at least an influential minority of interpreters who were confident *"the signs of the times"* showed the nearness of Christ's return.

As the first thousand years came to an end there was an acceleration of prophetic activity; the apocalyptists took up their themes with renewed vigour. The "Cosmic Week" was recalculated to bring its terminus to the year 1000, and it was thought that the 11th century would introduce Christ's Millennial reign on earth.

The idea that there would not be a further millennium was widespread in Europe. Many people gave away all their goods, so that nothing would harm their readiness to meet Christ. Thousands perished on pilgrimages to the Holy Land. On the "last day" of the year 999, crowds climbed Mt Zion eager to see the returning Christ. They went home disappointed.

However (as McGinn shows), there was not as much apocalyptic activity, or alarm, as might have been expected. People generally were not much disturbed as the turn of the Millennium drew near. The world was generally peaceful. No major disasters were threatening. And at such times people tend to remember all the mistaken predictions of the past and not to give much attention to the doomsayers. So when the year 1000 came the apocalyptists were not able to capture the mass audience for which they had no doubt hoped. Nonetheless they remained active and influential. [198]

My main source for these centuries has been McGinn. I commend his excellent study to anyone who wants to gain a

---

(198)   McGinn, pg. 88-93.

comprehensive picture of the various streams of apocalyptic hopes that were then prevalent. McGinn shows the roots of those hopes, how they developed across the centuries, and the effect they had on the larger society, both in religion and politics. Here, though, I have selected only those references dealing with an expectation of the imminent return of Christ.

So let us now go back to the beginning of this period.

The continuation of the eastern branch of the empire, with its capital at Constantinople (known also as "New Rome" and later as the "Byzantine Empire"), had helped to solve the problem of why the fall of old Rome had not brought the End of the World. It was possible to argue that after all Rome had not truly fallen. The richest, most populous, and most cultured part of the empire was still thriving under a succession of Christian emperors. Constantinople rivalled old Rome in its magnificence. The territories of the empire were sadly diminished, but not its pomp and glory. Indeed, under Justinian I, middle 6th century, the empire was nearly as extensive as it had been of old.

In church life, the patriarch of Constantinople was second in prestige only to the pope in Rome, and indeed was above the pope in his political and social influence, especially in the east. So people now began to say that "New Rome" was the city that would last to the end of time. The Byzantine [199] monarchy now became the *"fourth kingdom"* of Daniel's vision – *"the iron kingdom"*, the last empire, that would survive until it was struck by *"the stone from the mountains"*, and so on.

---

(199) The Roman emperor Constantine I, built his new capital, Constantinople, upon the site of an ancient Thracian town called Byzantium, which then gave its name to the whole empire. The Byzantine Empire endured through many vicissitudes for another thousand years, until it was finally overrun by the Ottoman Turks in 1453. The modern era of European hegemony is commonly said to date from that time.

Thus the authority of scripture was saved – or rather, the authority of the apocalyptic way of reading the biblical oracles – and people were able to maintain faith in the traditional interpretation of the prophecies. An example is found in

- ***Joachim of Fiore*** (1135–1202); a monk, philosopher of history, specialist in eschatology, and bishop.

His writings were for a time prodigiously influential. He predicted the beginning of the Millennial age would occur in 1290 –

> *In the course of the 13th century the Franciscan Order and its satellites were deeply influenced by the apocalyptic, eschatological prophecies of Joachim of Fiore, the millenarist prophet of the 12th century. The second coming of Jesus was widely expected, and special dates were assigned to the future transformation of the world.* (200)

Another commanding preacher of the 11th century was

- ***Peter the Hermit***, who greatly influenced the mounting of the First Crusade to rescue the Holy Land from the Muslims.

He saw the Crusade in apocalyptic terms, and was certain it was a sign of the approaching End of the World, preparing the way for Christ to return to Jerusalem.

> *One of the underlying beliefs of the 11th century was that Domesday would arrive at the millennium – its date not known precisely, but believed to be 1000 years since the completion of the New Testament – and that the scene of*

---

(200)   Popular Religion in the Middle Ages; Rosalind & Christopher Brooke; Thames & Hudson, London, 1984; pg. 154.

> *Judgment would be Jerusalem, in Christian hands. This was one of the great beliefs that motivated the first Crusades.* (201)

To solve the problem of the supposed constant failure of the predictions, other expedients were also called upon. For example –

- The Millennium began with the resurrection of Christ, which bound Satan and guaranteed victory to the believing church; but the year 1000 would bring that period to an end and would usher in the events predicted in *Revelation* (ch 20, 21, & 22).

- *"Gog and Magog"* were identified with the Mongol hordes, when they began to appear from the depths of Asia.

- The stunning rise of Islam in the 7th century gave great impetus to the apocalyptists.

The Muslims swiftly conquered vast tracts of formerly Christian territory (in Africa, Egypt, Syria), and they even placed Byzantium under threat. Seers and interpreters sprang forward to show how all of these terrors were foretold in the Bible and were sure signs of *"the last days"*.

- The rise of the Frankish kingdom under Charlemagne (742–814) provided a useful way of restructuring the prophecies.

The new empire was seen as a revival and continuation of the original – hence its later name, "The Holy Roman Empire." Once again it could be argued that Rome had not actually fallen, but had been merely humbled, to prepare the way for the

---

(201) From <u>Chronicles of the Crusades</u>; ed. Elizabeth Hallam; Weidenfeld and Nicolson, London, 1989; pg. 60.

new Christian empire. Hence the prophecies of *Daniel, John,* and the others, still remained to be fulfilled.

This identification of old Rome with the new empire became especially necessary when the Byzantine empire finally collapsed in the 15th century.

The "Holy Roman Empire" endured in one form or another until 1806, when it was finally abolished by Napoleon; but by then people no longer felt it necessary to link the End of the World with the fall of Rome. (202)

"THE COSMIC WEEK"

Hardly a generation went by without some attempt to update the method of computing the time when the sixth millennium would end and the final Millennium begin. McGinn gives a number of examples. (203) There are also numerous references in the Fathers. (204)

In my time, going back 70 years to when I first became interested in Bible prophecy, those who used the "Cosmic Week" device were sure that the sixth millennium would terminate with the year 2000. That day is now some years behind us, and the heavens remain silent. The clouds are undisturbed by battalions of advancing angels, and Christ has not appeared. I have observed since then a rather singular silence on the matter of the "Cosmic Week". Perhaps at last they are learning wisdom. But I suppose there will always be some who find the idea too compelling to resist. It will be interesting to see how our modern prognosticators compare with their ancient colleagues in date-adjusting ingenuity!

---

(202) Except for "The Fifth Monarchy Men" – see below, under the "17th Century".
(203) Pg. 77, 78, and others.
(204) See ANF 1/146(b)(xv); 557(b)(3); 7/211(b); 8/734. Also PNF/1, 2/426(b); 6/477(b); 8/15(b).

THE ANTICHRIST

Various forms of the Antichrist legend were promulgated during the Middle Ages, including the idea, from time to time, that he had already been born. Hence **Joachin of Fiore**, an immensely influential visionary, told **King Richard Lionheart** of England (in 1191) that the Antichrist had already been born in Rome. [205] Just over a century later, **Bernard Gui**, an Inquisitor, condemned as heretics some apocalyptists who had opposed the pope. In his accusation against them he recorded that they had taught that the Antichrist

> *had already been born, and will run his course according to some of them, in the year of our Lord 1325. Others say that it will be in the year 1320; while still others put it later in the year 1335 . . .* [206]

It was inevitable that the year 1335 should figure in apocalyptic speculation, as also did the years 1260 and 1290 (see Daniel's cryptic words, 12:7, 11, 12). The arrival of each of those years created a great ferment among students of prophecy. But they all passed without any significant change in human affairs. If Christ should delay his return for so long (as he may well do), it is thoroughly predictable that a new batch of apocalyptists will be waiting eagerly for the 24th century (Da 8:14)! But perhaps I am too pessimistic. Perhaps they will all have learned wisdom by then. But the record of the past twenty centuries does not instil much confidence!

THE MILLENNIUM

I have already mentioned above that various new ways were developed, both before and during the 9th century, to show how

---

(205) McGinn, pg. 314.
(206) McGinn, Pg. 220.

the year 1000 would usher in a Millennium of bliss on earth. That sweet hope, of course, failed to materialise. But as the 14th century drew near, a thousand years after Constantine, an opportunity arose to reinterpret the prophecies. It was now argued that the Millennium predicted in *Revelation 20* had in fact begun with the first Christian emperor, whose conversion had brought about the ascendancy of the church. A thousand years had now passed since Constantine, hence the appearance of Gog and Magog and the day of final judgment must be imminent. If you think such arguments were ingenuously foolish, I agree with you; but they were no more ill-informed than many similar arguments I have heard in recent years.

DREAMS AND VISIONS

During the Middle Ages, some exponents of Bible prophecy kept reasonably close to the scriptures, but there was a growing trend toward using very obscure passages in very strange ways. There was also a growing readiness to add things to the Bible, such as personal dreams, visions, revelations, and the like. The end result was a weird combination of Bible verses, arcane images, mysterious parables, and citations of various strange authorities. The Greek and Roman **Sybils** were cited, and even the British wizard, **Merlin**, whose fame was widespread. Passages of scripture, ripped wildly out of context, were applied to current events. The whole enterprise of interpreting Bible prophecy became swathed in mystery, crammed with esoteric symbols, and accessible only to those who were party to the secret "keys".

Happily, the Reformation cleared away most of those mythical and imaginary accretions. Apocalyptic teachers once again became more closely bonded to scripture and more responsible in their efforts to understand precisely what the biblical writers were intending to say. That did not mean (as we shall see) that the Reformers were any more reliable in their interpretations than their forebears had been; but they were at least trying to stick to the words of scripture.

"THE NUMBER OF THE BEAST"

Another common enterprise during the Middle Ages was the ancient quest of trying to calculate the significance of the number *"666"* (Re 13:8). That quest had been a favourite pursuit among the Fathers, who devised many ingenious applications, and it remained (and still is) a popular enterprise. The savants of the Middle Ages, however, gave the quest some new twists. For example, the emperor **<u>Frederick II</u>** (died 1250) became (in the opinion of some) the first man ever to apply *"666"* to the papacy. He calculated that the Latin name of his papal adversary, **<u>Innocent IV</u>**, had a numerical value exactly equalling the infamous *"Number of the Beast"*. Frederick thus set a precedent that the Protestant reformers, some 300 years later, were not slow to follow. But in the intervening centuries many others who fell foul of the papacy did not hesitate to make similar calculations. The popes, in turn, were just as clever in finding colourful and improbable ways to apply the dread *"666"* to *their* foes.

And some modern writers are still finding ways to apply the number to current persons or events, and thus show that the Second Advent must be near!

PERSECUTION

One unhappy development during and after the late 13th century was the rising opposition of the establishment against apocalyptic teaching. This led to increasingly violent persecution of those who adopted or spread apocalyptic ideas. The point was reached where crusades were actually launched to stamp out whole colonies of people who had gathered to await the End of the World, or to protect themselves from their enemies. Their leaders were imprisoned, some were cruelly tortured, scores were burned at the stake – all in the name of Christ. The sufferers died while denouncing, with good reason, their papal foes as Antichrist.

Despite the most ruthless efforts to silence the apocalyptists, and indeed because of those persecutions, many thousands of people, pastors as well as lay people, continued to cling to their fervent hope that prophecy was being fulfilled around them and that the "End of the World" was near. How could it be otherwise when, in the reckoning of many of them, *"the abomination of desolation"* (the pope) spoken of by Daniel was already *"standing in the holy place"* (the church)?

The modern papacy, happily, is more benign, and I doubt that anyone would turn to the present pope to discover a sign of the end of the age. But perhaps that is too optimistic. I suppose even now there are people who delight to name the Pope as the *"false prophet"* spoken of in the Apocalypse (Re 16:13; 19:20; 20:10).

PREDICTIONS

A continuing motivation among apocalyptists has been a desire to discover the place each succeeding generation has occupied in God's universal scheme. Indeed, it is the need to give meaning and importance to life's seeming absurdity and injustice that provokes people to think of their own as the last and most significant generation. Only thus, for many, can sense be made out of wars, pestilence, brutality, persecution, famine, and so on. These otherwise obscene and awful happenings gain a cosmic value when they are read as *"signs of the times"*, the last upheaval of wickedness prior to the dawning of God's new age of beauty and peace.

So the apocalyptist is always busy, striving to collate history with prophecy – sometimes showing original and powerful thought; sometimes merely updating the schemes of the past; sometimes resorting to mythical and mystical symbols; sometimes near to scripture; sometimes distant from it; but in the end, coming to the same conclusion: "These are the Last Days! The return of Christ is at hand!"

Hence the following collection of sayings that so closely resemble the things that modern apocalyptists are still saying (the page numbers refer to McGinn) –

> *The rumour had filled almost the whole world that when the Feast of the Annunciation coincided with Good Friday without any doubt the End of the World would occur.* (**Abbot of Fleury**, 11th cent., pg. 89/90.)

> *The world with all its powers now weakened and oppressed by many hardships and calamities is bowed down to its End.* (The prophetess **Hildegard**, 12th cent., pg. 102).

> *The Second Coming of Christ himself is approaching or already soon imminent.* (**Geroh of Reichersberg**, 12th cent., pg. 106).

> *The End of the World approaches.* (**Hugh of St. Victor**, 12th cent., pg. 111).

> *If the church wished to study the sacred text and the holy prophecies . . . she would find . . . a greater certitude about the time of the Antichrist.* (**Roger Bacon**, 13th cent., pg. 156).

> *There remain only two 30-year periods in which everything said about the Antichrist and the End of the World must be fulfilled.* (From an anonymous letter, 13th cent., pg. 161).

> *In the last days, at the End of the World, as we believe without any doubt, (God has) raised up our two orders in the ministry of salvation.* (**John of Parma**, 13th cent., pg. 164).

The emperor **Frederick II** was thought by many to be the final Roman monarch –

> *The sceptre will not be taken from the hand of the Lord Frederick . . . until he who is sent comes (that is, until Christ comes for the Last*

> *Judgment)* (**Nicholas of Bari**, *13th cent., pg. 172.)*

When Frederick, at the height of his power, died suddenly in 1250, and the last of his heirs was executed in 1268, without any great change taking place in the world – except an increase in papal power – it caused much dismay in some apocalyptic circles. Some abandoned the whole enterprise of trying to predict the End; others struggled to recast their predictions to match the new events –

> *Many wise men . . . have thought that the days of the Antichrist would come in this period. (That is, the mid-13th century.* **Roger Bacon**, *pg. 190/191).*

> **Bonaventure** *thought that his own time was witnessing the climax of the sixth age, which would usher in a time of peace just prior to the End of the World. (Late 13th cent., pg. 197).*

> *The time of the persecution by the Antichrist will fall within the 14th century from the birth of Christ.* (**Arnold of Villanova**, *14th cent., pg. 224).*

> *Wandering prophets preaching imminent destruction appeared in 1472, 1484, 1490, 1492. (Pg. 277).*

And last, but certainly not least:

> **Christopher Columbus** *thought that his own divinely inspired mission to open up a new path to Asia . . . would herald an age of universal conversion that would precede the End of the World. (Late 15th cent., pg. 284).*

To the above I add the following by ***Lalage Pulvertaft*** –

> *(In the Middle Ages) there was an absolute belief in Hell fire; the End of the World was a real fear: when it had not arrived at 1000 A.D. it was expected at 1500 . . . The old world seemed corrupt, and ready for the vengeance of God to destroy it and to replace it with a new world . . . In 1525 the constellations moved into Pisces, and the Deluge was imminently expected. People took lodgings in the tops of houses; there was serious talk of moving the government into the mountains.* (207)

In a sense, of course, the apocalyptists were right. God *was* about to judge the whole world, and to change the face of human society. But he used, *not the tool of the <u>Second Advent</u>, but that of the <u>Reformation</u> and all that sprang from it* – including the founding of the USA. Perhaps the same is true of modern apocalyptic expectations. The apocalyptists may be correct in sensing that God is about to intervene powerfully in human affairs, but incorrect in predicting what the Divine action will be. Perhaps the return of Christ *is* near. But perhaps it is still far distant. Only the Father knows.

Feb 1st, <u>1524</u>, was a special date. Astrologers were widely agreed that the End of the World would begin on that day. Scores of families left London and fled to higher ground. In at least one place, a church built a hill-top fortress and stocked it with enough food for two months. (208) When nothing

---

(207) <u>International History Magazine</u>, #6, June 1973, pg. 59, 60, 63.

(208) I have no reference for this information, or for other pieces scattered through this book that are not annotated. But notice how little things have changed. In our own time various groups of Christians have built desert or mountain hideaways, and stocked them with food, hoping they will be able safely to weather the time of "great tribulation", which they are sure is about to break loose upon us.

happened, the astrologers simply went back to their calculations, discovered a mistake, and pushed the date forward a century, to 1624!

The selections given above are brief and arbitrary. But they do establish the point that throughout the Middle Ages there was always at least a significant minority of Christians who lived in fervent hope that Christ would soon return. Their hopes proved vain. Did their children learn wisdom, and stop the practice of trying to predict when the End would occur? I regret that many of them did not.

THE REFORMATION

The amount of apocalyptic literature produced during the past 500 years is almost measureless, and during the past 100 years it has been like an overwhelming flood. Even to survey briefly the available material would be almost impossible. I won't even try. But I do want to show you that the kinds of prediction being made today in many evangelical and charismatic circles (e.g., *"these are assuredly 'the last days' and many 'signs' point to the nearness of Christ's return"*) are not unique to our generation. They have been common since the time of the Reformation.

THE 16TH AND 17TH CENTURIES

- **_Martin Luther_**; the great Protestant Reformer, wrote –

    The day of judgment is not far off. Christ's words and these signs move me so to believe. For whatever chronicles we may read of the time of Christ until now, we shall not find a parallel to the present century ... The world has reached its culmination in what relates to temporal interests, or what Christ called the cares of this life . . . Whoever considers must acknowledge that this cannot hold much longer. ... [209]

O my Lord Christ, do come soon from heaven with fire and brimstone to put an end to such mockery and blasphemy! How most unbearably and intolerably men are outdoing themselves in wickedness! [210] ... *Grant, dear Lord God, that the blessed Day of thy holy advent may come soon, so that we may be redeemed from this bad, wicked world, the devil's dominion* ... [211]

One is not obliged to expect any other Antichrist. To have a worse regime on earth, one that kills more souls than does that of the pope, is impossible ... He is the real, head Antichrist, whom, God willing, our Lord Jesus Christ will very shortly thrust into the abyss of hell by his advent ... [212]

(The Devil) raised false prophets and erring spirits and filled the world with heretics and sects until the coming of the pope, who has utterly ruined it with sects and heresies, as behoved the final and mightiest Antichrist ... [213]

Oh! Let everyone who can do so call and cry ... And especially in these terrible last days, so

---

(209) The original source of this quotation is unknown to me.
(210) <u>What Luther Says</u>, ed. E. M. Plass; Concordia Publishing House; 1959; vol.3, pg 1108, sel. # 3541.
(211) Ibid. # 3542.
(212) Ibid. vol. 1, # 100, 104.
(213) Ibid. # 1163.

> *close to the End of the World ... Therefore let us watch and call without ceasing.* (214)

There are many places in his writings where Luther makes statements that pre-suppose a short time to the "End of the World". An example –

> *It is certainly true that the need for prayer has never been greater than it is at this time, and it will be still greater from now on until the End of the World.* (215)

Richard Bauckham (216) has shown that a number of leading Puritan divines in the early 16th century were deeply convinced that theirs would be the "last" generation on earth, the one spoken of by Jesus in *Matthew 24:34*.

During the Reformation, a number of Christian leaders taught that the Second Coming and the establishment of the 1000-year reign of Christ on earth was closer than a hair on their heads. A Calvinist named

- **_Johann Heinrich Alsted_**

argued from *Daniel* and *Revelation* that Christ would return in 1694. About the same time, in England and elsewhere, groups of radical Christians were selling all they had and setting up communal agricultural projects in preparation for Christ's imminent arrival and the establishment of God's Kingdom. (217)

The horrors of the Thirty Years War in Germany led students of prophecy to believe that *"the last days"* had come, and a rash of books were published warning people to prepare for the End of

---

(214)   Ibid. vol. 2, pg. 1090.
(215)   Ibid. pg. 1084.
(216)   In his book, Tudor Apocalypse, Sutton Courtenay Press, Oxford.
(217)   Owen Salter, in On Being, October 1978, pg. 6.

the World. It is said that by 1649 more than 80 books dealing with the Millennium had been published in England alone. Some of the more radical Puritans were convinced that the Millennium was about to be established –

> *They interpreted the prophetic symbols as contemporary figures in British political life, and pictured themselves as the instruments of God that would tear down the existing structure in order that God might establish this new kingdom of heaven. This is a curious contrast to the 20th century pre-millennialists who tend to be pessimistic, fatalistic, non-political, and non-activists . . . King Charles I was adversely identified by various writers as the little horn of Daniel 7:8, as one of the ten horns of the Beast of Revelation 17:12-15, and as the King of the North of Daniel 11:15-19.* (218)

- **F.F. Bruce**, the noted church historian, points out that the Protestant leaders of the Reformation were deeply convinced –

> *that they were living in the last days . . . (and) with this conviction they looked around for the Antichrist of the last days, and had no difficulty in finding him in the Papacy.*

However, not to be undone, the friends of the pope took up the argument and, as Professor Bruce writes –

> *There were eschatological stirrings in the (Catholic) camp as well, and there it was not overlooked that Luther's name lent itself rather*

---

(218) Dwight Wilson, <u>Armageddon Now</u> - *The Premillennarian Response to Russia and Israel Since 1917*; Baker Book House, 1977, pg. 17, 18.

easily to numerical analysis which yielded a total of 666. (219)

Luther's followers thought that he was probably the promised *"Elijah"*, and Professor Bruce quotes a hymn about this, written by Nicolaus Hermann –

> Elijah, ere the last great day,
> On earth should we be hearing,
> Proclaiming to this evil world
> That Christ is soon appearing;
> But our beloved man of God
> Has sounded late his voice abroad:
> The End must now be nearing! (220)

Another Lutheran preacher named

- ***Melchior Hoffman***

    came to Strassburg in 1529, where he met Anabaptists for the first time. He quickly became one himself. He left Strassburg again the following year, taking his new views northward to the Netherlands and North Germany . . . He was a fiery preacher and baptised many converts. Numerous groups of Melchiorites emerged in the fertile spiritual soil of the Netherlands.

    Hoffman had a special interest in the future events of the Second Coming and the Millennium when Christ would reign as King. He was also much occupied with the place of these events and fastened on Strassburg as the New Jerusalem.

---

(219) <u>Answers to Questions</u>, Paternoster Press, 1972, pg. 153/154.
(220) Ibid.

> *For this reason he returned there and in 1533 cheerfully went to prison because he believed that his imprisonment would set in motion the sequence of the last events of human history. Instead, he died in prison ten years later.* (221)

Among the various Anabaptist groups there was widespread belief in the nearness of Christ's return. A good example of this can be found in the Anabaptist leader

- **_Hans Hut_** (c. 1520) –

    > *(In 1525, Hut came to the conclusion that) Christ would return on Pentecost 1528, three and a half years later . . . (So he) embarked on a feverish missionary journey, baptising and using the cross as a sign upon the forehead in order to recruit the 144,000 saints needed for Christ's Millennial kingdom . . . Hut was captured, and he died on 6th December, 1527, of smoke inhalation in his prison cell.* (222)

The same article goes on to say –

> *Both peasants and townfolk, like all people in those times, interpreted the Turkish threat to European civilisation and even planetary movements as ominous signs of the impending end-times.* (223)

- **_John Donne_** (1572-1631); English divine, metaphysical poet, and the most famous preacher of his day.

In one of his poems he reflects the common view of his

---

(221) *Christian History* magazine, vol. 14, # 1, pg 9.
(222) Ibid. pg. 14.
(223) Ibid. pg. 18.

contemporaries that the world was in decline, and would soon end –

> *If the world's age, and death be argued well*
> By the sun's fall, which now towards earth doth bend,
> Then we might fear that virtue, since she fell
> So low as woman, should be near her end. (224)

Astronomers had noticed a variation in the sun's path, which persuaded some thinkers that the sun was coming nearer the earth year by year. This was taken as a sign that the world would soon be consumed. He uses the same analogy in his poem *Fair, Great, and Good*, in which he describes "the world's subsidence toward chaos" (A. J. Smith) –

> ... now when the sun
> Grown stale, is to so low a value run ...
> Since now, when all is withered, shrunk, and dried,
> All virtue ebbed out to a dead low tide,
> All the world's frame being crumbled into sand ...

Then, in his elegy upon the death of Prince Henry, Donne even more clearly declares his belief that the End was near –

> Was it not well believed, that he would make
> This general peace, th' eternal overtake,
> And that his times might have stretched out so far
> As to touch these, of which they emblems are?
> For to confirm this just belief, that now
> The last days came ... (225)

The idea is this: it was expected that Henry would carry the present peace of England right on into the Millennium; that "his times might have stretched" to the eternal kingdom, of which the present felicity was but an "emblem". His sudden

---

(224) *Man to God's Image*, lines 17-20.
(225) *Look to Me Faith*, lines 35-40.

death cast a shadow over such bright expectations, and raised a question about whether it really was a "just belief" that "the last days" had come. However, the question was merely a poetic device. Donne no doubt remained convinced, as did his fellows, that the sands of time were rapidly dissipating.

In the mid-17th century, an apocalyptic group gained prominence, called

- **_The Fifth Monarchy Men_**

They saw the execution of **_King Charles I_**, and the inauguration in England of the Commonwealth, as the first stage in the final ruin of Daniel's *"Fourth Kingdom"* (Da 2:40-43). They identified the *"Fourth Kingdom"* (as had many before them) with the Holy Roman Empire, plus the other states of Europe that had once been part of the ancient Roman Empire. The *"Stone Kingdom"* (vs. 35, 44-45) was called the *"Fifth Monarchy"*, and it was identified with Christ's Millennial reign upon the earth.

The "Fifth Monarchists" believed that the Second Advent was immediately at hand, and that it was the duty of all Christians to prepare Britain for the coming of its King. This was to be done by persuasion if possible, by force if necessary. They proclaimed Christ as King of England, and were initially enthusiastic supporters of **_Oliver Cromwell_** and his Roundheads. They saw themselves fighting with Cromwell to purge the kingdom of a corrupt monarchy and of everything contrary to the rule of Christ, thus making the land fit for his return. But they were infuriated when Cromwell usurped the Commonwealth and established his Protectorate. The Fifth Monarchists tried to foment an uprising, but their leaders were arrested and the movement sternly suppressed. However, it was not obliterated. Two hundred years later, it was still a recognisable cult in English church life. (226)

The great poet **_John Milton_** (1608-1674) was among those who reckoned that the oracles of Esdras were being fulfilled in his time, and that the return of Christ could not be far distant.

THE EIGHTEENTH CENTURY

- **_William Whiston_** (1667-1752)

He was a London mathematician, and theologian, who succeeded Sir Isaac Newton as professor of mathematics at Cambridge University. He is most famous today for his translation of "The Works of Josephus." In 1736 he predicted that the End of the World would occur on October 13th of that year. As a consequence,

> once again Londoners headed for the high ground. It was reported that pickpockets did especially well among the throngs at Hampstead Heath and Islington Fields. (227)

Later on, arguing that "the Tartars were the lost tribes" (of Israel), Whiston declared that "the Millennium would begin in 1766." (228) Furthermore,

> he drew up a list of ninety-nine "proofs" that the end of the age was at hand. One third of these signs come from 2 Esdras and are quite general, resembling similar predictions in the canonical scriptures. . . . Much more specific was Whiston's interpretation of the significance of

---

(226) Articles on the "Fifth Monarchy Men" can be found in most encyclopedias, or church histories. See also below, under the "19th Century".

(227) I have lost the source of this quote.

(228) From the Preface by W. S. LaSor to a 1960 edition of <u>Josephus</u>; Kregel Publications; pg. xi.

> *the rumour, circulating in 1726, that an illiterate farm woman of Surrey, named Mary Toft, had given birth to a litter of rabbits. . . . (He) was convinced that here was a signal fulfilment of (the prophecy of Esdras) that at the end of the age "women shall bring forth monsters" (5:8).* (229)

- **_Johann Bengel_** (1687-1753); Lutheran pastor, theologian, and hugely influential commentator, some of whose writings are still in print.

He penned several apocalyptic works, in which he strove to establish dates for the appearing of the Antichrist and the beginning of the Millennium – which he reckoned would begin in 1836. This posed some problems for editors of later editions of his commentaries, obliging them to revise drastically Bengel's notes on the *Apocalypse*. One of those editors wrote an "Introduction" to Bengel's "Word Studies in Revelation" –

> *(Bengel) assumes that, in spite of the multiplicity of failures hitherto, it is possible to expound the* Apocalypse *correctly, even before it is entirely fulfilled . . . (He) thought the most important task to be the explanation and application of the prophetic sense, and the deciphering of its chronology; both of the predictions already fulfilled, and that which is yet future. He brought to his task wonderful resources of knowledge and intellect; but how sad it is that a spirit so noble, so richly endowed in many things, so far in advance of his age, should in this respect be so enslaved as to waste*

---

(229) The Old Testament Pseudepigrapha Vol. One; ed. J. H. Charlesworth; Doubleday & Co, New York; 1983; pg. 523.

> *such vast scholarship, labour, and genius, on what, after all, was only a blunder!* (230)

What is perhaps even sadder is the multitude of preachers and writers since Bengel, far below him in genius and learning, who nonetheless have refused to learn from his folly. They are still drawing up charts, setting dates, making predictions, with even less substance behind their conclusions than Bengel had.

The astonishing thing about Bengel is that a man so brilliant and usually so sober in scholarship, should have turned so wild when he dealt with Bible prophecy. Caution was altogether discarded –

> *Among the results of his system were these. The final rage of the Antichrist for three and a half years extends from A.D. 1832 to 1836. The fight with the beast from the abyss, and his overthrow by Christ's appearing, were to occur in June 18, 1836. From then to 2836, Satan was to be bound, and then loosed for a season, until 2947. From A.D. 2836 to 3836, would be the millennial reign of the saints in heaven, and the latter year the date of the end of the world, and the last judgment . .*
>
> *It were wrong to mock at the blunder of such a noble Christian spirit, to whom Theology and the Church owe so much . . . .* (231)

Well, I have no wish to mock Bengel, or anyone, but it does seem like wilful blindness to keep on pursuing a method of Bible study and interpretation that has been proved again and

---

(230) <u>New Testament Word Studies</u>, a 1971 reprint of a 19th-century abridgement of Bengel's Gnomen on the New Testament; pub. by Kregel Publications; vol. 2; pg. 831-832.

(231) Ibid.

again for two millennia to yield false results!

- **_Matthew Henry_** (1662-1714); Puritan divine, preacher, commentator, renowned for his "Commentary on the Bible."

Among the pious, both ancient and modern, Matthew Henry was rare in his cautious approach to biblical eschatology. He gave some apt advice in the early 18th century, which is just as appropriate today –

> *As to the "end of the world", do not enquire when it will come, for it is not a question fit to be asked, for "of that day and that hour, knoweth no man"; it is a thing at a great distance; the exact time is fixed in the counsel of God, but is not revealed by any word of God, either to "men" on earth, or to "angels in heaven"; the angels shall have timely notice to prepare to attend in that day, and it shall be published, when it comes to the children of men, with sound of trumpet; but, at present, "men and angels" are kept in the dark concerning the precise time of it, that they may both attend their proper services in the present day.* (232)

How surprising it is that such sound thinking has not long since swept away all the groundless speculations that continue to bedevil the study of eschatology. But sobriety has never had much appeal for those who yearn to *"know the times and the seasons"*, and who refuse to accept the Lord's rebuke (Ac 1:7).

---

(232) Matthew Henry's Commentary on the Whole Bible; in 6 volumes; reprinted by Marshall, Morgan and Scott, London, 1953; vol. 5, pg. 544; commentary on Mk 13:32-33.

THE MODERN ERA

THE 19ᵀᴴ CENTURY

In the early 19th century a famous apocalyptic preacher **Richard Brothers**, made numerous predictions about the last days, including an extraordinary pronouncement that William Pitt's grand daughter, Lady Hester Lucy Stanhope, would become *"Queen of Jerusalem"*. (233) The oracles that continued to pour from the lips of enthusiastic preachers throughout the remainder of the century were little better!

- **Thomas Carlyle**, renowned 19th-century Scottish author.

In an essay called "Signs of the Times" (1829) he wrote –

> *How often we have heard, for the last fifty years, that the country was wrecked, and fast sinking . . . public principle is gone; private honesty is going; society, in short, is fast falling in pieces; and a time of unmixed evil is come upon us.*

> *At such a period, it was to be expected that the rage of prophecy should be more than usually excited. Accordingly, the Millenarians have come forth on the right hand, and the Millerites on the left. The Fifth Monarchy Men prophesy from the Bible . . . (announcing) that the last of the seals is to be opened, positively, in the year 1860 . . .* (234)

---

(233) *Biblical Archaeology Review*; July/August 1984; pg. 71.

(234) Thomas Carlyle - Selected Writings; ed. by Alan Shelston; Penguin Books, 1971; pg 63. Mr Shelston, in a footnote, mentions that there was an upsurge of millenarianism at the time of the Industrial

Continued on next page ....

Would Carlyle, I wonder, be more amused, aggrieved, or amazed to find, nearly two centuries after the death of those "Fifth Monarchy" prophets, that little has changed? Using exactly the same scriptures, the same worn-out arguments, changing only the newspaper headlines they brandish, our latter-day seers are making the same irresponsible predictions. Will they never *learn* ?

- ### *Hippolytus Redivivus*

Some quite learned men, who observed the development of Europe during the 19th century into democratic states, were persuaded that the time had come for the predictions of Hippolytus [235] to be fulfilled.

Hence the following footnotes to "Hippolytus" in my 19th century edition of the *Ante-Nicene Fathers* –

> *The comments of (Hippolytus) on this book (Daniel) . . . deserve special attention, as from a disciple of St John himself.* [236]

Hippolytus, commenting on Daniel's vision of the *"Fourth Kingdom"*, said that *"the toes of the image turn out to be democracies"*; which elicited the footnote –

> *True in A.D. 1885. A very pregnant testimony to our own times . . . (Hippolytus) is deserving of special note. Who could have foreseen the universal spirit of democracy in this century (the 19th) save by the light of (Daniel's) prophecy? . . . Is not this treatise (by Hippolytus) a voice to our own times of vast*

Revolution – as indeed there has been, and continues to be, during every time of social crisis or upheaval.

(235)　See above, "2nd Century".
(236)　ANF, vol. 5, pg. 178.

significance?... All this is very significant to us of the "last days". (237)

- **<u>Margaret McDonald</u>**

In the year 1830, by a "prophetic" utterance, she became apparently the first person ever to suggest that the rapture of the church would be an event separate from, and several years prior to, the visible return of Christ.

Her suggestion was taken up by

- **<u>J. N. Derby</u>** (the founder of the Christian Brethren movement).

He developed an entire theology around the idea of a secret (that is, invisible) pre-tribulation coming of Christ for his church. Derby's theories were incorporated into the

- **<u>Scofield Reference Bible</u>**

and thence became widespread among evangelicals and charismatics. The constant presumption, of course, was that this "secret rapture" could, and probably would, occur at any moment. At least there was never any doubt that the "Last Days" were upon the church, and the Millennial Age must soon dawn.

Later editions of Scofield have considerably modified the original doctrines, to rid them of their sectarian character and make them more widely acceptable.

- **<u>William Miller</u>** (1782-1849).

He was a diligent Bible student, and avid reader, who began adult life as a sceptic, but was converted, in 1816, both to Christ and to a premillennial eschatology.

---

(237)   Ibid. pg. 178, 209, 219, 248.

After much study of the apocalyptic scriptures Miller "proved" conclusively that Christ would come in the year 1843. He did this by stating that the *"seven times"* of *Leviticus 26:18* represented 2520 years, which began in 677 B.C. (the year of King Manasseh's captivity). He also "proved" that 1843 was the terminal year for the 7-year war of *Ezekiel 39:9, 10*; the 7x7 number of *"Jubilees"*; the 3 *"days"* of *Hosea 6:1-3*; and the 2300 *"days"* of *Daniel 8:14*. Miller's date was later corrected by some of his followers to Oct 22, 1844, on which very day they were sure Christ would return.

When that date also passed without incident many of Miller's disciples fell away, disillusioned. Others, however, argued that Christ in fact had come, as predicted, except that he returned, not to an "earthly" sanctuary, but to a "heavenly". There, in the heavens, he "cleansed" the sanctuary in preparation for the final denouement at the very end of the age. A segment of people who adopted the revised plan also embraced parts of the Jewish law, and became the group now known as Seventh Day Adventists. (238)

According to one authority, Miller

> *persuaded the "New York Herald" to publish his prediction of the destruction of the world by fire. A few fanatics murdered relatives and committed suicide, thinking the dead would get to heaven first. Thousands screamed and prayed on hilltops. When nothing happened, Miller kept moving the date up according to "new calculations". Meanwhile, he collected a fortune selling white ascension robes to believers. When he died in 1849, he had made*

---

(238) The information on Miller came from various sources. There is a large literature on the Adventist Movement.

> *3,200 speeches predicting the end of the world –
> on various dates.* (239)

Here is something for you to think about. Jesus undoubtedly understood scripture better than any person who has ever lived. He had access to the *Book of Daniel*, and to all the other O.T. prophets. He knew about the various mystical numbers recorded in Daniel. He was just as able to calculate dates, to add up the years, as any modern teacher might be. If the methods used by those moderns were accepted by Jesus, then he could easily have come to the same conclusions as they do. He could have predicted with fair accuracy the terminal points for each of Daniel's prophecies.

Therefore, if those prophecies mean what some teachers claim they mean, Jesus would have *known* that his Second Advent and the End of the World were far distant. Yet he plainly knew nothing of the sort. He did *not* see in Daniel, or in any of the other prophets, what latter-day soothsayers see there. He declared emphatically that the time of his return was known neither by himself, nor even the angels, but only by the Father. If *angels* cannot take hold of Daniel's prophecies and use them to calculate the time of the End, how can anyone reasonably suppose that *we* can do so?

- **_John Cumming_** (1807-1881); a Scottish preacher and writer on Bible prophecy.

He wrote numerous essays and books on apocalyptic themes, all of them imbued with a strong expectation that the Second Advent would take place before the turn of the century. In 1855 he wrote two books that became almost a standard framework for numerous later premillennial volumes. He reckoned that 1864 would be a strong terminal date in prophecy, and that if the world did not actually end on that date, its ruin could not

---

(239)   I have lost the source of this passage.

long be delayed.

Indeed, during the early part of the 19th century there was an avalanche of books on Bible prophecy nearly equal to that of the late 20th century. All those writers would have been dismayed, and astonished, if someone had told them that 150 years after their books and sermons were long forgotten, the church would still be waiting for the return of Christ!

- **_H. Grattan Guinness_** (1835-1910); Irish evangelist and writer.

  (He) was a cautious scholar, who spoke disparagingly of those who glibly set dates, nevertheless (in 1880 he declared) that the latest possible year for the return of the Lord was around 1923. He wrote a book of nearly 700 pages to substantiate his view . . . (Likewise) in 1890 the Christian Herald, *a journal with nearly a quarter of a million circulation, suggested that the year 1900 was the latest possible date for the consummation of the age.* (240)

- **_"Things to Come"_**

In the late 19th century, a monthly journal was published in England called *Things to Come*. It was the official organ of a group of "prophetic conferences", hence its message was focussed on the nearness of the Second Advent. Its editors and authors reckoned that *"the signs of the times"* proved that the return of Christ must soon take place. The copies of the magazine that I have seen suggest that its main readership was among Baptists and other evangelicals.

The issue of July, 1896, contains the following –

---

(240) The Return, by Winkie Pratney & Barry Chant; Sovereign World, England, 1988; pg. 72.

> *(The) signs of Christ's near coming seem to be multiplying on every side . . . we believe that the end of the world is approaching (pg. 7)*

In the same issue, under the heading *Signs of the Times* (pg. 10), a number of items are listed, taken from contemporary political and religious events, that were said to show the nearness of Christ's return. The same heading, with similar lists of "signs" occurs in each edition of which I have a copy (July 1896 through June 1898, plus January through December 1913).

The issue of January 1897 has this –

> *(Thank) God, we feel that our Lord is very near and that everything done for the conversion of souls at home and abroad is rapidly hastening his coming. Some of us believe that we can almost hear the sound of the chariot wheels of our King! In any case, expectation is intensified and zeal increased a thousand-fold by the conviction that at any moment the last soul may be saved out of the number foreseen by God to complete his church – and when THAT hour strikes, what remains but the Coming of the Lord to receive his people to himself?" (pg. 79).*

And from February 1897 –

> *The signs of the times are bringing the Lord to the doors. The fig tree (Mt 24:32-33) is putting forth her leaves."*

And from March 1897 –

> *The light, then, which prophecy sheds upon the present crisis is this. We may be about to witness the opening act in the stupendous drama. It may be postponed for a time, but it does not seem likely. . . . If indeed the first act is*

about to begin, then we are within seven years of the establishment of the millennial kingdom!"

- **W. B. Yeats** (1865-1939); Irish poet, nationalist, and mystic.

In his poem "The Second Coming", he wrote –

> . . . Things fall apart; the centre cannot hold;
> Mere anarchy is loosed upon the world,
> The blood-dimmed tide is loosed, and everywhere
> The ceremony of innocence is drowned;
> The best lack all conviction, while the worst
> Are full of passionate intensity.
> Surely some revelation is at hand;
> Surely the Second Coming is at hand.
> The Second Coming! . . .

THE LAST 100 YEARS

What shall I say about this tormented age? How can I select even a few passages from the mountainous heaps of apocalyptic literature that continue to pour from evangelical presses?

So far in these pages I have presented quotes from nearly every century; but now, not even every decade would suffice. This entire volume could be filled with failed predictions that have been made since the 20th century began – indeed, since the past few decades began, continuing into this present century!

Date after date has been calculated, trumpeted confidently, then abandoned or revised as the predicted time came and passed, with no change. Since the World War alone, countless books on Bible prophecy, when their forecasts failed to materialise, have been consigned to extinction. Hundreds more are joining them as the years unfold, tossed on the musty heap of two millennia of obsolescent prophetic writings.

My first intention was to include here a group of quotes from every decade across the past 100 years. But there were too many of them. In any case, just walk into any evangelical book shop, or scan the advertisements in any popular Christian journal, and you will soon have in your hands enough examples to fill this whole book!

Let me mention just a handful, quickly gleaned from my shelves, and put here just as they came to hand, without regard to date –

- A British evangelist, **_Brian Williams_**, in 1963 published *Jesus is Coming Very Soon*, in which he claimed: "That we are living in 'the last days' and 'the time of the end', there can be no doubt . . . With all my heart, I believe that Jesus is coming very soon."

- In 1917 the **_Balfour Declaration_** was issued by the British government, declaring Palestine a home for the Jews, and committing Great Britain to help achieve that goal. This event caused a great flurry of excitement among prophecy buffs. Thousands of them were convinced that within a generation of the liberation of Jerusalem from the Turkish yoke, Christ must return (Mt 24:32-34). It is proving so far (2013) to be a long generation!

- **_A. J. Ferris_** in his writings used the various *"seven times"* oracles in scripture to calculate that 1936 was a terminal year, and in several booklets, which I have in my library, he asserted that the return of Christ was near at hand.

- In 1973 **_John Strong_** wrote *The Doomsday Globe*, in which he predicted that Armageddon would begin in October 1979, and that the Second Advent would occur 12 months later. His book was so well written, and his arguments so persuasive, that scores of people sold everything and went far out into the country. They carried with them piles of food and other necessary items, along with weapons for self-defence, and sat down to wait in safety (they hoped) until Christ appeared.

- In *The Nearness of Christ's Return*, **Basil Mowll** wrote in 1948 that the year 1917 was a terminal date in prophecy. He calculated that several predictions had been fulfilled in that year – the 1335 days of Da 12:12; the seven times of Le 26:18; and others. He then added a 40-year period of "testing", to arrive at the year 1957. He felt that the return of Christ could be delayed beyond that date by at most a short time.

- In 1956, **Herbert Armstrong**, in *The Middle East in Prophecy*, identified various contemporary events in Bible prophecy, and then said of the Second Advent, "It is now near, even at the doors." He later wrote another booklet, *1975 In Bible Prophecy*, in which he predicted the onset of a terrible drought that would be the beginning of the *Great Tribulation*. This in turn, he said, would herald the nearness of Christ's return.

- In 1970 **Hal Lindsey** published *The Late Great Planet Earth* in which he asserted that the return of the Jews to Palestine "would occur shortly before the events which will culminate with the personal, visible return of the Messiah, Jesus Christ" (pg. 52). The Jews were re-established in Israel in 1948, which caused Lindsey to quote *Matthew 24:34*, and then write: "within forty years or so of 1948 all these things could take place (pg. 54) . . . With the Jewish nation reborn in the land of Palestine . . . the most important prophetic sign of Jesus Christ's soon coming is before us" (pg. 57-58).

- In 1987 **Edgar Whisenant** published a booklet, *88 Reasons Why The Rapture Could Be In 1988*. It sold several million copies, but its predictions still failed. The 88 arguments proved to be fallacies. The very next year he wrote another book to demonstrate that Christ would surely come in 1989, which staggeringly also sold well. After that, his popularity rapidly declined.

- And then, in perhaps one of the most astonishing of all examples of nonsensical oracles, there is the anonymous pamphlet, *God's Judgment Day is Near*, published in 1991. It made the ludicrous claim that Jesus would come again at 1.00 a.m. (Sydney time) on the 29th October, 1992; or, *in the event of Daylight Saving*, at 2.00 a.m!

With what enthusiasm all those writers (and scores like them) have called upon the familiar and hoary *"signs of the times"* to show that the End is near! But their fathers have done the same every year across the past 100 years. Every folly from the previous 1900 years, and worse, has been repeated in our lifetime.

Despite a growing frenzy, the year 2000 came and went, just as the year 1000 did, without bringing the End of the World. For a few more years yet, an angry reaction may survive against the prophecy preachers who stirred up all the excitement, and eschatology will fall into disfavour. But not for long! A new crop of biblical soothsayers will come along, and probably already has, with newly updated calculations, once more to lead the unwary astray.

Of course, Christ may well return before the end of this week! Perhaps this very day. I hope so. With all true believers I am always *"looking for and hastening toward the day of his coming!"* What else can a Christian do, except live with joyful anticipation, on the very edge of eternity, watching, waiting, eager for the Lord's return?

But the fact remains – *"no one knows the day nor the hour"*, (241) and only *"a fool pretends to know the future, and*

---

(241) Matthew 24:36, 42-44, 50; etc; Acts 1:7; etc.

spins many words about it. ⁽²⁴²⁾ The end of the age may be close; it may still be far distant. Let us then be done with trying to predict that which cannot be known. Let us be content simply to be found always *"watching and ready, for we do not know when our Lord will come;"* and, *"he will assuredly come at a time when you least expect him!"*

FINAL COMMENTS

You will realise, of course, that the list of predictions collected in these pages is a minuscule selection compared with the vast number that could be assembled. I have drawn only from my quite modest personal library, and even then, to avoid pointless repetition, I have left out many quotes. If one were to do an exhaustive search through some of the world's great libraries and archives, thousands more such passages could be found.

You might have noticed that the same set of biblical references are quoted over and over again, generation after generation. Nothing changes, except the news headlines quoted by the unwise wielders of the biblical oracles!

Surely it must be obvious that *a method of handling scripture that has been so wrong for so long* ought to be rejected. The biblical predictions are safe enough. Their truth, inspired by the Holy Spirit, can be absolutely trusted. But the manner in which they have been interpreted across the centuries is highly suspect. We need to find a better way of reading and understanding the sacred oracles. Perhaps the arguments in this book will help at least some people to achieve that goal.

In the meantime, I join my prayer with all God's children: *"Even so, come, Lord Jesus!"* (Re 22:20).

---

(242) Ecclesiastes 10:14.

BIBLIOGRAPHY

BOOKS

Assyria, Its Princes and People; The Religious Tract Society: London, 1926.

Berkouwer, G. C. *Studies in Dogmatics, The Return of Christ*. William B. Eerdman's Pub. Co., Grand Rapids, Michigan, 1975.

Bettenson, Henry, tr. and David Knowles, editor. *City Of God* (Augustine)Penguin Books: London, 1977.

Braaten, Carl E. *Eschatology and Ethics*. Augsburg Pub. House Minneapolis, Minnesota, 1974.

Bullfinch, Thomas, *Bullfinch's Mythology*. The Modern Library: New York, undated reprint.

Chant, Ken, *The Cross and the Crown*. Vision Publishing.

Donne, John, Poem. "Go, Catch a Falling Star." *The Complete English Poems*. Edited by A. J. Smith. Penguin Books:1982.

Dostoyevsky, The Brothers Karamazov.

Esdras 2; The Apocrypha

Eusebius, Church History.

Historicity and Chronology in the New Testament 1965.

History of the Worthies of England; Fuller; Folio Society; London, 1987.

Hobson, Christine, *The World of the Pharaohs*. Thames & Hudson: New York, 1987.

Hoople R. E, R. F. Piper, and W. P. Tolley, editors. *Preface to Philosophy, A Book of Readings*; Macmillan Co., 1947.

James, William, *Principles of Psychology*.

Know Why You Believe. Scripture Press Pub. Inc., Wheaton, Illinois, 1968.

Longfellow, H. W. Poem "God's Acre" *Poems of Henry Wadsworth Longfellow*. 1895

Maccabees Two; The Apocrypha

McGinn, Bernard, *Visions of the End*. Columbia University Press: New York, 1979.

Morris, Ivan, tr. *The Pillow Book of Sei Shonagon*. Penguin Classics:

1967.

Orr, Robert, *Victory Pageant*. Pickering & Inglis: London, 1972.

Payne, J. Barton, *Encyclopedia of Biblical Prophecy*. Hodder & Stoughton: London, Sydney, 1973.

_____. *The Imminent Appearing of Christ*. Eerdman's Pub. Co., Michigan, 1962.

Pratney, Winkie and Barry Chant, *The Return*. Sovereign World: 1988.

Pritchard, James B. editor. *The Ancient Near East Vol One*. Princeton University Press: reprint 1973.

Sirach; The Apocrypha.

Whitman, Walt, Poem. **"Song of Myself"** (from Leaves of Grass, first published in the 1855 edition).

ARTICLES

Feyman Richard P. art. National Geographic. March 1990.

Luther, Martin, *Quote*. Plain Truth. December 1973.

Maeir, Paul, art *The Empty Tomb as History*. Christianity Today. March, 1975

Pulvertaft, Lalage, *art*. International History Magazine. June, 1973.

Ross, Bob. Book Review. Christianity Today. April 13, 1973.

Thomson J. S. Essay. *Death and Immortality*. Christianity Today. August 3, 1962.

Tenney, Merrill C. Essay *The Glorious Destiny of the Believer*. Christianity Today.

Yamauchi, E. M. Quote Christianity Today. March 29th, 1974.

_____. art. *Easter - Myth, Hallucination, or History*. Christianity Today March 15, 1974.

BIBLE COMMENTARIES

Anders, Max., editor. *Holman New Testament Commentary*. B & H Publishing Group: Nashville, Tennessee, 2004.

Barnes, Albert (1798-1870) *Notes on the Bible*.

Bible Background Commentary. Intervarsity Press: Nottingham, U.K., 1993.

Calvin, John (1509-1564) *Calvin's Commentaries*.

Clarke, Adam (1715-1832) *Commentary on the Bible.*
College Press NIV Commentary, The. Joplin, Missouri, 1996.
Excell, Joseph S. and Spence-Jones, H. D. M., editors. *The Pulpit Commentary.* 1881.
Gaebelein, Frank E., editor. *The Expositor's Bible Commentary.* Zondervan Publishers: Grand Rapids, Michigan.
Gill, John., (1690-1771) *Exposition of the Entire Bible.*
Hawker, Robert., *The Poor Man's Commentary On The Whole Bible.* 1850.
Henry, Matthew., *Commentary On The Whole Bible.* Marshall, Morgan, and Scott: London, 1953
Hodge, Charles., (1797-1878).*A Commentary on Ephesians.* Intervarsity Press.
Interpreter's Bible, The. Abingdon Press: New York, 1952.
Ironside, H. A., *Expository Commentary* (1876-1951).
IVP New Testament Commentary Series, The. Intervarsity Press: Nottingham, UK.
Jamieson, R, A.Fausett and D. Brown., *A Commentary on the Old and New Testaments,* 1871.
Johnson B. W., *The People's New Testament.* 1891.
_____. .*The People's New Testament Commentary.* Word Search Corporation: Nashville, Tennessee, 2010.
Macdonald, William., *Believer's Bible Commentary.* Thomas Nelson Publishers: 1989.
Nelson's New Illustrated Bible Commentary. Thomas Nelson Inc., New York, 1999.
New Testament Commentary, The. Baker's Publishing House: Grand Rapids, Michigan, 1987.
Poole, Matthew., *Matthew Poole's Commentary.* 1685
Preacher's Commentary, The. Word Inc., Nashville, Tennessee, 1992.
Preacher's Outline and Sermon Bible. Word Search Corporation: Nashville, Tennessee, 2010.
Robertson A. T., *Word Pictures in the New Testament*; 1933.
Stern, David H., *Jewish New Testament Commentary.* Jewish New Testament Publications Inc.,Clarksville, Maryland; 1982.
Trapp, John., *Commentary On The Old And New Testaments* (1601-1669).
Vincent, Marvin R., *Vincent's Word Studies.* 1886

Walvoord, John and Zuck, Roy., *The Bible Knowledge Commentary*. Cook Communications: Colorado Springs, Colorado, 1989.
Wesley, John., *Explanatory Notes on the Whole Bible* (1703-1791).
Wiersbe, Warren W., *Wiersbe's Expository Outlines*. Pub. David C. Cook: Colorado Springs, Colorado
Wiseman, D. J., General editor. *Tyndale Old Testament Commentaries*. Intervarsity Press.

BIBLE VERSIONS

In addition to the *KJV* or *Authorised Version* of the Bible, the following versions or translations are cited, or were consulted by the author of this work.

CEV – *Contemporary English Version*; the American Bible Society, New York, NY; 1995.
ESV – *English Standard Version*; Crossway Bibles, a publishing ministry of Good News Publishers; Wheaton, Illinois; 2001.
GNB – *Good News Bible*; Second Edition, by the American Bible Society; New York, NY; 1992.
GW – *God's* Word; God's Word to the Nations Bible Society; Cleveland, Ohio; 1995.
JBP – *The New Testament in Modern English;* J. B. Phillips; Geoffrey Bles, London; 1960.
JPS – *The JPS* Bible; the Jewish Publication Society; Philadelphia, PA; 1995.
ISV – *International Standard Version*, v. 1.2.2; The ISV Foundation, La Mirada, CA; 2001.
NEB – *The New English Bible*; Oxford University Press, New York; 1972.
NET – *The Net Bible*; Biblical Studies Press; Richardson, Texas; 2006.
NIV – *New International Version*; Zondervan Bible Publishers, Grand Rapids, Michigan; 1978.
NJB – *New Jerusalem Bible*; Doubleday & Co. Inc; Garden City, New York; 1985
RSV – *Revised Standard Version;* Thomas Nelson Inc., New York; 1959.
NRSV – *New Revised Standard Version*; the Division of Christian Education of the National Council of the Churches of Christ

in the USA; 1989.
REB – *Revised English Bible with Apocrypha*; Oxford University Press; 1989.
YLT – *Young's Literal Translation*; by NJ Young; 1898.

www.ingramcontent.com/pod-product-compliance
Lightning Source LLC
Chambersburg PA
CBHW070442170426
43201CB00010B/1187